Outward

Outward

Adrienne Rich's Expanding Solitudes

Ed Pavlić

University of Minnesota Press
Minneapolis
London

The University of Minnesota Press gratefully acknowledges the financial assistance provided for the publication of this book by the Willson Center for Humanities and Arts at the University of Georgia.

Frontispiece photograph of Adrienne Rich courtesy of Eamonn McCabe/ Popperfoto via Getty Images.

Published by the University of Minnesota Press
111 Third Avenue South, Suite 290
Minneapolis, MN 55401-2520
http://www.upress.umn.edu

ISBN 978-1-5179-1077-8 (hc)
ISBN 978-1-5179-1078-5 (pb)

Library of Congress record available at https://lccn.loc.gov/2020058642

Printed in the United States of America on acid-free paper

The University of Minnesota is an equal-opportunity educator and employer.

28 27 26 25 24 23 22 21   10 9 8 7 6 5 4 3 2 1

For Stacey Cecile

A kind of mind
That would address
Duress
Outward in larger terms

—Adrienne Rich, "Fragments of an Opera"
(2012)

Contents

"how we are with each other"

"useless without the other end"
The Journey Outward

In the foreword to her first volume of collected poems, *Collected Early Poems: 1950–1970,* published in 1993, Adrienne Rich looked back on the beginnings of her career as a poet: "I was like someone walking through a fogged-in city, compelled on an errand she cannot describe, . . . holding one end of a powerful connector, useless without the other end." The powerful connecter could be understood as poetry or, alternatively, as consciousness itself. Over the decades Rich would come to explore how profoundly both depended on what she called "the other end," a sense of experience, a shifting reality inextricable from the situation of her body—a body among bodies—in history. The remembered character-self in her 1993 foreword sees how experience must lead outside "neighborhoods already familiar." Rich's sense of an outward beyond the familiar involved questions at every level of her life, aesthetic questions, experiential necessities, and political confrontations.

In her lyrical essay "Permeable Membrane" (2006), Rich scripted a concise and expansive description of the "connector" she had found herself coming into somewhat foggy possession of as a teenager in the years following World War II: "The medium is language intensified, intensifying our sense of possible reality." Thus equipped and mobilized, the "poetic imagination," Rich wrote, is "radical, meaning root-tangled in the grit of human arrangements and relationships: *how we are with each other.*" From the first, Rich's poems evince an awareness that "human arrangements and relationships" are bracketed and policed by complex systems. Those systems operate within, between, and around people. Her experience of motherhood in the 1950s, as she put it years later, radicalized

1

her, alerted her to a complex politics of human relationships, a politics informing, even controlling, *"how we are with each other"* even in the most private and intimate reaches of life.

Outward guides a nuanced encounter with the shape and texture of Rich's quest for "the other end" in poems, a journey that transformed a prodigiously talented midcentury formalist lost in a "fogged-in city" into arguably the most socially sensual and expansively radical ("radical" as defined immediately above) American poet of the twentieth century. Over the course of that journey, Rich's speaker moves toward a historically constituted vision of a collective "we" (and at times more than one), positioning and repositioning herself, but always situated within that vision. Rich's poems explore *how* the dimensions and dynamics of collectives fluctuate— indeed, *radically*—over the decades as class, war, race, gender, sexuality, geography, and economics appear and tangle together as factors en route to "the other end," to a living sense of *"how we are with each other."*

Adrienne Rich's poems are rarely direct and never simple. But they are also almost never more indirect or complicated than they need to be. Via a developing instrument, the poet feels her way out beyond the tips of her fingers, sensing the always-changing dimensions of her—which is also our—urgent, relational capacity for being. To travel over this vast and intricate terrain is to encounter the protean thrusts of a consciousness attempting to take itself and its world seriously. The result amounts to a phenomenology of experience in which the goal is a practical distillation of our social and sensual—our radical—situation: mutuality.

Outward traces the arc of Rich's turbulent quest for "the other end," for consciousness in its most intense and practical relevance, for poetry's role in successive phases of progressive human realization. Prose and other media play supporting roles here. Excerpts from critical readings of Rich's poems appear when necessary, as do passages from Rich's essays, a few of which become touchstones—refrains, almost. But my first concern is the heart of the matter, the poems themselves.

"radical, meaning root-tangled"
Preparing to Read Rich's Career in Poems

As the best book-length studies of the poet's work make clear, scholars and reviewers have rigorously engaged with the first half of Adrienne Rich's career. A celebrated 1950s formalist (*A Change of World*, 1951; *The*

Diamond Cutters and Other Poems, 1955), Rich defied the formal constraints of the poetry she was trained to write (*Snapshots of a Daughter-
in-Law*, 1963) by writing poems from a subjective and at times gendered
location and from a new proximity to her *own* personal and private life
(*Necessities of Life*, 1966). In the late 1960s she embraced an aesthetics
of process and opened her gendered, lyrical work to explicitly political
events and concerns, connecting Black liberation to the struggle against
the war in Vietnam (*Leaflets*, 1969; *The Will to Change*, 1971). In the early
1970s she became a celebrated, consciously feminist poet (*Diving into the
Wreck*, 1973). Through that decade and into the early 1980s, developing
into a publicly visible poet and racially aware author-activist (*The Dream
of a Common Language*, 1978; *A Wild Patience Has Taken Me This Far*,
1981), Rich was a principal architect of a lesbian-feminist revolution in
women's consciousness. Focused on the quest for relation that informs
all of these stages, *Outward* adds new textures and emphases to our encounters with these crucial intervals of Rich's career in poems. But it
leaves the existing narrative basically in place.

In order of publication, the best studies of Rich's career are Claire
Keyes's *The Aesthetics of Power: The Poetry of Adrienne Rich* (1986); Craig
Werner's *Adrienne Rich: The Poet and Her Critics* (1988); Alice Templeton's
The Dream and the Dialogue: Adrienne Rich's Feminist Poetics (1995);
Cheri Colby Langdell's *Adrienne Rich: The Moment of Change* (2004);
and Jeannette E. Riley's *Understanding Adrienne Rich* (2016). The most
basic stakes in *Outward* become clear based on the two best critical narratives of Rich's career up to the early 1980s and the extensions projected
by the structure of their conclusions. In *The Aesthetics of Power*, Keyes
traces Rich's process (early 1950s to the mid-1960s), working beyond her
position in the dominant masculine modes of poetry in which she had
been immersed as a young writer. The major tension between Keyes's account of Rich's career (which ends with Rich at the apex of her lesbian-
feminist identification) and the discussion presented here stems from
Keyes's concept of an individualized integrity and the inward-looking,
autonomy-based lyric process that serves it: "Poetry, at least in our age,
depends upon the individual voice. Our poets are condemned to the
personal." Given that point of view, it makes sense that Keyes considers
Rich's poems weakest when "trapped in a shared reality" and engaged
in political action. Drawn from images across Rich's full career, my
mapping of the poet's work in this volume pretty much reverses Keyes's

values, a difference that becomes essential to the structure of explicitly relational and politicized solitudes that Rich explored in the second half of her career.

Werner ends his account in *Adrienne Rich: The Poet and Her Critics* at almost precisely the same stage of Rich's career as does Keyes, but with inverse conclusions. Far more attuned than Keyes to the cultural and political (even revolutionary) stakes of Rich's poems and public persona, Werner stresses how Rich's poems reach beyond conceptions of integrity understood as "self-conscious individual assertion." Instead, he reads Rich's work as a search for "an integrity based upon relationships rather than solipsism." In a conclusion sounding deep affinities with the way *Outward* charts the structures of Rich's full career, Werner finds that, at its best, Rich's poetry "implies an alternative means of conceiving the self as a conscious *manifestation* of ever-shifting relationships." I think it is important to note that these are not racially neutral emphases. Werner's grounding in the African American literary and cultural tradition positions him to approach Rich in ways that engage her emphasis on relational in addition to (and at times as opposed to) individualized assumptions and goals. Subsequent book-length studies of Rich's career have tended to follow the structure of Keyes's readings more closely than that of Werner's. Because of the key role played by an ever-expanding radius of relation and radical political engagement in Rich's later poems, Keyes's white-leaning emphasis on individuality and on the self as an *owned* quantity presents difficulties for tracking Rich's career through the 1980s and beyond.

Without a relational basis on which to ground critical explorations of Rich's later works, many critics have relied heavily on the author's essays as guides to her decisions. Readings of her later career have focused on the "public" nature of her poetry (as in Riley's *Understanding Adrienne Rich*), often emphasizing her role as a "citizen poet" (as in Miriam Marty Clark's "Human Rights and the Work of Lyric in Adrienne Rich," 2009). Other scholars (such as Langdell, in *Adrienne Rich: The Moment of Change*) have read Rich's works in strictly feminist terms across her full career, an approach that of course identifies key veins of importance. In *The Dream and the Dialogue*, Templeton traces dialogic patterns in Rich's later work in ways generally compatible with my focus on relation in this volume. With attention to the closely intimate nature of images in her "public" poems, the fugitive and dissident energies in her "citizen poet's" work, and implications that include but also go beyond ones associated with feminism per se, my readings here do not deny these important facets of Rich's later works, but I also strive for a deeper and more distinctive set of observations based on close readings of evolving structures in and between her poems.

Most critical perspectives on Rich's work have remained grounded in conceptions of personal and artistic integrity generally compatible with Keyes's readings in *The Aesthetics of Power*. For many reasons, most of which orbit this central tendency, the well-acknowledged itinerary of Rich's career weakens after *A Wild Patience Has Taken Me This Far* in 1981. Again for many reasons, but mostly because fewer critics have seriously engaged Werner's emphasis on "an integrity based upon relationships" in Rich's work, the second half of her career has not received adequate attention. The nine collections of poems that Rich published across the last three decades of her life have certainly been noted, and features of her radically shifting voice and approach have found praise or criticism depending on the politics guiding the wide array of scholars and reviewers who have been positioned to comment. But none has really examined the sustained and searching relational structures in the second half of Rich's career in poems. At times, indeed, it appears that the point has been not to engage. Reviews of the collections *Later Poems: Selected and New, 1971–2012* (2012) and *Collected Poems: 1950–2012* (2016) illustrate this reality with stark clarity.

Both of these books enabled and encouraged (and, for reviewers, *required*) serial or global readings of Rich's later works. Judging by the reviews and essays dedicated to these volumes, this is a task that critics were unprepared to undertake. The published reviews of these volumes differ quite drastically from one another in all ways except one: nobody really seems to know what to make of Adrienne Rich's poems from 1981 to 2012. The two most extensive reviews of *Later Poems* betray their authors' intolerance for what they understand to be Rich's politicized view of poetic vocation. Cynthia Haven's "The Suffering of Others: On Adrienne Rich" (2013) compares Rich's later poems' supposed artlessness with a "Twitter feed" and their "heavy rhetorical baggage" with "aesthetic toxicity." Ange Mlinko's "Diagram This: On Adrienne Rich" (2013) argues that Rich's "impact on poets of the last couple generations has been weak," in part because Rich's stress on meaning misaligns with the training that writers now receive in academic workshops. Mlinko quotes Cathy Park Hong's observation that many later writers have been "raised on a diet of negative capability" and taught that poems "should quiver with equivocation."

Contrasting sharply with the barbed, takedown tone in reviews of *Later Poems,* a chorus of celebration greeted the posthumous appearance of Rich's *Collected Poems.* Maybe readers (and editors who assign such essays) had had time to prepare themselves for a respectful send-off appropriate for a poet of Rich's stature. Still, even Dan Chiasson's perceptive "Boundary Conditions" (2016), published in the *New Yorker,* characterizes Rich's career largely in terms of negative gestures: "She grew as a poet by self-repudiation . . . disowning, with real pain, her delegated roles as wife, mother, straight woman, and privileged white American." There's truth there. But it misses the overwhelmingly affirmative nature of Rich's career: the ever-shifting record of self-creation, of solidarities and intimacies (and pain) embraced, of political and moral dangers engaged and clarified in poems over six decades. In "As in Tendrils a Transparency" (2006), Roberto Tejada counters such one-dimensional accounts of Rich's supposed "grim intellectuality." He argues that her poems are "powerful reminders that it is still possible to address the catastrophe of the historic present and to resist its harrowing world effects with a sensual optimism of body and language." *Outward* focuses on how the various tendrils of Rich's critiques, studies, and affirmations are woven together in her attempts to, in Tejada's words, "reclaim an exhausted body and . . . make syllables smolder anew."

Rich's constantly evolving longevity makes global statements about her career elusive. Chiasson links Rich to Yeats, and there is certainly a connection—especially early in her career—but it wears a mask. According to Chiasson, "The key to Rich's genius, in fact, is Yeats's famous aphorism, maybe the best thing anybody ever said about the art: 'We make out of the quarrel with others, rhetoric, but of the quarrel with ourselves, poetry.'" Though presented as a compliment, this remark quarantines Rich's poems—and the lyric or poetry in general—in a way that Rich actively resisted and eventually overcame. In the foreword to her collection of essays *Arts of the Possible* (2001), reiterating an explicit theme in her poems dating to the early 1970s at least, Rich warns against essentializing the personal element in her poetry: "For more than fifty years I have been . . . a poet of the oppositional imagination, meaning that I don't think my only argument is with myself." In his compliments, in effect, Chiasson enlists Rich's work as a character witness against its own core intentions. The results reinforce our impression of the lyric as an essentially inward-looking device. As Craig Werner notes in "Trying to Keep Faith: Adrienne Rich's 'Usonian Journals 2000'" (2006), Rich's career attests powerfully otherwise. Werner highlights how, more than arguing with herself, Rich's later poems combine "her rejection of conventions predicated on patriarchy and white supremacy" with "her belief in the value of embodied political passion."

In his likewise laudatory review of *Collected Poems* for the *New York Times Book Review* (2016), Wayne Koestenbaum presents an alternative to the critical claims of artless rhetoric in reviews of *Later Poems*. He trains the ear to "physiologies" of Rich's language in her "revolt against tamed sound." In ways like Chiasson, Koestenbaum reads Rich as an architect of discreet (if politically resonant) lyrical bursts: "She founded a perpetually astonishing body of work" that moved in "illuminating flashes." This is important for sure. But, as if playing one side of a dialectic, this praise reins in a career of poems that—beginning possibly with "Apology" (1961) and intensifying all the way until the end—pushed beyond epiphany and astonishment to build bridges of connection along a disenthralling rhythm reaching toward clarity. Once more, the clarity Rich sought in poems grew increasingly mutual. She came to understand, in effect, that people in real danger—from threats interior, personal, and political, local and global—cannot afford to depend on flashes of astonishment and quiverings of equivocal disquiet, no matter how negatively capable the instructor lauds them for being. Koestenbaum, reading poems that Rich arranged in rigorously chronological terms over decades, still relies on single statements that propose to cover the whole of her career, as if her songs of "long vowels and keen consonants" floated along in a space dislodged from the place of the poet's (and reader's) body in successive eras of history. Increasingly throughout her career, Rich disavowed this kind of lyrical free-floating in principled and unmistakable terms. The music of Rich's most powerful work tunes itself into subversive, relational solidarities and sounds its way toward engaged mutual presences in contest with (not detachment from) history's dangers and trials. This book is a detailed map of that journey.

Unlike reviews of *Later Poems* that warn us away, reviews of *Collected Poems* invite us on a journey, and a long one. But these readings of

Rich's career offer at best untrustworthy signposts and almost no map at all for half of the trip. As such reviews accumulate, the message seems to be this: if we can't avoid a long conversation with Adrienne Rich's poetry, here's how we might navigate her career without having our sense of poetry—and experience—disrupted too profoundly. Let's look for astonishing moves in phrases while understanding that, in the end, Rich is really arguing with herself. At best, this is a profoundly insufficient approach. At worst, these readings, whether caustic or celebratory in tone, amount to a cover-up, repudiation by omission.

On the other hand, major essays about Rich's *Collected Poems* by Claudia Rankine and Sandra M. Gilbert testify to a profoundly shared sense of connection and purpose that arose in their readings of Rich's work. The connections were not about similar arguments these poets just happened to have with themselves. A few reviewers—all of them women—understood that the key was a deepening and widening sense of mutuality. In "A Life Written in Invisible Ink" (2016), published in the *American Scholar,* Gilbert quotes Ruth Whitman's remark about the collective (social and political) capacity of Rich's work: "in one woman the history of women in our century." Gilbert, recalling her "own feminist awakening" illuminated in Rich's poems in the 1960s and 1970s, and rereading those works in the *Collected Poems,* "realize[d] how much of what she said I didn't really grasp, even as I'm more than ever astounded by her body of work." But the clarity of Gilbert's identification with Rich's feminism, too, dissolves after 1980.

In "Adrienne Rich's Poetic Transformations" (2016), which appeared in the *New Yorker* and also serves as the introduction to the *Collected Poems,* Rankine extends the impact of Rich's work beyond the brackets of gender/sexuality in the 1970s:

As a nineteen-year-old, I read in Rich and [James] Baldwin a twinned dissatisfaction with systems invested in a single, dominant, oppressive narrative. . . . Rich claimed, in "Blood, Bread, and Poetry: The Location of the Poet," from 1984, that Baldwin was the "first writer I read who suggested that racism was poisonous to white as well as destructive to Black people." It was Rich who suggested to me that silence, too, was poisonous and destructive to our social interactions and self-knowledge.

Rankine describes how Rich's career created a public terrain for writers whose work "questioned paternalistic, heteronormative, and hierarchical notions of what it meant to have a voice," so that these writers would not have to "experience their own work as 'sporadic, errant, orphaned of any tradition of its own,' to quote from her foreword to her 1979 book *On Lies, Secrets, and Silence*." Eavan Boland, in her perceptive review of *Later Poems* for the *New Republic* (2012), offers one useful global statement: Rich "re-united the public poem with the political one . . . an enormous achievement."

While the reviews noted above and a few other scholarly essays do highlight important aspects of Rich's later work, we still lack a structure that would enable readers to engage the deep logic of the poet's development in the true sense of a full career. A range of scholarly essays engage the public, political nature of Rich's later poems. These essays position the author as a radical "citizen poet," a poet whose work plays a self-consciously activist, public role in the world beyond its strictly literary and traditionally inward-looking lyrical domain. Among the best of these essays about Rich's later work are Mark Nowak's "Notes toward an Anti-capitalist Poetics" (2006); Werner's "Trying to Keep Faith"; William S. Waddell's "Where We See It From: Adrienne Rich and a Reconstruction of American Space" (2007); Lin Knutson's "Broken Forms: Land, History, and National Consciousness in Adrienne Rich's Poetry: 1989–1995" (2007); Maggie Rehm's "'try telling yourself / you are not accountable': Adrienne Rich as Citizen Poet" (2017); and Jeannette E. Riley's "'questing toward what might otherwise be': Adrienne Rich's Later Work" (2017). As I read the scholarship and reviews of Rich's later career, two pieces stood out: Clark's "Human Rights and the Work of Lyric in Adrienne Rich" and Cynthia R. Wallace's brief review "Adrienne Rich: *Later Poems*" (2013). With its archival sources and specificity, Michelle Dean's essay "The Wreck" (2016) is particularly noteworthy, because it provides a valuable account of the forces at work in one key era of important change in Rich's life and career (late 1960s–early 1970s). Despite these contributions, we still lack an adequate vision of how the structures in Rich's poems shifted over the final three decades of her career. This dilemma is relational. It weakens our ability to respond intensely and coherently to the series of crucial calls made in her later works. The result is a diminishment of our capacity for presence, for what Muriel

Rukeyser called the "moving relation between the individual consciousness and the world."

So it is precisely at that point (chronologically, aesthetically, and politically) where *Outward* makes the balance of its contribution. In the
present account, during the first half of her career, Rich's poems betray
shifts at the core of what is known as lyrical, shifts away from the introspective (focused within a person) to what I'll term the "interspective"
(focused between people). Setting up the trajectory of her later career,
as they play out across the decades, these moves profoundly alter the
nature of creative solitude, an alteration that radiates through Rich's career as she sought ways to grow more radical with each decade. More
radical? What might that mean? Rich's later work answers that question
in waves of left-verging and delving images across decades, images that
seek and salvage living connections between people while thwarting the
evolving means of quarantining and dividing people's lives. Along these
lines, *Outward* charts a radical geography: Rich's creation of an ever-
shifting, subversive, and socially engaged sense of creative "solitude."

To understand the sinuously subversive scope of Rich's career in
poems, it helps to have a basic sense of the tradition she entered and
a precise sense of where her work engages and expands that tradition.
Generally speaking, the traditional lyric has been an inward-looking device. In the preface to the 1802 edition of his *Lyrical Ballads,* William
Wordsworth defines poets as those who, "from the motions of their
own minds merely," create sensations in writing that "nearly resemble
the passions produced by real events." The nature of lyrical creation for
Wordsworth turns exactly on the poet's *own* powers of re-creation set
apart from the surrounding world. The poet, according to Wordsworth,
composes using "especially those thoughts and feelings which, by his
own choice, or from the structure of his *own* mind, arise in him without
immediate external excitement" (italics mine). In short, as employed by
poets, Wordsworth's concept of lyrical solitude is meant to convey freedom from external constraint and social limitation: autonomy. In Rich's
reading, however, intensified by modern industrial and social structures,
by the mid-twentieth century, even—maybe especially—for those privileged enough to have rooms of their own in which to encounter it, lyrical solitude means becoming "unavailable to others"; it represents isolation more than freedom. At times, Rich thought, such lyrical solitude
proposed isolation *as* freedom.

The first step in Rich's reconception of lyrical solitude resists this sense of isolation, which she increasingly considers to be a pillar of patriarchal ideology. Indeed, images in her early work ("An Unsaid Word," 1951; "Ghost of a Chance," 1962) betray traces of what Rich would initially term the "estranged intensity" of masculine isolation. By the early 1970s, and imprinted by the suicide of her estranged husband in the fall of 1970, she identifies isolation as a potentially lethal affliction, a key symptom of patriarchal design. Isolation was woven into the cultural and political norms of the time; it operated as a badge of cultural attainment and sophistication. In "The Ninth Symphony Of Beethoven Understood At Last As a Sexual Message" (1972), Rich hears the "music of the entirely / isolated soul." In addition to the cultural prestige isolation carries, Rich reads it as a masculine social legacy in a militarized history. In "Dien Bien Phu" (1973), isolation extends the violence of warfare as a nurse moves among men who are "terribly alone." Like malfunctioning military ordnance, figures stricken in these ways are prone to antisocial outbursts: "each man she touches / is a human grenade / an anti-personnel weapon." When it operates with the force of a principle, isolation becomes, as Rich writes in "Merced" (1972), a dangerous feature of "a world masculinity made / unfit for women or men."

By the mid-1980s, Rich suspects that, together with class privilege, whiteness intensifies the isolation of the men—and women—whom she meets, whose stories and poems she reads. Recounting a litany of gendered isolations, Rich pauses, in section IX of "An Atlas of the Difficult World" (1990–91), to interject: "I wonder if this is a white man's madness." If it is, she concludes, "I honor your truth and refuse to leave it at that." She meant that. As she depicted in poems such as "Virginia 1906" (1983), Rich found that racial isolation afflicts white women—even feminist activists, herself among them—separating them from their nonwhite counterparts and (at least potentially) from compatible artistic and activist traditions. Her poems from the 1990s and up until the final weeks of her life, in fact, leave a detailed and engaging record of precisely how, in "refus[ing] to leave it at that," she took it from there.

Outward attends to how Adrienne Rich's career remade the lyric into an ever-evolving public and political—as opposed to strictly private and personal—vehicle. Resources for lyrical invention and social momentum were not essentially one's *own*. Some inventions and momentum, in fact, could not be created by secluded geniuses who were white men

with wealth. Many forces could be—even had to be—generated mutually and collectively; very often they were the products of relationships.
Thus, the surviving substance of this lyrical force could not be owned,
it had to be shared. Along these lines, this book maps a series of shifting
solitudes in which Rich expanded and extended the nature of the lyric,
of poetic process, and of the space (the solitude of reading and writing)
in which it takes place.

There are identifiable stages in this process. The first two chapters
trace contours in the first half of Rich's career, the second chapter concluding with Rich's realization of a lesbian-feminist "relational solitude"
in *The Dream of a Common Language* and *A Wild Patience Has Taken Me
This Far*. In these books she explores the power and complexity of a creative solitude patterned by mutual energies. The importance of mutuality resonates publicly from Rich's acceptance of the 1974 National Book
Award on behalf of fellow finalists Alice Walker and Audre Lorde, and
on behalf of all silenced women. From there Rich's career proceeds in
ways beyond the brackets of feminism as such. That she worked beyond
the brackets of feminism should not be taken to imply that Rich became a postfeminist or left important ongoing solidarities and critiques
of feminism behind. She never did that. Instead, successive phases of
her career in poems from the early 1980s onward make it increasingly
obvious that, as Marilyn Hacker puts it in "The Mimesis of Thought"
(2006), because "Rich took a woman's worldview to be emblematic, her
inquiries did not stop—as they had not started—at questions of gender."

The third chapter charts an expansive "social solitude" in the 1980s
(*Your Native Land, Your Life*, 1986; *Time's Power*, 1989; *An Atlas of the
Difficult World*, 1991) that culminated with Rich's most politically extensive, racially inclusive poetic sequence, "An Atlas of the Difficult
World." In social solitude, relational patterns cross borders between
inherited racial, classed, and geographic (in addition to gendered and
sexual) territories and identities. While no one has explored these signal elements of Rich's later career adequately, at least two scholars have
noticed their centrality. In "Human Rights and the Work of Lyric in
Adrienne Rich," Miriam Marty Clark highlights the searching relational openness in Rich's later poems. She notes the intensity and power
of Rich's "attention to the join between her own experience and the
experience of others" as a feature linking the eras of her full career, in
fact, eras that change as the poet fathoms "figurative strategies of affilia-

tion" in ways that shift across the decades. In her brief review "Adrienne Rich: *Later Poems,*" Cynthia R. Wallace observes how complex and at times competing urgencies toward mutuality provide the basis for how Rich's approach to the lyric developed. Wallace writes: "Rich's poems do not tend to be narratives or mellifluous lyrics: more frequently they are snapshots, speeches, questions stacked on questions. . . . The result of these various voices, insistent questions, and second-person pronouns is a certain air of *populatedness* in *[Later Poems]*. Read together, the poems suggest the multiplicity of human life, the negotiations of relationship, the responsibility implicit in dialogues both intimate and public." In these ways Rich's poems seize upon the relational textures of creative solitude that she realized under self-conscious feminist auspices and adapt those textures to resist increasingly broad and complex social and political predicaments.

The fourth chapter focuses on the experiential results of relationships that cross and challenge historical divisions. I call the first of these "fugitive solitude" (*Dark Fields of the Republic,* 1995). In the mid-1990s Marxism became a major factor in Rich's search, in poems, for politically vibrant relationships. As it turned out, paradoxically, the experience of figures who achieved connections to each other across historically policed borders took on a "fugitive" or "outlaw" quality. Images in these poems feature figures who steal away to sustain a sense of mutuality that violates norms enforced by identities as chartered by dominant social custom and institutions. As these fugitives come to terms with the mutual implications of their marginal status, they eventually find ways to cooperate in resisting the systems of division and quarantine that surround them. In these spaces, in the late 1990s, Rich's poems evoke a new energy: "dissident solitude" (*Midnight Salvage,* 1999; *Fox,* 2001). In 1997, Rich signaled this stage of her career publicly by refusing the National Medal of Arts bestowed by the Clinton administration. In ways that included but expanded on the terms of her acceptance of the 1974 National Book Award on behalf of all silenced women, Rich refused the National Medal of Arts on behalf of all laborers—artists such as herself included—whose work was demeaned and whose lives and communities were imperiled by the neoliberal policies of the Clinton administration.

The fifth chapter features images of a twenty-first-century "radical solitude" (*The School among the Ruins,* 2004; *Telephone Ringing in the Labyrinth,* 2007; *Tonight No Poetry Will Serve,* 2011). Radical solitude establishes images of mutuality among speakers threatened by alienation from themselves and isolation from each other in ways more subversively subtle and tactile than those for which American discourses of "identity" can account. In images of radical solitude that bristle with futurity, the liberal tradition of autonomy collapses as subjects connect with each other, suffused in the practical methods and media of resistance smuggled into the twenty-first century via the preceding succession of solitudes. Structured in this way, the itinerary of readings in *Outward* traces and distills Rich's career in poems along a path of outward-radiating engagement between subjects, the lyric, and their ever-shifting historical situation.

Finally, I want to include a note about my relationship to Adrienne Rich. We met when she chose my first book of poems for the American Poetry Review/Honickman First Book Prize. We first spoke just before New Year's Day in 2000. We began to exchange letters in early 2001, when she was drafting a foreword for that book. At the end of that exchange she encouraged me to stay in touch, which I did. In short order, we became friends and colleagues, partners, of a sort, maybe of a strange sort. I was in my early thirties and navigating the early years of marriage, parenthood, and what appeared to be a writing career; in this respect Adrienne understood the various pressures my wife, Stacey, and I were under better than we did. As for writing, I came to literary arts out of experience more than out of academic study. And I'd never had any connection to the field of "creative writing" at a university. Born to an immigrant, bricklayer father in the Midwest, I'd also lived (what might now be called) a racially nonbinary life athwart the divisions of American apartheid from the time I was a child. Adrienne and I shared a deep love of and respect for music, especially Black music. In the foreword to my book she wrote: "Mr. Pavlić has listened closely to our most profound American art, the blues and jazz, and that music has . . . allowed him to explore a mesh of experience extraneous to literary theories." Somewhere in the midst of these forces in our lives, and in our work, Adrienne and I found much to discuss.

At the time we met, I knew her work—a few essays more than poems—only slightly, though of course I knew *of* her work. I found that she was game to discuss poems, ideas, life, music. My early impression was that she seemed willing to engage anything except foolishness. We wrote each other about our work, mine just beginning, hers picking up just before the publication of *Fox,* a copy of which she sent to me. By 2003 or so we were exchanging pretty much everything we wrote and notes about much that we read; we wrote notes and letters to each other multiple times each week, a correspondence that lasted up until the last weeks she was alive. I've never met a person more willing—in fact, driven—to engage in conversations and meditations on what living here on the planet is all about. Adrienne was uniquely *able* to be present in nonreductive but still coherent ways. Knowing her as I did, that was my accumulating impression over the years.

The one thing we didn't talk about much was her previous work, though her previous life came up often enough. We dealt with each other as much as possible as contemporaries, which we both kind of were and most certainly were not. What is important to share, I think, is that for those years I was reluctant to go back and "study" her career. It felt like it would be strange to research the life of a friend I was writing to and talking with all the time. But when she died, I decided to read and reread all she had written, especially the poems, which, as she had made very clear, constituted the most meaningful element of her work. Adrienne said that she wrote essays on assignment, and of course she was extremely good at it. Her essays are important. But she always maintained that the poems came from a denser and more necessary place. Poems made things possible in unique ways. So in a way to continue our relationship after she died, I started to read and reread her books of poems in sequence, keeping quotes and notes in unlined notebooks. I also read the books of essays, but I went back to reread the poems in first editions, and again in selected volumes, and finally in *Collected Poems.* I called these readings an "underwater itinerary." I told people I was trying to learn some of what she taught me, or teach myself some of what I'd learned through knowing her. After a few years I began to sense a structure wound into the textures and rhythms of the images, passages, and stanzas. I was conscious that part of what I sensed was there on the pages and part of it was in memory from our conversations and letters. In order to check and clarify my sense of structures as they emerged from my readings, I began to write essays; those essays eventually became this book.

To the extent possible, I did not want this book to be about Adrienne, and certainly not about our friendship and the ways we worked together over those years. That's for elsewhere, maybe. But in a way similar to how most of Adrienne's poems are simultaneously about her and about much more than her, inevitably there are many connections between the structures in the poems identified here and the sense I make of them and the ways Adrienne and I knew each other. There are things I know that come directly from knowing, writing, and talking with Adrienne. I note some of them as they arise in the discussion, but I include only those moments that seem crucial to the substance of what this work is about.

What is this book about? I think of it as a geography, or maybe something like an MRI. In the chapters that follow, I trace the deep, ligatory structures of Adrienne Rich's career in poems. I remember Adrienne once told me that her therapist stopped a session to interject, "You have a thirst for relation." Much of what this book charts grows from the way Adrienne's life and work were driven by that need. But this book is also about one friend trying to know another through poems and, through that effort, to learn something about shared dimensions of the world. And in that effort, I'm trying to be as nonreductive and coherent as possible. This book is about how such an effort can uncover, clarify, and intensify what we can think of as possible, what we can know about the lives within and between us: *how we are with each other.*

"Our words misunderstand us."
Poems toward an Aesthetics of Experience, 1951–1970

"And we by now too wise"
Formalist Years

In the elite world of Ivy League poetry where Rich found herself ("fogged-in") as a teenage poet, the rules were as clear as they were rarely stated. In *A Change of World* (1951), her first book, chosen for the Yale Younger Poets Award by W. H. Auden, time and nature present themselves as unswerving and unanswerable brackets to human action. The job of the poet is to describe the nature of the human predicament responsibly and ably within those given parameters. As in Rich's poem "The Ultimate Act," nothing can be learned that is not instantly stabilized, no desire can be left prey to "the world's corruption." The students and poets who populate the book, as the detached and responsible inheritors of the impartial duties of the elite, must "do the things left to be done / For no sake other than their own." But is this the poet's own sake or the poem's? Turns out it's both, each detached from the other and the poet safely separate from the person. Poems for the sake of poetry and each person at the helm of his or her own future, a destiny cast about by powers that may be noted but never directly addressed.

In *A Change of World*, both experience and poems are essentially individual quantities best articulated in a transcendent solitude. In "Unsounded," "Every navigator / Fares unwarned, alone. . . . These are latitudes revealed / Separate to each." The individuated speakers in these poems are uneasy about their obligations to detached stability, but the poems are careful to assure that they speak on behalf of a new generation that understands its assignment. In "A View of the Terrace," "two furtive exiles" watch "the porcelain people" carrying out the elite social theater in which they will soon take their roles. Rich writes: "And almost we imagine / That if we threw a pebble / The shining scene would craze." Almost, maybe. But in ways no less than Ralph Ellison's would-be disruptor in *Invisible Man* (1952), who resigns himself to "a socially responsible role to play," Rich's poem ends in the pose of a maturity resigned to the stability of social structure, a poet who pledges allegiance to the conservative, stabilizing role of poetry:

> But stones are thrown by children,
> And we by now too wise
> To try again to splinter
> The bright enamel people
> Impervious to surprise.

After graduating from Radcliffe, supported by a Guggenheim Fellowship, Rich studied at Oxford and traveled in Europe. Much of her second book, *The Diamond Cutters and Other Poems* (1955), which she would later disavow as derivative, concerns her sojourn in Europe. By appearances, the poet Adrienne Rich was rolling along largely in sync with the formalist norms of the poetry she was raised (first by her father, later at Radcliffe) to write. But that path was about to change.

"Dear fellow-particle"
Beyond Formalism, Awakenings

Written from 1947 through 1954, the poems contained in Rich's first two books cover about one hundred pages in *Collected Poems: 1950–2012*. Marriage and the births of three sons (in 1955, 1957, and 1959) would drastically alter Rich's writing. The pace fell off markedly; poems from the next four years total less than six pages. Two poems, each one page in length, date from 1954, one from 1955, one from 1956, and another from 1957. When Rich regained her writing rhythm in 1958 and 1959, it is clear that a career was reinvented, not merely resumed. The changes are immediately apparent. Initiating a habit that would last throughout the rest of her life, Rich arranged the poems in her third collection, *Snapshots of a Daughter-in-Law: Poems, 1954–1962* (1963), chronologically, dating each with the year of its completion. The prosody is much less regular than in her earlier work, and, although Rich's lines would always be con-

sciously sculpted and finely tuned to her musical purposes, the first letters of lines are no longer capitalized.

But the most important changes are not strictly formal. *Snapshots of a
Daughter-in-Law* begins to recast the poetic project at every level. This
"bright enamel" poet has begun to splinter her world. The surprises start
with herself. The poems no longer advertise the "detachment from the
self and its emotions" that Auden had praised—"without which," he
confirmed, "no art is possible"—in his foreword for *A Change of World*.
The pose of universal vision and knowing has started to fracture, and
some of the figures and speakers in the poems are women. As Claire
Keyes observes in *The Aesthetics of Power*, it would take Rich another
decade to work her way out of the male-identified position she had inherited in poems and to link the voice speaking in her poems directly
to herself. But that process surfaces in *Snapshots*. Gone, too, are the un-
challenged notions of time as a metaphysical quantity and of thought
as a matter of unbroken, secluded concentration. Her life as a wife and
mother had bludgeoned Rich with the realization that all those supposed universals were really male (later she would explore the gendered,
classed, and racialized nature of such assumptions as well). Near the
close of the title sequence of the collection, the speaker informs: "Sigh
no more, ladies. / Time is male." For the speakers in *Snapshots*, time
doesn't fall upon the shoulders like a knighthood. It arises in the packed
and pressurized rhythms of the day: "Reading while waiting / for the
iron to heat, / *this is the gnat that mangles men.*" (In this poem's republi-
cation in *Poems: Selected and New* in 1975, and thereafter, Rich swapped
out the italicized quote from Emily Dickinson about time *"that mangles
men"* for one that identifies with a woman's frustration: *"My Life had
stood—a Loaded Gun—."*)

Still, Rich sensed that there was more to these immediate time zones
than a degraded version of male time. There was a unique kind of power
(and poetry) to be derived from forcing one's immediate circumstances
to feel, to think, and to speak. By 1960, in "Readings of History," we see
the poet studying her twin, a woman balanced against the minute-by-
minute pressure of her situation in life, in *her* life, which is a *woman's*
life: "The present holds you like a raving wife, / clever as the mad are
clever." In that space, thinking is not a matter of transcendental musing,
it is more immediate, less predictable. Subjectivity itself has been recast
in the moment: "What are you now / but what you know together, you

and she? // She will not let you think." Thought isn't the polished out-come of a stable route between being and knowing, first, because one doesn't *have* all day every day to get there.

A year later, in "A Marriage in the 'Sixties" (1961), the speaker attempts to address her husband and finds herself trying to communicate across a divide in their conceptions of experience: "They say the second's get-ting shorter—/ I knew it in my bones—." But the husband, in the spot-light of history's favor, goes ahead as if time is unbroken. The speaker observes: "Time serves you well." The poem ends with the wife reach-ing out to the husband, looking for a partner in a changed worldview, speaking from a radicalized experience:

> Dear fellow-particle, electric dust
> I'm blown with—ancestor
> to what euphoric cluster—
> see how particularity dissolves
> in all that hints of chaos. Let one finger
> hover toward you from There
> and see this furious grain
> suspend its dance to hang
> beside you like your twin.

The poet has been thrust out of the so-called universal (what turned out to be male) perspective and the kind of time and thought it entails, elements Rich had been raised to think of as natural and, naturally, to call her own. While addressing her immediate self-twin and taking ac-count of the company of other women—Jeanne d'Arc, Emily Dickinson, Mary Wollstonecraft—by allusion, she wonders if the new energy can transform for everyone those institutions cast in patriarchal mode, such as universal point of view, time, and marriage.

Rich's impulse to splinter the system controlling the structure of aes-thetics and experience would play out, by increments, in the long term. In the near term, the poet and her twin, the daughter-in-law, watch as the would-be partner in change, the husband/father, stays in the old, secluded mode. In "Ghost of a Chance" (1962), however, rather than a man facing forward on his pedestal of patriarchal power, the image is of a perilous and thwarted struggle to change, to evolve. The partner can't go forward. Instead, he is swept backward. Operating at the level of impulse, even the speaker's urge to protect her struggling partner re-inforces his seclusion:

You see a man
trying to think.

You want to say
to everything:
Keep off! Give him room!
But you only watch,
terrified
the old consolations
will get him at last
like a fish
half-dead from flopping
and almost crawling
across the shingle,
almost breathing
the raw, agonizing
air
till a wave
pulls it back blind into the triumphant
sea.

It's as if the speaker has borne sons who have come from elsewhere, from underwater, and learned to speak, crawl, and walk as demands of (the institution of) motherhood radicalized her apprehension of experience as well. Meanwhile, instead of transforming himself along with them, the husband/father is swept backward into the blindness of "old consola-tions" inherent in the patriarchal structures. At the time, these ideologi-cal structures were masked as natural (if not metaphysical) forces, "the triumphant / sea."

The poet's clarity of vision has been hard-won over several years in the new, more immediate, more phenomenological, element of womanhood foisted on her by the institution of motherhood in the 1950s. For her part, in "Apology" (1961), the poet records her reckoning in unmistak-able terms. Addressing her own version of "old consolations," rational-izations embedded in the so-called nature of womanhood that covered the bleary confusions brought on by the ceaseless labors entailed by the institutional role of the mother, she determines:

> I've said: I wouldn't ever
> keep a cat, a dog,
> a bird—
> chiefly because
> I'd rather love my equals.
> Today, turning
> in the fog of my mind,
> I knew, the thing I really
> couldn't stand in the house
> is a woman
> with a mindful of fog
> and bloodletting claws
> and the nerves of a bird
> and the nightmares of a dog.

In her mirror, but even more in her partner, she is looking for an equal to love but finds herself addressing a perilous fissure. In "The Lag" (1962), she figures the distance between the would-be partners in a conversation across time zones. Ostensibly calling back to the United States from Europe, but also addressing her husband from a threatened and transformed subject position, she writes: "I'm older now than you . . . / My words / reach you as through a telephone / where some submarine echo of my voice / blurts knowledge you can't use." For more than a decade, Rich's poems contended with just such a chasm in the world, in her life, a division encoded in the structure of the language itself.

Most important of all the transformations initiated in *Snapshots* is the notion of relational truth. Rich discovered that truth could be a social process rather than a preexisting form discovered by a detached and solitary thinker. To fathom such meanings was itself a process, a participation in rhythms of flux and transformation. These poems search for truths created mutually by the poet and her would-be partner/husband, her immediate self-twin, her ancestors, and contemporary women writers. At first in the submarine echoes and images of the voice appears a search for collective movement capable of refashioning what is known and how knowledge is produced and enacted in the world. Engaged with the immediate nature of time and in search of a relational truth, the speaker in "Double Monologue" (1960) says:

> I now no longer think
> "truth" is the most beautiful of words.
>   Today, when I see "truthful"
> written somewhere, it flares
>
> like a white orchid in wet woods,
>   rare and grief-delighting, up from the page.

The dimming vision of a solitary, possibly alienated, singular truth rests against the opening vista of a collective search, "unwittingly even," for ways "we have been truthful." The burgeoning mass movements of what would be remembered as "the sixties" and the collective spirit of protest and change that Rich would first engage in books like *Leaflets* (1969) and *The Will to Change* (1971) lay far ahead, at least for her. And, as we'll see, one by one, the impediments to relational truth-sensing are, like the orchid, coded white.

While still in Rich's future, models for the potential meanings and powers of collective movements were not totally out of sight. In "Rustication" (1961), set in the family summerhouse in Vermont, a place that recurs at intervals throughout most of Rich's career, we run across an image of an unforeseen form of power arriving on the American scene: "Marianne dangles barefoot in the hammock / reading about Martin Luther King." It's tempting to imagine the woman reading James Baldwin's article "The Dangerous Road before Martin Luther King," published in *Harper's* in February 1961. No matter what particular piece it is, the image makes it clear that a truthfulness of another structure, and emanating from another source of power, is in the world as well as in the "submarine echo" of the poet's quest. In the final years of the decade, Rich would connect means to power through collective action to the poet's submarine echo. But that's getting ahead.

Snapshots of a Daughter-in-Law scripted an awakened sense of self and a ruptured and altered sense of poetic craft and mission. Rich's next book, *Necessities of Life: Poems 1962–1965,* published in 1966, charted recalibrations by turns daring, driven, and careful. Also, acquired by

Denise Levertov for the list at W. W. Norton, *Necessities of Life* initiated Rich's association with the publisher of all her subsequent work published in the United States. The title poem is the first poem in the collection; it announces that the duties of decorum and renunciation at the core of *A Change of World* no longer apply: "I used myself, let nothing use me . . . // What life was there, was mine." This is by no means an easy declaration for a mother of three boys who loves her husband; nonetheless, the poems seek "to name / over the bare necessities" of engaged subjectivity initiated in *Snapshots*.

This claiming of experience, however, entails an opening outward more than a turning inward. Refusing to refuse feelings and perceptions at odds with the vision of life she had been raised to think into existence, in "Two Songs" (1964), the poet opens herself to stirrings at the thought of a young man she'd seen the previous day on a train, "touchingly desirable, / a prize one could wreck one's peace for." The poem concludes with a sensualist's nod to human drives considered low-down by the high-minded. In the mainstream of the early 1960s, for wives and mothers, these urges were coded in deepest privacy when admitted at all. In contrast, Rich acknowledges,

> I'd call it love if love
> didn't take so many years
> but lust too is a jewel
> a sweet flower and what
> pure happiness to know
> all our high-toned questions
> breed in a lively animal.

In this account, "pure happiness," of necessity, depends on an anarchic element that cannot be pinned down or contained.

In "Storm Warnings" from *A Change of World*, freedom is a shuttered, private enclave where one hides from unanswerable forces in "troubled regions" of the world. In "Double Monologue" from *Snapshots of a Daughter-in-Law*, "truthful" is a single "white orchid," isolated, rooted, set against the encroaching loam of the woods. In "In the Woods" (1963) from *Necessities of Life*, Rich openly resists assumptions about safety and fixity that control the meaning of terms such as

Happiness! how many times
I've stranded on that word,
at the edge of that pond; seen
as if through tears, the dragon-fly—

Against confining safety and stability, the vitality in *Necessities of Life*
depends on dynamic moments when "my soul wheeled back / and burst
into my body. // Found!" The two approaches appear to be incompatible. As if noting the fork in the road ahead, in "The Parting" (1963)
Rich measures the available routes toward poetic and experiential truth:
an active if vulnerable openness versus a fixed, defended safety. Of the
former openness, she writes:

You can feel so free, so free,
standing on the headland

where the wild rose never stands still,
the petals blown off

before they fall
and the chicory nodding

blue, blue, in the all-day wind.

And of safety provided by fixedness:

Barbed wire, dead at your feet,

is a kind of dune-vine,
the only one without movement.

Every knot is a knife
where two strands tangle to rust.

Occurring as they do in accord with the gendered ideology cloaked
in the guise of a natural, feminine inheritance, the needs of family, of
children, at times clearly operate in league with the barbed wire. As
constituted, family becomes a kind of women's quarantine. In the next
poem, "Night-Pieces: For a Child" (1964), Rich writes: "Your eyes /
spring open, still filmed in dream. / Wider, they fix me—." The poet watches

the protector/mother/wife transform into an angry and dangerous presence: "sphinx, medusa? / . . . Mother I no more am, / but woman, and nightmare." A year later, in "The Knot" (1965), she achieves a terrace of at least metaphoric clarity. "For years I never saw it," says the speaker, eyeing the red spot at the center of a blossom of Queen Anne's lace, "sitting in the whiteness of the bridal web." Echoing the stone throwers who threaten the "bright enamel people / Impervious to surprise" in "A View of the Terrace" from *A Change of World*, the red within the blossom becomes a spider who had been "there, all along, . . . // waiting to plunge his crimson knifepoint / into the white apparencies." The process of splintering vision with clarity won't be covered by any epiphany, however. And much of the process involves changes that are difficult to distinguish from injuries to self and others. Nonetheless, Rich's speaker is in for the long haul: "Little wonder the eye, healing, sees / for a long time through a mist of blood."

"Any Husband to Any Wife" (1965) follows "The Knot." The husband, any husband, sees the tumult as the natural ebb and flow of life. He sees his wife, any wife, like "the sea . . . / grinding and twisting, a turmoil of wrecked stuff." The husband stands in his role as provider of stability: "the pier stands groaning / as if the land depended on it." In the end, the storm passes and, "in aftercalm," the whole returns to its supposedly naturally unfocused state, "the black, blurred face to something we can love." But Rich's speaker does not feel bound to return to "aftercalm." By the end of *Necessities of Life*, in "Moth Hour" (1965), at least some part of the poet—attempting to break free of the rust and tangle seizing her in the image of mythic wife and mother—has taken to the wind: "I am gliding backward away from those who knew me / . . . When you put out your hand to touch me / you are already reaching toward an empty space." Still the cultural coding comes clear in images of whiteness as well as the speaker's impulses to seek freedom in individual flight ("I am gliding backward away") and claims of autonomy achieved through ownership ("what life was there, was mine").

Near the end of *Necessities of Life*, "Spring Thunder" (1965) is the first of Rich's poems to turn its lyric lens toward overtly political subject matter. Responding to President Johnson's escalation of the war in Vietnam with Operation Rolling Thunder, which began in March 1965, the poem connects Rich's consistent themes of nature, domestic life, and private life to warfare and to the image of the United States as a global empire: "Thunder is all it is, and yet / my street becomes a crack in the western hemisphere, / my house a fragile nest of grasses." The United States exhumes and embraces the extinct story of empires:

The power of the dinosaur
is ours, to die
inflicting death,
trampling the nested grasses:

Echoing her preference for the openness of poetic and free-blown personal truths over closed shutters, rooted flowers, and barbed wire, Rich gestures toward a rising horizon of counterintuitive political power:

power of dead grass
to catch fire
power of ash
to whirl off the burnt heap
in the wind's own time.

Snapshots of a Daughter-in-Law ends with "The Roofwalker" (1961), a poem in which the speaker openly seeks freedom from personal, domestic entrapment, "a roof I can't live under? . . . / A life I didn't choose." A kind of draftee herself—as a wife and a mother, at least in her mind, analogously conscripted—Rich identifies with the drafted soldier in "Spring Thunder": "No criminal, no hero; merely a shadow / cast by the conflagration." "Spring Thunder" joins the woman to the citizen, the strangling confines of domestic shelter to the overarching power of empire. Echoing "The Roofwalker" almost verbatim, the poem depicts a trap of global scale: "Over him, over you, a great roof is rising, / a great wall: . . . // Did you choose to build this thing?" At the close of the poem, the political rhetoric and military machinery of Operation Rolling Thunder unite in the image of a nation that casts a murderous shadow on the earth:

It is the first flying cathedral,
eating its parishes by the light of the moon.
It is the refinery of pure abstraction,

a total logic, rising
obscurely between one man
and the old, affective clouds.

Written in five sections that overlay the personal on the political, "Spring Thunder" gestures toward the next phase of Rich's career. In that phase, she will develop signals of personal recalibration such as those in *Snapshots of a Daughter-in-Law* and *Necessities of Life* into an experientially and politically engaged—and ultimately radical—poetic form.

"all these destructibles"
An Aesthetics of Experience

In 1964, apparently as a preface to a reading she did while working on *Necessities of Life*, Rich made a statement signaling her awareness that her approaches to her work and life were changing, converging, opening:

> I find that I can no longer go to write a poem with a neat handful of materials and express those materials according to a prior plan: the poem itself engenders new sensations, new awareness in me as it progresses. . . . I have been increasingly willing to let the unconscious offer its materials, to listen to more than one voice of a single idea. . . . In the more recent poems something is happening, something has happened to me and, if I have been a good parent to the poem, something will happen to you who read it.

About four years later, as she neared completion of her next book, *Leaflets: Poems 1965–1968,* Rich became involved in a translation project that helped her assemble a form matched to her intensifying need to expand and deepen her approach to encounters in (and between) her work and her life. She worked with Aijaz Ahmad on translations of ghazals by Mirza Asadullah beg Khan, known as Ghalib, a nineteenth-century poet who wrote in Urdu and lived most of his life in Delhi. In a letter to Ahmad, Rich described the importance of the experience of translating Ghalib's ghazals:

> *I needed a way of dealing with very complex and scattered material which was demanding a different kind of unity from that imposed on*

it by the isolated, single poem: in which certain experiences needed to find both their intensest rendering and to join with other experiences not logically or chronologically connected in any obvious way. . . . What I'm trying for, not always successfully, is a clear image of articulation behind which there are shadows, reverberations, reflections of reflections.

Taken together, these two statements chart the logics that contributed to a drastic shift in the form and scope of Rich's poems in the second half of the 1960s. After moving to New York City with her family in 1966, Rich began to access energies of political awakening and social action that further mobilized her work and life. She lectured at Swarthmore and Columbia University, and then, in 1968, began teaching in the SEEK program at the City College of New York (part of the City University of New York system). SEEK (which stands for Search for Education, Elevation, and Knowledge) was designed to help first-generation immigrants and people of color gain access to higher education, and Rich's work with the program brought her out of the elite perch of private northeastern universities and into close contact with the experience and intelligence of working-class and nonwhite New Yorkers. In her 2016 *New Republic* essay "The Wreck," Michelle Dean quotes from a letter Rich wrote to poet Hayden Carruth in which she said that applying to SEEK was "the only thing I've ever done from a political motive." Rich told Carruth that she had "applied for the job after King was shot, as a political act of involvement, from which I've gained such a sense of doing something practical and effective." That new sense of experience (political, practical, and effective) would provide a flexible grounding against which she would measure her life and work thereafter.

Rich's experiences in working on planning and preparation with SEEK colleagues such as June Jordan, Audre Lorde, Barbara Christian, Aijaz Ahmad, Toni Cade Bambara, David Henderson, and Addison Gayle were as transformative for her as what happened in the classroom, if not more so. Her activities in the program were among her first consciously political acts. Crucially, Rich's early work with SEEK took place during a period of radical change within the CUNY system as it entered the chaotic open-enrollment era, in which the classed, racialized, and gendered structures and goals of higher education were exposed and challenged. Throughout her life, she would remember her work with students and colleagues in SEEK as transformative.

Known as the first of Rich's radical books, *Leaflets* is really a transitional work. The cover of the first edition notes, below Rich's name,
"Author of *Necessities of Life*." In form and subject matter, the poems of
the first section, "Night Watch," resemble those in *Necessities of Life* more
closely than they do the latter poems in *Leaflets*. The war in Vietnam
lingers over the poet's family life, and images of empire and a failing patriarchy seem to appear from beneath the print of formally conventional
poems early in the book. In "Orion" (1965), the speaker addresses the
constellation as it stares

> down from that simplified west
> your breast open, your belt dragged down
> by an oldfashioned thing, a sword
> the last bravado you won't give over
> though it weighs you down as you stride
>
> and the stars in it are dim
> and maybe have stopped burning.

The poems have discovered new truths. New necessities have renewed the very nature of truth. The poet now searches about her for sur-
roundings that might further her quest. Instead, she finds relationships
seemingly designed and people seemingly compelled to hold the new
truths in check. Dissatisfaction intensifying, in "In the Evening" (1966)
she writes: "We stand in the porch, / two archaic figures: a woman and
a man." Insecure on new footing, "the old masters, the old sources /
haven't a clue what we're about, / shivering here in the half-dark 'sixties."
Rather than fulfilling the role of intrepid partner, her companion holds
on to her hand as if it were "a railing on an icy night." Turns out, as in
"Holding Out" (1965), the life she has helped build isn't about renewal
and furthering; instead, "the point is, it's a shelter." The early poems in
Leaflets script a painful stasis; in "The Key" (1967), she asks, "How long
have I gone round / and round, . . . I've covered this ground too often."
The poems know, have known, where they are headed; the poet can't
make the move.

In "5:30 A.M." (1967), a poem that is a kind of rewriting of "Apology,"
quoted above, Rich forswears the accoutrements of her shelter. First to
go are the drugs: "They've supplied us with pills / for bleeding, pills for

panic. / Wash them down the sink." Finally, her totemic animal, "The fox, panting, fire-eyed, / gone to earth in [her] chest," emerges as she prepares to defy the new truth, whose first appearance masquerades as mortal danger:

> No one tells the truth about truth,
> that it's what the fox
> sees from his scuffled burrow:
> dull-jawed, onrushing
> killer, being that

In order to survive, she'll need another image for the new truths. Something "gone to earth in [her] chest" knows that seeing the old way, "being that / inanely single-minded / will have our skins at last." Still, as in "Two Poems" (1966), the riddle of a self-interest that works somehow, dangerously, against itself brings her to what feels like the border of her right mind, "There's a secret boundary hidden in the waving grasses: . . . // The crazy ones push on to that frontier / while those who have found it are sick with grief."

Early in the second section of *Leaflets,* titled "Leaflets," we find the poet where we left her. In "Implosions" (1968): "My hands are knotted in the rope / and I cannot sound the bell // My hands are frozen to the switch / and I cannot throw it." Switch thrown or not, the quest continues almost without her, coming at her from every direction, as in "Continuum" (1968):

> and that poster streaking the opposite wall
> with the blurred face of a singer whose songs
> money can't buy nor air contain
> someone yet unloved, whose voice
> I may never hear, but go on hoping
> to hear, tonight, tomorrow, someday,
> as I go on hoping to feel
> tears of mercy in the of course impersonal rain.

Controlled by impersonal codes, as in "On Edges" (1969), she still involuntarily translates new ideas into portents of betrayal and doom. A woman seeking liberation from ideological duties she's told are natural "types out 'useless' as 'monster'"; an American-born Jew bent on leaving shelter to enter public protests and make change still types "'history' as 'lampshade.'" By the end of the poem, she is done with the premeasured tutelage of self-interest and the careful duties of the caregiver:

> Is this all I can say of these
> delicate hooks, scythe-curved intentions
> you and I handle? I'd rather
> taste blood, yours or mine, flowing
> from a sudden slash, than cut all day
> with blunt scissors on dotted lines
> like the teacher told.

One line break from "Continuum" hovers over Rich's poems from the late 1960s: "alive, whatever it is." If it's not all about private security—as she had put it at the outset of "Necessities of Life" (1962), "What life was there, was mine"—what *does* it mean to live? If freedom is something that can't be owned, something "money can't buy," then what? As we'll see, this question will find its answer in relational terms in 1974 and radiate defiantly outward throughout the rest of Rich's career.

Maybe it's right, then, that in 1968, as a teacher who feels almost murderously embittered by what she has been taught, Rich encounters the new truth in the form of a student, almost certainly a nonwhite student from her work in the SEEK program at CUNY. Responding directly to her challenge in "5:30 A.M.," she determines to tell "the truth about truth" without turning away. In broken stanzas, her second totally unpunctuated poem, "Gabriel" (1968), announces the new direction:

> There are no angels   yet
> here comes an angel   one
> with a man's face   young
> shut-off   the dark
> side of the moon   turning to me
> and saying: I am the plumed
>   serpent   the beast
>   with fangs of fire   and a gentle
>   heart

But he doesn't say that   His message
drenches his body
he'd want to kill me
for using words to name him

Back in her "bare apartment," the poet reviews American poetry for
lessons that can address Gabriel's presence. While she reads with this
student in mind, nothing answers the immediacy of the message that
"drenches his body":

words stream past me   poetry
twentieth-century rivers
disturbed surfaces   reflecting clouds
reflecting wrinkled neon
but clogged   and mostly
nothing alive left
in their depths

The call for a new truth meets with a new resolve, and the poet determines not to look away this time: "I get your message Gabriel /
just.   will you stay looking / straight at me / awhile longer." In the title
sequence, "Leaflets," the poet resets the goals of poetry: a new aesthetic
in which the living energies, not the objects themselves, are made to last,
to last by joining the unchanging fact of change. This would be a poetry
made for thinkers in motion, not seated, staring at the ground with the
elbow on the knee, the fist under the chin:

life without caution
the only worth living
love for a man
love for a woman
love for the facts
protectless

that self-defense be not
the arm's first motion

The poet is determined to liberate herself from the lethal safety of shelter. So the dashed-off and passed-on "leaflet" replaces Keats's timeless

urn as the aesthetic model, and, as if addressing her student's message-drenched dark body, in the final section of "Leaflets" she writes:

> I want to hand you this
> leaflet streaming with rain or tears
>   but the words coming clear
> something you might find crushed into your hand
>   after passing a barricade
> and stuff in your raincoat pocket.
>   I want this to reach you
> who told me once that poetry is nothing sacred
>   no more sacred that is
> than other things in your life—
>   to answer yes, if life is uncorrupted
> no better poetry is wanted.

With "Leaflets" the point of living is no longer a question of private possession—it is already inherently and openly relational even before these important changes are consciously understood, necessities shifting faster than understanding can track. The poem tracks:

> I want this to be yours
> in the sense that if you find and read it
>   it will be there in you already
> and the leaflet then merely something
>   to leave behind, a little leaf
> in the drawer of a sublet room.

Far from privately owned and possessed as it seemed to Rich in 1962, the room where what it meant to be alive flared into being was sublet; one's name wasn't even on the lease.

All of these successive, often colliding, shifts in her life and in her work prepared Rich to engage directly and deeply with one of the most important lessons that would emerge (no matter how tattered and embattled) from the twentieth century: neither the conscience nor the survival of the species can be entrusted (or subordinated) to the institutions established to the tune of the rational self-interest of modern individuals. Sleeping, waking, feeling, marching, and working collective energies would end the twentieth century and begin the twenty-first as the living, moral reservoir of redemptive action. Long brewing in working-class and nonwhite communities, those energies appeared to the middle-class (mostly white) mainstream—no small portion of which immediately began to mobilize into what ultimately became the Reagan reaction—in the 1960s.

Rich's first formal foray into the new poetry took its cues from the new necessity to respond immediately and with immediacy to extensions in her experience, from her work with SEEK students and colleagues, and from her exposure to the ghazal form. The final section of *Leaflets,* "Ghazals (Homage to Ghalib)," leaps forward. It has much more in common with the poems to come in *The Will to Change* than with anything else Rich had written to date. Written from July 12 through August 8, 1968, Rich's first set of seventeen ghazals constitutes the form of what would be, throughout the rest of her career, the spine of her most powerful and fully realized work: the extended poetic sequence. In a kind of preface to the final section of *Leaflets,* Rich explains her attraction to Ghalib and to the ghazal form in the translation project with Ahmad. She then adds:

> My *ghazals* are personal and public, American and twentieth-century; but they owe much to the presence of Ghalib in my mind: a poet self-educated and profoundly learned, who owned no property and borrowed his books, writing in an age of political and cultural break-up
> I have left the *ghazals* dated as I wrote them.

With the aesthetic and experiential presence of "Gabriel" still palpable, Rich's first ghazals continually push the readers' attention beyond the page, out through the window, down into the street, and into a much more immediate connection to their own lives—and, crucially, to each other's lives as well. Cued by the epigraph in *The Will to Change* from Charles Olson, Claire Keyes identifies traces of Olson's "projective verse" in Rich's new poetic openness. But the effects are already in the ghazals at the end of *Leaflets.*

This lyrical language exists *between* people and calls for words that as yet do not exist: "When I look at that wall I shall think of you / and of what you did not paint there." Concluding the opening ghazal: "When you read these lines, think of me / and of what I have not written here."

Rich opens the poetic island of what is said to the vast oceans yet unsaid, speakers gesture to the textures of darkness and shadow beyond the
white spotlight of the conscious mind. And everywhere in the ghazals
appear images of the *interactive* urge to relational speaking, thinking,
dreaming, and being: "Sleeping back-to-back, man and woman, we were
more conscious / than either of us awake and alone in the world." The
antiformalist's form draws everything said into the interactive processes
of a voice whose permanence is ephemeral, whose truthfulness is measured in the language—always different from itself—that comes next:
"These words are vapor-trails of a plane that has vanished; / by the time
I write them out, they are whispering something else." That interactive,
constant variability goes beyond the restricted possibilities of the indi-
vidually constituted, definitive statement, the dinosaur's aesthetic: "For
us the work undoes itself over and over: / the grass grows back, the dust
collects, the scar breaks open." And the new openness, the forward-,
outward-, inward-looking and *veering-into-next* (if we like, "projective")
orientation of each poetic moment, seeks its mirror in the social landscape, in relationships that insist upon risk, growth, and innovation.
The poet has had enough of relationships designed to rehearse human
confinement in the name of safety: "In Central Park we talked of our
own cowardice. / How many times a day, in this city, are those words
spoken?" She has learned that enclosed shelters are lethal. And openness
is dangerous. The poet seeks associations that will further growth rather
than rationalize fear: "The friend I can trust is the one who will let me
have my death. / The rest are actors who want me to stay and further
the plot."

In her foreword (June 2000) to *Arts of the Possible,* Rich notes that in
the 1970s, "gender was just beginning to be understood as a political cat-
egory." So at this point, race serves as a more explicit political touchstone
than gender. As if veering back to the metaphor of the threatened and
restrictive "white apparencies" in "The Knot," the second ghazal, dated
July 26, 1968, connects the dangerous restricting force of traditional relationships directly to American racial apartheid. Rich's language also
echoes her translation of Ghalib's "Ghazal XV" in the collection edited
by Ahmad. In its original, Ghalib's fourth couplet in "Ghazal XV" identifies the power of Islam to heal divisions and forge connections between
disparate tribes. In Rich's American translation, she converts the question of tribalism into one of racial division: "We are the forerunners;

breaking the pattern is our way of life. / Whenever the races blurred
they entered the stream of reality."

The ghazal she authored elaborates and intensifies its attention to the
American racial dilemma, focusing on white people's immediate need
for—as well as the risks, dangers, and errors inherent in—cross-racial
interaction. This was Rich's most explicit address to racial apartheid up
to that time, and it warrants quotation in full:

7/26/68: II

A dead mosquito, flattened against a door;
his image could survive our comings and our goings.

LeRoi! Eldridge! listen to us, we are ghosts
condemned to haunt the cities where you want to be at home.

The white children turn black on the negative.
The summer clouds blacken inside the camera-skull.

Every mistake that can be made, we are prepared to make;
anything less would fall short of the reality we're dreaming.

Someone has always been desperate, now it's our turn—
we who were free to weep for Othello and laugh at Caliban.

I have learned to smell a *conservateur* a mile away:
they carry illustrated catalogues of all that there is to lose.

By late summer 1968, the assassinations were in full swing at the highest
levels: King, Kennedy. All the casualties of the fast-radicalizing times
were not literal. In her essay "The Wreck," Michelle Dean notes that
Rich, clearly persuaded by the urgent criticisms of "LeRoi!" (Jones,
later Amiri Baraka) and "Eldridge!" (Cleaver), wrote to Carruth: "James
Baldwin is as dead as Medgar Evers. Was he always, or did he die a slow
death? I haven't reread any of the early essays or that first novel that
seemed so good to me five years ago." In a letter written within weeks
of Robert Kennedy's assassination, Rich wondered how to signpost the
volatile changes taking place within and around her. She concluded her
thought to Carruth: "Maybe our perceptions are getting sharper. Maybe
[Baldwin] sharpened them, blunting himself in the process." Years later,
Rich would return to Baldwin, judging him a necessary voice worthy of

repeated rereading. She would also return to Baraka's work, especially
his book *The Dead Lecturer* (1964). At the time, however, the stakes were
dire, the needs acute in both social and personal terms; the necessity
and reality of interactive meaning operated at every level of experience,
an intimacy that was psychological, intellectual, and even biological:
"When your sperm enters me, it is altered; / when my thought absorbs
yours, a world begins."

This is lyrical interspection, a process free from the ownership of individuals, quite beyond the capacity of what Wordsworth considered
the autonomous action of the poet's "own mind merely." As Rich paused
to note, Ghalib "owned no property and borrowed his books." She knew
well by then how the social and personal reinforced or conflicted with
each other, how easily one could be one's own worst-best friend: "To
resign *yourself*—what an act of betrayal! / —to throw a runaway spirit
back to the dogs." Enacting the personally and socially interactive insur-
gency she had in mind would require forging much anew. This would
entail mistakes, approximations, and translations; in a situation where
the reigning powers held sway over all faculties of stable understanding,
moments of blurred vision and half-developed truths passed back and
forth between people amounted to a kind of mutually intuitive counter-
intelligence. Perceptions and ideas in-and-of process were key, the end
results were often not the point: "In the red wash of the darkroom, I see
myself clearly; / when the print is developed and handed about, the face
is nothing to me." "If these are letters, they will have to be misread. / If
scribblings on a wall, they must tangle with all the others." "When they
read this poem of mine; they are translators."

In the darkrooms where extended and connective processes developed—processes taking place both within the person and between
people—refined and perfected ideals would be discarded or overthrown.
But that didn't mean utopian impulses would be forsworn: "I long ago
stopped dreaming of pure justice, your honor— / my crime was to believe we could make cruelty obsolete." Rich knew very well that the
existing psychological and political structures would not give way easily, or peacefully: "There's a war on earth, and in the skull, and in the
glassy spaces, / between the existing and the non-existing." At the end
of *Leaflets,* in the final ghazal, dated August 8, 1968, and dedicated ("for
A.H.C.") to her husband of fifteen years, from whom she would separate in 1970, she speaks to the real possibility of casualties in the battle

between "existing and non-existing" forms: "I'm speaking to you as a woman to a man: / when your blood flows I want to hold you in my arms." The ghazals that conclude *Leaflets* veer forward. The dangers were very real and some of them very nearby. By the time her next book, *The Will to Change: Poems 1968–1970,* was published in 1971, Rich's husband, Alfred Conrad, was dead by suicide, and the poet was deeply immersed in pursuing the path into an opening and deepening encounter with herself and her world.

Easily her most formally various and politically engaging book to date, *The Will to Change* takes its title from a line in Charles Olson's poem "The Kingfishers" and is dedicated to Rich's three sons. The formal variety in this volume would become the norm for Rich's future collections. *The Will to Change* does include a few single-page poems that appear to resemble those from previous works. But several multipage sequences constitute the spine of the book: "Pierrot Le Fou," "Letters: March 1969," "Pieces," "The Will to Change," "Photograph of the Unmade Bed," and "Images for Godard." To these Rich adds another series of precisely dated ghazals, "The Blue Ghazals," and the collection concludes with an extended, ghazal-like series similar to the one at the end of *Leaflets.* Titled "Shooting Script," this series includes Rich's translation of one of Ghalib's ghazals.

As the titles "Pierrot Le Fou" and "Images for Godard" indicate, the virtuosic filmic career of Jean-Luc Godard provided Rich certain cues for radical aesthetic development across turbulent times. From *Breathless* in 1960 to *Weekend* in 1967, Godard made fifteen feature films in the 1960s, leaving a politically charged and aesthetically anarchic streak across the consciousness of the decade. Famous for his declaration that "the cinema is truth 24 frames per second," Godard reinvented possibility in film, providing a case study for risk and renewal that matched and led (although he said it followed) the increasing speed of political and cultural change. In "Gabriel," Rich surveyed "twentieth-century" poetry looking for a vitality to speak to the times and the lives of her CUNY students in the SEEK program. She found the streams "clogged and mostly / nothing alive left / in their depths." In Godard she found an artist whose interrogations of his art and political critique provided a challenging and liberating guide for what might be possible. Godard's influence is nowhere more important than in the single most strikingly different work in *The Will to Change*. Among Rich's greatest single poems, "The Burning of Paper Instead of Children" (1968) operates much like a short film by Godard. Its direct engagement with the Vietnam War and antiwar protests and its mix of prose and burning lyricism, together with language quoted from a student's work, give this five-section series a new kind of power. The power is evident in responses from readers across generations as well as in the work's echoes throughout Rich's career.

From the first poem in *The Will to Change*, "November 1968" (1968), Rich's speaker is newly exposed and situated in unsheltered space. The collection opens: "Stripped / you're beginning to float free." The shifts away from the detached and objective pose initiated in *Snapshots of a Daughter-in-Law* have made certainties nearly—if not completely—impossible. If, by the end, *Leaflets* leaps ahead, *The Will to Change* charges headlong: "once the last absolutes were torn to pieces / you could begin." Addressing herself in the second person, the speaker is obscured by the new mode of being, even to herself:

> my ignorance of you amazes me
> now that I watch you
> starting to give yourself away
> to the wind

No longer cowering from new truths, the poet is now exhilarated by arrivals from the unknown and depends on them.

The third poem in *The Will to Change*, "Planetarium" (1968), marks a major event in Rich's career. The poem explores the career of the astronomer Caroline Herschel. In her essay "When We Dead Awaken: Writing as Re-Vision" (1971), Rich notes that "Planetarium" "was written after a visit to a real planetarium, where I read an account of the work of Caroline Herschel, the astronomer, who worked with her brother William, but whose name remained obscure, as his did not." The poem notes Caroline Herschel's overshadowed accomplishments, "in her 98 years to discover / 8 comets." Twinning interstellar space with the interior life, the charting of astronomy with the interior sounding of the lyric, the poem scripts a new lyrically expansive discovery. Transforming "sight" from an intellectual faculty back into an embodied sense, Rich connects the quest for discovery and the will to change: "What we see, we see / and seeing is changing." This has been true all along, but only now does the poet arrive at the realization that to be seen by the world is also to be *changed* by the world: "I have been standing all my life in the / direct path of a battery of signals." Such signals are responsible for the shape-shifting of women's images in the mirror, in the sky, and in the social/political imagination of a society: "A woman in the shape of a monster / a monster in the shape of a woman."

In "When We Dead Awaken" Rich remarks a much nearer discovery in "Planetarium." Noting the convergence of the poet and the speaker, a connection she had been aiming at since the early 1960s, Rich writes: "At last the woman in the poem and the woman writing the poem became the same person." Intuitively, the identity of poet and speaker as one might suggest closing down, closing in, closing off. But instead the poem describes a vast opening. The close of the poem sketches an opening and newly dimensional self, a woman of vast expanse and yet-to-be-determined shape, scant traces of which have as yet been charted:

> I am a galactic cloud so deep   so invo-
> luted that a light wave could take 15
> years to travel through me   And has
> taken

The two syllables "luted," after the line break midway through the word "involuted," place an emphasis on the musical complexity of the task at hand. And, via its homonym, a key word of the times, "looted," Rich emphasizes the brutal robbery of self perpetrated by the "battery of signals" that recast her image (and self-image) "in the shape of a monster." But looting also stood for the "liberation" of private property. Forswearing the detached objectivity of observation in a poem about a woman who works in an observatory, "Planetarium" and other poems in *The Will to Change* mean to stare back at the world and refigure the self in order to further the possibility of its active, protean reality. This will be invo-luted music to be sure, but also work with a pragmatic purpose that requires it be played as plainly as possible, though never simply:

> I am an instrument in the shape
> of a woman trying to translate pulsations

into images   for the relief of the body
and the reconstruction of the mind.

The emphasis on translation underscores the process-driven, interactive nature of the medium Rich envisions; the ghazal form as well as the antiformalist and open aesthetic she achieved through it at the end of *Leaflets* play key roles in *The Will to Change*.

Rich's pursuit and tracking of change required that she translate her aesthetic into a much more active role in her experience and extend it beyond the pages of the book. The material form of the book itself became an impediment to the goals of change. "The Burning of Paper Instead of Children" marks the complex goals of the new aesthetic. In three of its five sections, the poem contains the first prose sections to appear in Rich's poetry. In the poem's opening, one of the speaker's sons and his friend, a neighbor's son, have burned their math textbooks after the last day of school. The neighbor, "a scientist and art-collector," calls the speaker in horror: "'The burning of a book,' he says, 'arouses terrible / sensations in me, memories of Hitler; there are few things that upset / me so much as the idea of burning a book.'" The poem's events take place during the time of protest against American napalm strikes in Vietnam, and the speaker is not impressed by the neighbor's objections. She most certainly is not aroused. She imagines the ambiguous function of books in the lived intensity of human lives, the coexistence of books with the urgencies of living. In section 4, she writes:

We lie under the sheet
after making love, speaking
of loneliness
relieved in a book
relived in a book [. . .]

What happens between us
has happened for centuries
we know it from literature

still it happens

Literary form is no match for human passions:

sexual jealousy
outflung hand
beating bed

dryness of mouth
after panting
there are books that describe all this
and they are useless

No matter the content of a book, fetishizing the material object, she reasons, is part of "the oppressor's language." At times, so is reason itself: "*burn the texts* said Artaud." The speaker concludes: "The burning of a book arouses no sensation in me." People are the point: "I know it hurts to burn." Poems can sharpen and enliven life and intensify one's sense of the stakes. Otherwise, what's the point? "The typewriter is overheated, my mouth is burning, I cannot touch you and this is the oppressor's language."

During the period when this poem was written, as Michelle Dean notes, Rich had begun psychotherapy with noted psychiatrist Leslie Farber. She was also immersed in her teaching in the SEEK program at CUNY. Strung between these venues of discovery, Rich began to realize the boundaries inherent in using language (whether in poems or in psychotherapy) for the "relief of the body" and the "reconstruction of the mind." In this case it is the bourgeois subject's body and mind. The problems afflicting most people's bodies and minds, in fact, cannot be addressed through "a woman trying to translate pulsations." People's bodies won't be relieved by acts of translation. Their lives need *material* transformation, and the language furthering that *action* is not—to Rich's knowledge, has not been—at home in books. Such embodied energy defies translation into the oppressor's language. The middle section of "The Burning of Paper" records Rich's first fingerings of this reality. Apparently quoting from—rather than translating—a SEEK student's work, Rich transcribes verbatim:

"People suffer highly in poverty and it takes dignity and intelligence to overcome this suffering. Some of the suffering are: a child did not had dinner last night: a child steal because he did not have money to buy it: to hear a mother say she do not have money to buy food

for her children and to see a child without cloth it will make tears in
your eyes."

Like Rich says of Frederick Douglass's voice, the poem implies that perhaps this student's voice in life, maybe even in print, employs "an English
purer than Milton's." The section ends with the lyric parenthetical:

> (the fracture of order
> the repair of speech
> to overcome this suffering)

Exploring needed fractures in the surrounding structures and their
implications for Rich's subject, the poems in *The Will to Change* reach
out, and down. They beckon their borders, their limits, and seek out a
form that can engage the sight of a reader in order to throw a changed
vision back into the world when the eyes come back up off the page. In
these poems, *reading,* like seeing, is changing. As in "Letters: March
1969," this is a high-velocity—even higher-intensity—aesthetic: *"send
carbons* you said / but this winter's dashed off in pencil / torn off the pad
too fast." Engaged lyric craft depends on turning the gaze of the poem
(traditionally inward, introspective) inside out, mastering "that trick of
reaching outward." As in "The Blue Ghazals" (September 21, 1968–May 4,
1969), the tableau is interactive, every exchange politicized:

> City of accidents, your true map
> is the tangling of all our lifelines.
>
> *The moment when a feeling enters the body*
> is political. This touch is political.

The fracturing has only begun, but Rich has responded to the need
and begun to reach outward beyond the pages in defiance of "the oppressor's language." But, of course, much lies ahead. One instructive
moment comes in "Our Whole Life" (1969), which begins, "Our whole
life a translation / the permissible fibs // and now a knot of lies." Without
new instruments, the poet finds herself in the position of "Trying to
tell the doctor where it hurts." In this she identifies with a postcolonial
subject,

like the Algerian
who has walked from his village, burning

his whole body a cloud of pain
and there are no words for this

except himself

Maybe she has Albert Camus's existential subject in mind? Or perhaps
one of Frantz Fanon's patients? In a way, she is right. For his condition,
there are no words spelled with all "those dead letters / rendered into
the oppressor's language." But the individualistic, existential vocabulary
doesn't cover it. Still, one can be sure—as is the case in section 3 of "The
Burning of Paper"—that a language *does* exist to articulate shared valences
of such suffering. Those structures are not yet a part of Rich's poems.

Such a language understands that a person's body may be likened
to a *drop* of suffering. But, unlike the subject of psychoanalysis, the
"cloud of pain" leads elsewhere, is not centered in the self. And there are
most certainly words for that: brother, sister, neighbor, family, community. Sentences in this relational (or communal) language would most
likely bear the assumption found in "Ghazal 5" by Ghalib, translated
by Rich in the final sequence in *The Will to Change,* "Shooting Script"
(November 1969–July 1970). The key couplet attaches the need to speak
with a language for the collective-in-resistance, a noun conspicuously
missing from the oppressor's dictionary. Translating Ghalib, Rich writes:
"Grief held back from the lips wears at the heart; the drop that / refused
to join the river dried up in the dust." Rich had felt the pulse of collective action in the politics of the time, and she had long been aware of it
in the Black freedom movement, but she had not yet felt such a pulse in
the veins of her poet-speaker, who, as of "Planetarium," was now herself.
That would come to her, and she to it, in the mid-1970s as women's
movements came together and articulated themselves in words and in
action. Rich would play an important role in all of that. In 1971, that
was still a few years away from the poems.

Addressing the "battery of signals" coming at the poet amounts to
an act of continuous translation, indeed. The will to work, to *change,*
like this must operate at every level, to deal with a situation in which, as
in "Images for Godard" (1970), "all conversation / becomes an interview
/ under duress." The goal, the form, the verb, always displaced into the

next frame, each pulsation becomes an image that casts the eye beyond itself. By the time it comes back, it is no longer what it was: "To love, to move perpetually / as the body changes // a dozen times a day." Indeed, as it was in Godard's work from the decade, in which he often directed without a script, interviewing his characters—who were often enough his lovers—as the cameras rolled, *The Will to Change* casts a poetry in process, poetry *as* process, language come to life. There's little need and less time for copies, the carbons will not serve. "Images for Godard" concludes with the coda for the era, the logic furthering Rich into the next phases of her life:

> the notes for the poem are the only poem
>
> the mind collecting, devouring
> all these destructibles
>
> the unmade studio couch the air
> shifting the abalone shells
>
> the mind of the poet is the only poem
> the poet is at the movies
>
> dreaming the film-maker's dream but differently
> free in the dark as if asleep
>
> free in the dusty beam of the projector
> the mind of the poet is changing
>
> the moment of change is the only poem

Continuing would mean tuning her poems into a new kind of "submarine echo." Rich begins the next stage of her career as a diver mapping other pulsations, waves found deep in the psyche, as if along the bottom of the ocean.

"look at her closely if you dare"
Feminism and a Relational Solitude, 1970–1981

"answer me / when I speak badly"
Writing and Living beyond the Borders

At least since the poems of *Snapshots of a Daughter-in-Law,* Rich had followed moments of opening in her work often by backtracking or looping around to retrace her steps. A private—maybe a secret—moment of reckoning would fail to assert itself in her personal or social life; freeing energy from teaching in SEEK or found in public forums of protest and demonstration would evaporate in her domestic and interior life. This troubling stasis registered in her work, certainly provided topics for discussion with her therapists. Meanwhile, fearful of making irreversible changes, the *poet* waited for something to happen in her *life,* a *woman* watched for change on the *page,* a *wife* who loved her husband nonetheless marked needs most certainly not answered in her marriage and quarreled with a *mother* who loved her sons but profoundly dissented from her role in the institution of motherhood regarded as natural law by the patriarchal ideology of the world. These clashing dimensions of Rich's life appear in the structure of her poems.

The transition between the first (experientially awakened) and second (consciously feminist) eras of Rich's engaged career is possibly most clearly marked in the poem "Tear Gas" (1969)—written between *Leaflets* (1969) and *The Will to Change* (1971)—which again surveys the bridge between personal and social reality. The poem's epigraph refers to the deployment of tear gas against activists by military police during an antiwar protest at Fort Dix, New Jersey, on October 12, 1969. Against that backdrop, Rich measures her need to change her personal life, to end her marriage. In this she summons personal strength from the public sphere of political protest: "This is how it feels to do something you are afraid of. / That they are afraid of." She knows that fear marks a border—something like the phase change at which water boils and turns into gas—in the process wherein a person changes by moving between fields of experience:

> tears of fear, of the child stepping into the adult
> field of force, the woman stepping into the male field
> of violence, tears of relief, that your body was here,
> you had done it, every last refusal was over)

This change, however willed or desired, nonetheless feels differently threatening in personal space, space much more isolated than sheltered, space where shelter *is* the danger:

> and I am afraid
> of the language in my head
> I am alone, alone with language
> and without meaning

Finding herself at a familiar crossroads, the poet leafs back through her work. She quotes (in italics) a line from a previous poem—"Like This Together" (1963), in *Necessities of Life*—dedicated to her husband. In "Tear Gas," she writes: "coming back to something written years ago: / *our words misunderstand us.*" Tactically, the decade had shown her how to locate future meaning in the body, in *her* body situated in cooperative, progressive, politically engaged spaces such as those in the SEEK program at CUNY. The body, so situated, engaged with history, compelled the mind to follow:

> The will to change begins in the body not in the mind
> My politics is in my body, accruing and expanding with every
>   act of resistance and each of my failures
> Locked in the closet at 4 years old I beat the wall with my body
> that act is in me still

The needs informing poems are impossible to circumscribe in formal terms, they are experiential:

I need a language to hear myself with
to see myself in
a language like pigment released on the board
blood-black, sexual green, reds
veined with contradictions

Rich wrote "Tear Gas" while coming to terms with what it means
that lyrical creation is not essentially private, that part of experience can
be collective. She explicitly states the extraliterary priorities of this zone.
She measures the role of social speech against writing, which is still pre-
sumed to be a private, introspective act: "that things I have said which
in a few years will be forgotten / matter more to me than this or any
poem." Clearly Rich took poems and poetic form seriously; this resolu-
tion does not diminish that in the least. It does signal an intensified importance placed on experience—nonliterary life—and enjoins poems to
meet the needs and further the goals of experience in the life of a person
attempting to dispel an isolation she cannot fully name, shelter that she
cannot live within but fears to be without.

As if made possible precisely by the way this poetic voice can make
the speaker—as if standing in the shadow of the demonstrators—visible
to herself, "Tear Gas" solves the impasse between Rich's will to change
(pushing her forward) and her will to relation (which, up until now, has
been holding her back) so that, in life, both push in the same direction:

these images are not what I mean
(I am afraid.)
I mean that I want you to answer me
when I speak badly
that I love you, that we are in danger
that she wants to have your child, that I want us to have mercy
    on each other
that I want to take her hand
that I see you changing
that it was change I loved in you
when I thought I loved completeness

Just as the importance of a poem is no longer a strictly formal achievement, and the point of a poem may not (maybe should not) be on the

page at all, the most important communication is not, as Rich writes in "The Burning of Paper Instead of Children" (1968), a matter of "How well we all spoke." In "Tear Gas," she writes, "I want you to answer me / when I speak badly." So much depends on mistakes. These are hard lessons for a poet/daughter trained to be exceptional. "Tear Gas" reconciles the will to love with the will to change, the poem (or poet?) answers the power of fear by aligning love *and* change with the will to live:

> not in poems but in tears
> not my best but my worst
> that these repetitions are beating their way
> toward a place where we can no longer be together
> where my body no longer will demonstrate outside your stockade
> and wheeling through its blind tears will make for the open air
> of another kind of action

> (I am afraid.)
> It's not the worst way to live.

That doesn't mean one doesn't search for a different way to live and different ways to work.

In her essay "When We Dead Awaken" (1971), Rich began to assemble a categorical, feminist understanding of a terrain she had been dredging in poems since the late 1950s at least. An "imaginative transformation" required "a certain freedom of the mind . . . to enter the currents of your thought like a glider pilot, knowing that your motion can be sustained, that the buoyancy of your attention will not be snatched away." This kind of solitude was "in no way passive" and did *not* imply that a feminist creative imagination must "become unavailable to others, or . . . become a devouring ego. This has been the myth of the masculine artist and thinker; and I do not accept it." In relationships (intimate and collegial) with men, and in wide reading, Rich had come to understand that a certain "mood of isolation" pervaded "male poetic—or other— inspiration." Something often referred to as tradition had barred women from a healthy creative solitude. Something very similar, if not identical, and also called tradition had transformed masculine solitude into noncommunicative isolation. On behalf of women, Rich gestured toward an alternate structure and declared that there "must be ways, and we will be finding out more and more about them, in which the energy of creation and the energy of relation can be united." This transformative vision depended on a breaking of old patterns and a rewiring of complex new connections; it depended—as she wrote in "Tear Gas"—on "another kind of action." Newly conscious in Rich's prose, this search for creative relation had been at work in her poems for more than a decade.

"the truth / of the lies we were living"
Relational Beginnings

Diving into the Wreck: Poems 1971–1972 (1973) marks a shift in which Rich consciously ceases her accommodation of patriarchal structures and the "traditional female functions" they encode and begins an urgent search for alternatives. The poems immediately begin to resituate the energies of creation and relation. The poet explores a new space, a feminine depth that straddles the rational structures of the "traditional" world; crucially, in this creative depth, she finds that one can be alone but not isolated. In tandem with a connective solitude, the gestures and assumptions of relation also shift. For the first time, several of the poems feature conversations between women. In "Will, Change, and Power in the Poetry of Adrienne Rich" (2006), Hugh Seidman mentions a comment Rich made to him personally in the late 1960s that casts into valuable relief the new emphasis on conversations between women in her poems. Seidman recalls Rich telling him that "the only important subject for poetry was to define the relationship between men and women." Looking back on the first two decades of her poems, we can see that theme clearly enough, although it is by no means the only one. By the early 1970s, however, Rich had moved on, as she would many times.

The opening poem of *Diving into the Wreck,* "Trying to Talk with a Man" (1971), depicts the break. Conversations between men and women framed by the tradition are "condemned scenery." The couple arrives at a point of reckoning in order to talk, but silence surrounds and pervades their interaction. Tradition would appeal to a sense of security made possible by the sacrifices necessary to such relationships. But instead of security, the woman notices, "you look at me like an emergency" and "I feel more helpless / with you than without you." The next poem, "When We Dead Awaken" (1971), connects creative life and relational life in a world structured to keep them apart, a world in which "everything outside our skins is an image / of this affliction." The feminist work of reconnection starts in relational (re)creation of self and other:

> even you, fellow-creature, sister,
> sitting across from me, dark with love,
> working like me to pick apart
> working with me to remake
> this trailing knitted thing, this cloth of darkness,
> this woman's garment, trying to save the skein.

The feminine skein has been torn in many ways, in overlapping dimensions, but the rupture begins with "The fact of being separate." Such so-called facts work day and night, amounting to "disproof of what we thought possible" and fueling "doubts of another's existence." Even sensations of rupture, however, are useful because they bring women "closer to the truth / of the lies we were living." The newly connective, creative pulses are nascent, fugitive, endangered: "blue energy piercing / the massed atoms of a bedrock disbelief." But there they are.

A crucial reckoning begins at the forced recognition of the supposed "fact of being separate." This reckoning resonates in different dimensions across the rest of Rich's career. We will encounter its echoes many times in the remaining pages of this book.

In "Waking in the Dark" (1971), the new creators are surrounded by "the tragedy of sex." The spaces are isolated: "—the hermit's cabin, the hunters' shack— / scenes of masturbation / and dirty jokes." The old designs are powerful but even more endangered than the new creators: "A man's world. But finished. / They themselves have sold it to the machines." The new forager is a veteran, but she's no hunter; she walks in "the unconscious forest, / a woman dressed in old army fatigues." Even when alone and surrounded she is not isolated like the hunters who aim to kill; she follows a sense of living possibility:

> Nothing will save this. I am alone,
> kicking the last rotting logs
> with their strange smell of life, not death,
> wondering what on earth it all might have become.

The energies of cocreation are there, but submerged somewhere: "All night dreaming of a body / space weighs on differently from mine . . . / we move together like underwater plants." There must be a way to connect the dream possible to waking life, to "go on / streaming through the slow / citylight forest ocean / stirring our body hair." As yet, in the waking world known to the speaker, the gap still divides:

> But this is the saying of a dream
> on waking
> I wish there were somewhere
> actual we could stand

In "Incipience" (1971), the men are "asleep in the next room," while the new creators "sit up smoking and talking of how to live." They mark and move beyond the mode of masculine isolation:

> He has spent a whole day
> standing, throwing stones into the black pool
> which keeps its blackness
> Outside the frame of his dream we are stumbling up the hill
> hand in hand, stumbling and guiding each other
> over the scarred volcanic rock

Soon we'll meet climbers somewhat like these, but more radical, who, "hand in hand" and connected by a *cable of blue fire*," led Rich into her first realized image of relational solitude. But not quite yet.

Poems in *Diving into the Wreck* re-create sensual perception as a dialectical process of resistance and change. On one hand, the poems burn and blur feeling and awareness at various levels of consciousness into combinations disallowed by rational and social structures. In "The Mirror in Which Two Are Seen as One" (1971), verbs signify the non-identifiable and therefore uncontainable. The slippery action recovers lost feeling itself:

> She is the one you call sister
> you blaze like lightning about the room
> flicker around her like fire

dazzle yourself in her wide eyes
listing her unfelt needs
thrusting the tenets of your life
into her hands

In "Song" (1971), that straddling and uncontained existence "knows what it is," "knows it's neither / ice nor mud nor winter light / but wood, with a gift for burning."

On the other hand, as a counterpart to her sense of connective blurring and burning—and echoing poems such as "Apology" (1961) and "5:30 A.M." (1967)—Rich sharpens her will to cold clarity. In "From the Prison House" (September 1971), she begins:

Underneath my lids another eye has opened
it looks nakedly
at the light

that soaks in from the world of pain
even when I sleep

Steadily it regards
everything I am going through

But Rich is not describing a detached, journalistic pose of objectivity. Instead, she is after a visionary vision fitted with a politically resonant lens that perceives "detail not on TV" and focuses on "the violence / embedded in silence." This active, creative vision means not to be distracted or obstructed, least of all by itself, not even by the faculties of blurring and burning connection on which its twin seeing depends:

This eye
is not for weeping
its vision
must be unblurred

though tears are on my face

its intent is clarity
it must forget
nothing

The dialectical motion between nonrational burning-blurring and visionary vision that "nakedly" and "steadily" focuses things hidden by barriers
and silences keeps sensuality from fogging into sentimentality, clarity
from becoming simplicity, and certainty from solidifying into stupidity.

The result, as in "The Stranger" (1972), is a new kind of *force* capable
of a searching—if not yet consciously relational—solitude that does not
devolve into isolation. "Looking as I've looked before, straight down the
heart," Rich's speaker asserts a vision that can clarify without reduction,
that can assert itself without domination:

> walking as I've walked before
> like a man, like a woman, in the city
> my visionary anger cleansing my sight
> and the detailed perceptions of mercy
> flowering from that anger

This presence has a shifting but communicable relationship to itself,
clearly, and it is not to be found among the preexisting alternatives offered by the world:

> if they ask me my identity
> what can I say but
> I am the androgyne
> I am the living mind you fail to describe
> in your dead language

In "Tear Gas," the speaker remembers her bodily force from childhood, alone, beating against the walls of isolation. In "The Burning of
Paper Instead of Children," language is part of the wall of separation: "I
cannot touch you and this is / the oppressor's language." In "Dialogue"
(1972), the struggle with the language of isolation has become a *mutual*
endeavor, an action that soaks a barrier that is now permeable: "for
hours our talk has beaten / like rain against the screens."

"Diving into the Wreck" (1972) is one of Rich's most enduring and
famous poems. Its sense of submersion and descent has become nearly
synonymous with her work. As Rich told me once, the poem was written
during a period in which she was—or had recently been—gripped with
terror at the prospect of descending stairways. She had written about

divers before, in both cases in flight above water, and in both cases she had associated diving with a forfeiture of control. In "The Springboard," according to the formalist and deterministic assumptions surrounding *A Change of World* (1951), she wrote that "what makes the body shoot / Into its pure and irresistible curve / Is of a force beyond all bodily powers." In "Waking in the Dark," film footage of divers is set "at the Berlin Olympics" in 1936. No longer natural, the encounter with overwhelming force has been historicized, but still diving is a losing battle, "control; loss of control," followed by images of genocide:

> before the dark chambers
> with the shower-heads
> the bodies falling again
> freely

The final image of the section depicts the film of the divers as a dissent from rogue ideological power (Nazism) masquerading as natural law:

> A woman made this film
> against
>
> the law
> of gravity

(Here I reproduce the lineation used in printings of these lines after the first edition of *Diving into the Wreck*. In that edition, there was no open line between "against" and "the law." Given that the lineation quoted here recurs across Rich's subsequent volumes of selected poems and then in *Collected Poems,* I take it to be the version she preferred.) The film itself was made by Nazi collaborator Leni Riefenstahl, whose complex aesthetics and politics would draw Rich into a fascinating exchange of letters with Susan Sontag in the pages of the *New York Review of Books* in the winter of 1975.

In "Diving into the Wreck," Rich explores what she forecast in "Tear Gas" as "another kind of action," a new kind of diving. It is a risky encounter, part deliberate, part improvised, part blurred, part focused. It takes place in an element not under the ideological control of history and in which the figure can learn to navigate on terms unavailable in the "dead language" of stable structures and strict divisions between this and that. Likewise, the border between history and the diver's element is not marked or stable:

I crawl like an insect down the ladder
and there is no one
to tell me when the ocean
will begin.

Once the diver is submerged, terms shift: "the sea is another story / the sea is not a question of power." Unlike the divers in previous poems, who encounter "a force beyond all bodily powers" and fight battles against ideology masquerading as "the law / of gravity," Rich's new diver learns how "to turn my body without force / in the deep element." Early on, the sense of solitude is very clear in lines like "but here alone," "and there is no one," and "I have to learn alone." But the depth is also a story of connection: "it is easy to forget / what I came for / among so many who have always / lived here." In "After Twenty Years" (1971), Rich stresses the creative power of new kinds of conversations between women "in the prime of life," whose "babies are old enough to have babies." She likens the new talk to "a city where nothing is forbidden / and nothing permanent." In "Diving into the Wreck," Rich's speaker connects to a murky, connective solitude, a changing permanence. She reports: "I stroke the beam of my lamp / slowly along the flank / of something more permanent." Diving becomes social traveling across division and into the company of a submerged multitude for whom change is something more permanent than permanence. It seems that diving offers a way (a psychoanalytic way) of disputing "the fact of being separate."

Arriving to "the wreck and not the story of the wreck / the thing itself and not the myth," one enters a new realm ("This is the place") in which distinctions blur. The rational has taught that facts separate; in this depth-realm, separation is the myth, the facts connect. One moves and unmoves, falls and floats, and the self itself becomes a transsexual plurality, themselves: "I am here, the mermaid whose dark hair / streams black, the merman in his armored body." In the realm of power, language—and myths—articulates division and asserts "the fact of being separate." In this new realm, a depth derived from accepted

contradiction and the plural simplicity of complexity, Rich's diver navi-
gates a dimension of heretofore impossible possibility:

> We circle silently
> about the wreck
> we dive into the hold.
> I am she: I am he
>
> whose drowned face sleeps with open eyes

Rich's work as a lecturer in the SEEK program had made her aware
of ambiguous relationships between language and power, types of language and types of power. Years later, in her book *Errors and Expectations*
(1977), the director of SEEK, Mina Shaughnessy, discussed the entry of
working-class and nonwhite students into the classroom. She noted "the
intelligence of their mistakes" in standard grammar, the grammar directly implicated in what Adrienne Rich came to call "the oppressor's
language." In a statement she prepared for a faculty meeting at CUNY
in April 1969, Rich cautioned against the idea that poor people were
powerless: "We are admitting minds which, because they have lived,
in LeRoi Jones's phrase, as 'suffering intelligences,' have a concern for
justice, truth and freedom which many of our better-prepared students
unfortunately do not." In a cover note for *Errors and Expectations,* Rich,
hedging against romanticizing poverty and segregation, pointed out the
important role of "strategies by which intelligence imprisoned by lack of
skill can be released into articulation." This complex dynamic between
standard and vernacular speech, between the (standard) grammar of articulated power and the (vernacular) power of articulate grammar, and
between imprisonment and freedom resonates at key moments in this
era of Rich's career.

In "The Burning of Paper Instead of Children," the speaker notes
voices in need, in distress, and signals them (in section 3) in quoted vernacular speech: "a child steal because he did not have money to buy it."
A parenthetical follows to note the force (as opposed to the power) of
those voices: "(the fracture of order / the repair of speech / to overcome
this suffering)." At the close of the poem the speaker marks her edu-
cated distance from those vernacular voices of repair and overcoming:
"How well we all spoke. A language is a map of our failures." Within

that language, the (standard) grammar of well-spoken power, the poem ends in isolation: "I cannot touch you and this is the oppressor's language." The final section of "Diving into the Wreck" subtly echoes (in the third line below) the vernacular language of repair and overcoming from "The Burning of Paper." Rich thereby rebuts the divisions encoded in the standard grammar of power. In this she makes a first, halting step toward liberating the force of creative solitude from its imprisonment of isolation in the grammar of power:

> We are, I am, you are
> by cowardice or courage
> the one who find our way
> back to this scene
> carrying a knife, a camera
> a book of myths
> in which
> our names do not appear.

"[T]he one who find our way" fits perfectly into section 3 of "The Burning of Paper Instead of Children." But this is the author's voice. The teacher has learned from her students. Some years after we met in 2000, I sent Adrienne Rich a new essay I'd written on Robert Hayden's poems. The essay centered on Hayden's "The Diver." Rich wrote me that she had always recalled Jacques Cousteau's influence on her notion of diving, those historic images that popularized scenes from under the surface of the sea. But when she read my essay, she told me, too much was familiar. So she went to her bookshelf, where she found her copy of Rosey Pool's *Beyond the Blues* (1962), an anthology of Black poets in which "The Diver" was first published. There, Rich reported, she found her notes in the margins from repeated readings, readings she had returned to in her own work without remembering having done so. I think this historic connection bears remarking. Also, Rich's elaborate teaching notes on Richard Wright's "The Man Who Lived Underground" signal the Black roots of Rich's sense of what diving is all about as well as its dangers.

"I know it hurts to burn," Rich's speaker says near the close of "The Burning of Paper Instead of Children." Popular invocations to burning echoed in chants from civil unrest across the hot summers of the late 1960s and early 1970s. In the title sequence of his 1970 collection *Words in the Mourning Time,* Robert Hayden inscribed, "sing hey nonny no / sing burn baby burn." The second half of *Diving into the Wreck* smolders with desire and anger. But in a deeper way, as with Heraclitus's sense of fire as the key element of being that owes its essence to change, to the permanence of impermanence, Rich's images of burning in *Diving into the Wreck* mark a shifting border of contradictory transformations, a veil of heat cast by phenomena that remain themselves by changing into something else. Images of flame and burning appear again and again. Poems—such as in the book's central and most important sequence, "The Phenomenology of Anger" (1972)—depict "how we are burning up our lives." People must change, even vanish, to remain themselves and go on, as in "Living in the Cave" (1972): "candles see themselves disembodied / into gas / and taking flight."

Much of the heat in the book comes from friction between Rich's impulse to clarity and lucidity and her need to trace connections that burn and blur, defying the "fact of being separate." The two modes open "The Phenomenology of Anger":

1.   The freedom of the wholly mad
to smear & play with her madness
write with her fingers dipped in it
the length of a room

which is not, of course, the freedom
you have, walking on Broadway
to stop & turn back or go on
10 blocks; 20 blocks

Images of frustrated attempts to light fires juxtaposed with images of spontaneous combustion follow immediately. Rich isn't singing "hey nonny no" in public, but in private we find the poet beckoning fire: "huddled fugitive / in the warm sweet simmer of the hay // muttering: *Come.*" An erotics of flame. The dead language—disguised as natural elements, light—separating the world into "facts" reigns powerful across institutions and private life:

4.   White light splits the room.
Table.   Window.   Lampshade.   You.

The world of discrete phenomena obeys passively while the ruling, military-industrial ideology (disguised as human nature) goes on "computing body counts, masturbating / in the factory / of facts." Of the legalities that answer to those military and economic powers, powers dedicated to separation and classification, Rich asks: "Will the judges try to tell me / which was the blood of whom?" She focuses on the "white light" of power, the "dead language," the grammar that inscribes divisions and boundaries (genders, sexes, races, nationalities) and positions "facts" (such as the human individual) neatly within them. She announces:

I hate your words
they make me think of fake
revolutionary bills
crisp imitation parchment
they sell at battlefields.

In service to an essentially military version of reality, the twisted fakery of power inveighs against—even criminalizes—the possibility of healthy human action: "a conspiracy to coexist / with the Crab Nebula, the exploding / universe, the Mind—." "Translations" (1972) witnesses how that discourse of discrete "facts"—facts that, once differentiated, are set in competition with each other—creates a mutual suffering, a story of separation, of individuation, that keeps people "ignorant of the fact this way of grief / is shared, unnecessary / and political." These destructive regimes of meaning are not natural, they're ideological. In factualizing the myths of separation, complexly overlapping persons become autonomous individuals who suffer collectively while images of mutuality vanish as if under attack, which they are.

In *Diving into the Wreck*, the diver surfaces. The sleeper wakes and goes to work. The poet continues to blur, burn, and then clarify. In "Merced" (1972), she enacts the method in precise sequence: (1) blur:

Walking Amsterdam Avenue
I find myself in tears
without knowing which thought
forced water to my eyes

(2) burn, turning to immolation and suicide protests:

> I think of Norman Morrison
> the Buddhists of Saigon
> the black teacher last week
> who put himself to death

(3) clarify, offering a truly visionary vision of renewed clarity:

> Taking off in a plane
> I look down at the city
> which meant life to me, not death
> and think that somewhere there
> a cold center, composed
> of pieces of human beings
> metabolized, restructured
> by a process they do not feel
> is spreading in our midst
> and taking over our minds
> a thing that feels neither guilt
> nor rage: that is unable
> to hate, therefore to love.

The insensate result is "a world masculinity made / unfit for women or men." From the process of blurring and burning and the cold will to clarity, the poet rides above the system as it digests its human contents, metabolizes persons into individuals capable of acting only in accord with the manufactured facts. These metabolized people see only by the "white light" of numb separation and mute isolation. In "The Ninth Symphony Of Beethoven Understood At Last As a Sexual Message" (1972), the "music of the entirely / isolated soul" resounds in this space "where everything is silence and the / beating of a bloody fist upon / a splintered table." Everyone is angry. But so few have any coherent idea what they are angry about. So they turn on each other. Institutions then exert their authority, classifying the results in arbitrary ways. In "Rape" (1972), commenting on masculine-institutional violence at its worst, Rich notes that bureaucratic classifications and divisions are determined as if by "machinery" and "in the sickening light of the precinct." By such means, as in "The Phenomenology of Anger," bureaucratic authority imposes its arbitrary force, at times to determine culpability, relation, and even kinship: "Will the judges try to tell me / which was the blood of whom?"

Diving into the Wreck scripts the focused force of a feminist poet who has begun to remake solitude. She has made it sensual, alone in the "sweet simmer of the hay // muttering: *Come.*" But she has also prepared kindling for the blurring-burning that will soon enough make solitude a mutual, relational force and set it in motion against the powers of isolation. In "Meditations for a Savage Child" (1972), the book's final sequence, the poet traces language back into the evolutionary depths, to a point "back so far there is another language / go back far enough the language / is no longer personal." Unlike four years before in "The Burning of Paper," where the "repair of speech" sounded clearly enough in the "fracture of order," the force in this depth-language is more ambiguous:

> these scars bear witness
> but whether to repair
> or to destruction
> I no longer know

She continues on nonetheless. By then there is no turning back.

"The Phenomenology of Anger" established the stakes facing Rich's poetry clearly enough: "Madness. Suicide. Murder. / Is there no way out but these?" The question was not abstract in the least—it was far-flung and near at hand, as violence proliferated all around and within the poet. The war in Vietnam raged on. Nixon's landslide reelection hazed into Watergate. In cities like New York, street and domestic violence was at epidemic levels. Closer to home, Rich's estranged husband, Alfred Conrad, had killed himself in October 1970. Guides to lead the way out did not exist. In "For a Sister" (1972), dedicated to Natalya Gorbanevskaya, Rich casts existing models of authority aside: "I trust none of them." Against the judges, the police, and "the trained violence of doctors," she goes with the uncertain routes of a burning-blurring personal life, working with the resources that appear along the way: "Only my existence / thrown out in the world like a towchain / battered and twisted in many chance connections."

In the world around her and in her study of the historical and contemporary endeavors of women, Rich would create a relational solitude deployed against isolation, a language dedicated to the survival of people, a language "no longer personal" but capable of—if not dependent on— "chance connections" between persons. Addressed to Gorbanevskaya, the blurry images emerge into a burning, politically mobilized clarity: "Little by little out of the blurred conjectures / your face clears, a sunken marble / slowly cranked up from underwater."

By seeking lyrics that worked in terms "no longer personal," Rich furthered her mission of remaking the possibilities of experience for women in the 1970s and beyond. This included a commitment to be both as public and as private as possible. The one thing Rich's mission would *not* be mistaken for was an individual writer's will to a successful career. *Diving into the Wreck* was chosen as cowinner (with Allen Ginsberg's *The Fall of America*) of the 1974 National Book Award. In advance of the announcement, all but one of the finalists for the award who were women (Rich, Audre Lorde, and Alice Walker) agreed to coauthor a statement to be read publicly should one of their books be chosen to win. As it happened, Rich read the statement, in which the women dissented from the terms (commercial, competitive, individualistic) under which the award was offered. Rich, Lorde, and Walker made their reasons clear in an attempt to further instigate the remaking of possibilities: "We believe that we can enrich ourselves more in supporting and giving to each other than by competing against each other; and that poetry—if it *is* poetry—exists in a realm beyond ranking and comparison. We symbolically join together here in refusing the terms of patriarchal competition and declaring that we will share this prize among us, to be used as best we can for women." Rich's foreword to her *Poems: Selected and New, 1950–1974,* published in 1975, echoes this commitment and provides a useful frame for her poems through the end of the decade. At the height of Watergate (Nixon resigned the presidency in August 1974) and with the war in Vietnam spiraling into American defeat, Rich wrote:

As I type these words we are confronted with the naked and unabashed failure of patriarchal politics and patriarchal civilization. To be a woman at this time is to know extraordinary forms of anger, joy, impatience, love, and hope. Poetry, words on paper, are necessary but not enough; we need to touch the living who share our animal passion for existence, our determination that the sexual myths underlying the human condition can and shall be recognized and changed. My friends—above all, my sisters, the women I love—have given me the heat and friction of their lives, along with the needed clarity, criticism, tenderness, and the daring of their examples. Midway in my own life, I know that we have only begun.

A new "we" had begun. And Rich began to explore how collective action was greater than the sum of its parts.

"my own forces so taken up and shared"
Relational Solitude Realized

Rich's next books, *The Dream of a Common Language: Poems 1974–1977* (1978) and *A Wild Patience Has Taken Me This Far: Poems 1978–1981* (1981) explored the contemporary possibilities of relations between women (and the dangers that women faced) at many levels: as shadow twins of themselves; as sisters and family members; as targets of patriarchal patterning and violence; as lovers to each other; as colleagues and comrades. These poems also sought out instructive (inspirational as well as cautionary) historical backdrops against which women's present and future predicaments and possibilities could be focused.

The new poems from 1973–74 published in *Poems: Selected and New* provide a bridge between the underwater solitude and blurring-burning visions of *Diving into the Wreck* and the self-consciously relational and public-facing work in Rich's next two books. These new poems chart isolation in hospitals, prisons, and dreams, and in limited—possibly masculine-identified—conceptions of imaginative work. In "Dien Bien Phu" (1973), a poem that was unpublished until the release of Rich's 1984 volume of selected poems *The Fact of a Doorframe*, a battlefield nurse, "wounded herself," dreams

that each man she touches
is a human grenade
      an anti-personnel weapon
      that can explode in her arms

The men are "terribly alone." Echoing images of quarantine from the early 1960s, one man's hand reaches "out like barbed wire." Women who reach back toward men in that condition volunteer to run those risks themselves: "if she takes" a soldier's hand, "will it slash her wrists again"? But disengagement isn't the answer; merely walking away is almost as lethal:

if she passes it by

will she turn into a case
of shell-shock, eyes
glazed forever on the

blank chart of
amnesia

In "Essential Resources" (1973), the speaker speaks from "a ward of amnesiacs who can be trusted" but longs to "create something / that can't be used to keep us passive." One key is to address the forces of isolation: "I want to write / a script about plumbing, how every pipe / is joined / to every other." Meanwhile, "the keepers of order are screaming." The screams and enforced silences of the patriarchal order work against the future meanings that women hold in their bodies. In "Incipience," work on a web goes on "inside the spider's body / first atoms of the web / visible tomorrow." Likewise, in "Essential Resources":

I am thinking
of films we have made but cannot show
yet, films of the mind unfolding
and our faces, still young
sweated with desire and
premature clarity

In "Re-forming the Crystal" (1973), a conscious discrepancy between personal and legal identity is itself a form of resistance:

Tonight I understand
my photo on the license is not me,
my

name on the marriage-contract was not mine.
If I remind you of my father's favorite daughter,
look again.

Left inarticulate, however, this difference becomes a scene of forfeiture
and betrayal: "The woman / I needed to call my mother / was silenced
before I was born." In "For L.G.: Unseen for Twenty Years" (1974), Rich
recalls her thwarted connection to a gay male friend at a time when both
were lost, silenced by the script of monogamous heterosexuality: "But
we were talking in 1952 / of the fear of being cripples in a world / of per-
fect women and men."

Speakers in these poems all bear the scars of separation (from self,
from mother, from lover, neighbor) and long for even chance—at times
accidental—moments of connection. As in "Re-forming the Crystal,"
even an accident can be crucial for "the energy it draws on." In "The
Fourth Month of the Landscape Architect" (1973), the speaker waits:
"For now, I am myself, / like anyone, like a man / whose body contains simply: itself." But as with the spider's web in "Incipience" and
the yet-to-be-screened films in "Essential Resources," for the architect
of connection, "A city waits at the back of my skull . . . / for all of us
who are done / with enclosed spaces, purdah, the salon, the sweatshop
loft." In these poems Rich moves consciously beyond images of freedom
that depend on personal autonomy and ownership. Something says that
the difference between resistance and forfeiture lies in the avoidance
of simple singularities such as a selfhood that "contains simply: itself."
In "The Alleged Murderess Walking in Her Cell" (1973), the speaker,
accused of helping to "beat a man to death," avoids isolation even in
solitary confinement. The fact of her shadow twin's presence is beyond
purposes positive or negative, beyond what she has been taught about
right and wrong: "I don't know what / it means, that we have each other.
/ Do they mean to—can they use you / against me?" It doesn't matter.
Together with her shadow sister, she feels

more at peace than in any prison night
here or outside—
your warmth washing into my ribcage
your frail silken skull asleep against my throat

Neither pure nor innocent, relational solitude speaks to a deeper sense of justice and possibility: "the blue pulse of your life / with its blind stroke: *Not-Guilty.*" The connection is existential, beyond right and wrong. *This* is factual. So, then what?

These transitional poems conclude with the brilliant sequence "From an Old House in America" (1974), an imagistic manifesto of an incipient revolution in women's experience, a tradition of banked and smoldering possibility veering into actuality on terms it has forged athwart the white light in the precincts of power and the blueprints of isolation:

> we have done our time
> as faceless torsos licked by fire
>
> we are in the open, on our way—
> our counterparts
>
> the pinyon jay, the small
> gilt-winged insect
>
> the Cessna throbbing level
> the raven floating in the gorge

The vistas are newly opened, the vision is collective. These quests envision lives beyond the lethal shelters and the cells of enclosure articulated in the white light and precincts of the oppressor's language, as if floating "near and yet above the western planet." Risks are commonplace—"Such women are dangerous / to the order of things"—and are also beyond easy confinement: "yes, we will be dangerous / to ourselves." Patriarchal methods and partitions have been internalized:

> Isolation, the dream
> of the frontier woman
>
> leveling her rifle along
> the homestead fence
>
> still snares our pride

Nonetheless, no matter the threat or reality of violence in the transmission, newly articulate systems of connection, a feminist self in touch with what is within and beyond itself, herself, form the basic fabric of possibility:

> —a suicidal leaf
>
> laid under the burning-glass
> in the sun's eye
>
> Any woman's death diminishes me

The final poem of the sequence, "The Fact of a Doorframe," joins the ageless pain of apparent futility, of beating one's head against a wall, "one of the oldest motions of suffering," to a new song of liberation as "Makeba"—Miriam Makeba, at the time newly separated from her husband, Stokely Carmichael—"sings / a courage-song for warriors."

The Dream of a Common Language explores the possibilities, pleasures, and dangers of lives lived in searching accord with the connective force between women. Rich scripts the resulting force in opposition to the powers of separation encoded by patriarchal myths and enforced by the hierarchical and competitive structure of institutions. At the beginning of *The Will to Change,* in "Planetarium" (1968), Rich's speaker announces her discovery that so-called empty space or silence can be loaded with ideological content: "I have been standing all my life in the / direct path of a battery of signals." Working with and against these codes, the poet's job is to "translate pulsations / into images for the relief of the body / and the reconstruction of the mind." In the first poem in *The Dream of a Common Language,* "Power" (1974), Rich positions Marie Curie in similar but clarified circumstances: "she must have known she suffered from radiation sickness / her body bombarded for years by the element / she had purified." Curie becomes an emblem of the dangers of assimilation, of working *with* an element, a power, destructive to self and world:

> She died   a famous woman   denying
> her wounds
> denying
> her wounds   came   from the same source as her power

Emblematic of labor that contributes to the white light of separation, in the would-be heroic image of the silent mother and betrayer, Curie's figure in the poem silently passes on the legacy of self-destruction and assimilation to the next generations.

Immediately following "Power," Rich presents her nascent encounter with a source of strength alternative to the power encoded in the myth of the heroic individual. This key moment echoes through the rest of her career and becomes one of the refrains guiding our sense of Rich's work as it shifts from one era to the next. She finds that so much depends on a collective force that is greater than the sum of its parts. In "Phantasia for Elvira Shatayev" (1974), a poem that proved to be among the most pivotal in her career, Rich depicts women involved in a typically masculine endeavor, mountain climbing, who nonetheless actively engage its assumptions and structures. The women die in the effort, but their collective and articulate work offers a sense that, at least to a degree, traditions can (maybe must) be changed from within. Speaking from beyond the frozen grave to her husband, who had come behind to bury the women climbers, Shatayev furthers the language of plurality, beyond division: "If in this sleep I speak / It's with a voice no longer personal / (I want to say *with voices*)." She notifies her husband of the difference: "You climbed here for yourself / we climbed for ourselves." Implicating the powers of division and separation as the wounds themselves, she articulates the discovery and process of an alternate force: "*I have never seen / my own forces so taken up and shared / and given back.*" So the term "ourselves" is not simply a multiplied version of "yourself." Voices and presence shared back and forth bridge divisions between selves understood in individuated, opposed, and competitive terms: "*We know now we have always been in danger / down in our separateness / and now up here together but till now / we had not touched our strength.*"

Here Rich scripts a new—and ages old—force into her work: the power of mutuality. Twelve years earlier, in claiming an autonomy that the institutions of her world—beginning with marriage and motherhood—denied her, Rich declared in "Necessities of Life" (1962), "What life was there, was mine." This autonomy was crucial, but it was not a solution. Sensing a trap in the private, and seeking a sense of mutual quest on the page and in life, a relation that would not hold her back, in "Continuum" (1968) she paused: "alive, whatever it is." In "When We Dead Awaken" she identified the problem with autonomy: "The fact of being separate." Most of *Diving into the Wreck* makes forays into connections, often metaphorically submerged or in dreamscapes. The poems in *Poems: Selected and New* mostly diagnose the problem among men and for Rich herself as she realizes, as in "From an Old House in America," "I have lived in isolation / from other women." In "Phantasia for Elvira Shatayev," an alternative becomes clear, a way not just to live but *"to survive."* Freedom is a collective achievement. Survival is a mutual endeavor.

Early in *The Dream of a Common Language,* Rich subtly dissolves the strictures that resign women to living deaths in assimilated (meaning: individuated, isolated, silenced) lives. She measures personal risks against the possible force of collective action. Directly addressing the methods of individuation in "Phantasia for Elvira Shatayev," she writes:

> When you have buried us   told your story
> ours does not end   we stream
> into the unfinished   the unbegun
> the possible

Then, recasting the nature of the dangers as well as the means and meaning of survival, she concludes the poem:

> *What does love mean*
> *what does it mean   "to survive"*
> *A cable of blue fire ropes our bodies*
> *burning together in the snow   We will not live*
> *to settle for less   We have dreamed of this*
> *all of our lives*

Pushing beyond the detached universals of the elite world of poetry in the 1950s, to live had been, first, to have a life of one's own. As those walls closed in, it became necessary to contribute (even in death) to a story beyond oneself, to connect to experience so that, as Rich puts it in "Meditations for a Savage Child," "the language / is no longer personal." This kind of connective diving was healing but was also another kind of isolation. Now, *"to survive"* meant that the lives of other people, at this point, other women, lived inside one's life—no longer one's *own*—and one lived, likewise, in the lives of others. This was survival. Rich realized that restricting experience to individual terms amounted to death by isolation.

In the early 1970s Rich was realizing that whiteness, masculinity, individuality, and isolation worked together to obstruct the relational energies of what it could *"mean 'to survive.'"* In "Origins and History of Consciousness" (1972–74), she allows: "I can't call it life until we start to move / beyond this secret circle of fire." "No one lives in this room," she writes earlier in the poem, "without confronting the whiteness of the wall / behind the poems." No matter the risks—and no matter the type of endeavor—in order *"to survive"* one must pursue "the true nature of poetry. The drive / to connect. The dream of a common language." As a function of the history and origins of consciousness, it becomes possible to imagine a selfhood in which the essential terms are mutual instead of individual, social instead of natural or psychoanalytic. Women "did this. Conceived / of each other, conceived each other in a darkness / which I remember as drenched in light. / I want to call this, life." Survival entails rituals of mutual, and continual, reconception.

Here Rich finds herself on the cusp of a radical reformulation of creative solitude. Subtle in the beginning, its implications would resound throughout the rest of her career as she interrogated and extended its implications across the decades. In "The Burning of Paper Instead of Children," the presumably heterosexual lovers cannot scale the wall between them using the standard language: "How well we all spoke . . . I cannot touch you and this is / the oppressor's language." In "Splittings" (1974), relationships between women evince a capacity for presence that is not a function of distance and a notion of distance that is not a function of spatial relations. This capacity presents the means of relational solitude where distance measures emotional, even political, proximity and connectedness. In a newly "common language," a new physics of self and other becomes possible. Speaking from San Francisco of a lover in New York, by refusing "givens," such as "the splitting / between love and action," the speaker maintains:

> I will not be divided   from her or from myself
> by myths of separation
> while her mind and body in Manhattan are more with me
> than the smell of eucalyptus coolly burning   on these hills

Such connections could be factual. Maybe if facts were to become human realities, they *had* to be mutual. In effect, Rich warns against confusing feminist solitude with masculine isolation. Survival is relational, a mutual endeavor. No matter where the lovers' bodies are, joining "love and action" creates a presence unbound by myths of separation, the supposed "fact of being separate."

In "Hunger" (1974–75), a poem dedicated to Audre Lorde, Rich identifies the new force of a collective action that refuses to pass on the silent pain of assimilated life (as did betrayer-mothers such as Marie Curie in "Power"). She describes women who suffer articulately, who, even if "blunted by malnutrition," are

> yet sharpened by the passion for survival,
> our powers expended daily on the struggle
> to hand a kind of life on to our children,
> to change reality for our lovers
> even in a single trembling drop of water.

In principle, therefore, one key distinction between feminist and masculine modes is women's noncompetitive interaction with the lives of other people. At this point, and for the rest of the decade, for Rich this possibility was grounded in erotic relations between women.

The final sequence in the first section of *The Dream of a Common Language*, "Cartographies of Silence," echoes Rich's 1977 pamphlet *Women and Honor: Some Notes on Lying*, which explores the destructive power of silence and lies between women. As Rich told me, *Women and Honor* began as her reaction to having been subject to emotional manipulation by a woman therapist and ended up considering the issue in terms that were "no longer personal." Whether unconsciously inherited from the oppressor's myths or reinvented in the image of "the so-called common language," a lie in a conversation between women is particularly dangerous because it "Inscribes with its unreturning stylus / the isolation it denies." Masked as a form of connection, such a lie actually transmits, like a virus, the "loneliness of the liar / living in the formal network of the lie." Silences in conversations of bad faith entrap and endanger just as surely as out-and-out lies. This is likewise a tradition employed to guard and keep illegitimate power:

Silence can be a plan
rigorously executed

the blueprint to a life

It is a presence
it has a history a   form

Against the threat of lies and silence masquerading as conversations
and poems, Rich imagines a utopian sense in which poetry could attain
a physical form impossible to assimilate into that oppressive tradition:
"If at the will of the poet the poem / could turn into a thing." Rich
continues:

If it could simply look you in the face
with naked eyeballs, not letting you turn

till you, and I who long to make this thing,
were finally clarified together in its stare

Like the transformation of solitude from isolation to relation, the result of such a revolutionary modernist work might be a different kind
of silence that bears no resemblance to absence: "as silence falls at the
end // of a night through which two people / have talked till dawn." But
Rich already knew that such presence does not arrive by epiphany, it is
not the result of a healing, mystical astonishment or catharsis. As her
image of the all-night conversation suggests, relational presence comes
from the work of active, searching, and deliberate communication.
This takes a tenacity of commitment and real bravery. As she writes in
Women and Honor, relational presence involves "a process, delicate, violent, often terrifying to both persons involved, a process of refining the
truths they can tell each other." For subjects deeply conditioned, moving
beyond attachments to the shelter of autonomy is terrifying.

Relational truths are plural, Rich writes in *Women and Honor,* because such truth is "not one thing, or even a system. It is an increasing
complexity." The point is that the persons who create relational truths
"are trying, all the time, to extend the possibilities of truth between us.
The possibilities of life between us." In "Cartographies of Silence," in the
shadow of utopian longings for a material condition immune to dangers

in language and ideological manipulations of silence, Rich resolves to keep on doing relational work inch by inch, word by word:

> what in fact I keep choosing
>
> are these words, these whispers, conversations
> from which time after time the truth breaks moist and green.

Section II of *The Dream of a Common Language,* "Twenty-One Love Poems," tests the theory of lives lived athwart the structures of patriarchal separation. In "Meditations for a Savage Child," the closing sequence in *Diving into the Wreck,* language that became "no longer personal" was an introspective (maybe psychoanalytic) endeavor; to achieve such a language, one had to dive deep or "go back far enough" into an unconscious or even preevolutionary state. Those "no longer personal" connections existed beneath or behind the present, daily structures of separation and isolation. But "no longer personal" was not relational. Unbounded space, self, or speech did not automatically inspire new cartographies of relation. The connections in "Phantasia for Elvira Shatayev" and "Splittings" were made possible by the erotic presence of women with each other in defiance of the existing structures. Through the creation of relational solitude, the "no longer personal" language became actively social.

The near-sonnets in "Twenty-One Love Poems" encode the lives of real women attempting to live with, learn from, and love each other. They hone and enlist the forces of openness, relation, and articulation against the power of individuation, separation, and silence. The force is all about a movement *toward*—not away from—the world. "Twenty-One Love Poems" brings relation out of dream-depths, down from the mountain, and into the lives of actual women. The poetic aperture aligns and connects phenomena in an expanded array of experiential energy:

> We need to grasp our lives inseparable
> from those rancid dreams, that blurt of metal, those disgraces,
> and the red begonia perilously flashing
> from a tenement sill six stories high,
> or the long-legged young girls playing ball
> in the junior highschool playground.

Fueled by intensified encounters with disparate, at times ambiguous, even dangerous energies of urban life, the women work within the elements (ideology masked as natural law) encountered by divers, dreamers, and climbers in Rich's poems for decades. They embrace

> the desire to show you to everyone I love,
> to move openly together
> in the pull of gravity, which is not simple,
> which carries the feathered grass a long way down the upbreathing air.

The density of experiential references in "Twenty-One Love Poems" works beyond the theoretical recalibrations in "Cartographies of Silence." These near-sonnets pit the force from vivid particulars in women's relational truths (mutual lives) against the violence of competition, silence, and separation. No longer confined to rehearsals of ownership and autonomy, Rich's speaker is in love and more personally free than she has ever been: "Did I ever walk the morning streets at twenty, / my limbs streaming with a purer joy?" But forces of separation and violence loom near and far. Patriarchal gestures are likewise not theoretical, they are coded in bodily postures and everyday action:

>   I'm lugging my sack
> of groceries, I dash for the elevator
> where a man, taut, elderly, carefully composed
> lets the door almost close on me.—*For god's sake hold it!*
> I croak at him.—*Hysterical,*—he breathes my way.

Rich's speaker answers the will to closed doors with openings, "I let myself into the kitchen, unload my bundles, / make coffee, open the window, put on Nina Simone / singing *Here comes the sun*." Openings bring energy, "delicious coffee, delicious music," and mutual presence unbound by distance, "my body still both light and heavy with you." How far is this relational presence from the formally shuttered windows in "Storm Warnings" (1951) and the pain of isolation in "The Burning of Paper Instead of Children": "my mouth is burning. I cannot touch you." Still, violently shuttered suffering continues somewhere. Always ambiguous, openings—in this case the mail—bring the possibility of violence as well. As it had in "Merced," the "world masculinity made" rages on. In "Twenty-One Love Poems,"

> The mail
> lets fall a Xerox of something written by a man
> aged 27, a hostage, tortured in prison:
> *My genitals have been the object of such a sadistic display*
> *they keep me constantly awake with the pain . . .*

But even the scripts of violence carry their energies of rebellion: "*Do whatever you can to survive. / You know, I think that men love wars . . .*" And now Rich understood something new about what it meant "*to survive.*"

For more than a decade, Rich's poems struggled with the dominant discourse in steadily escalating terms: in "Like This Together" it was a curious impediment, "Our words misunderstand us"; in "The Burning of Paper Instead of Children" it was a systematic opponent, "This is the oppressor's language"; in the final section of "Hunger," caught amid complex skeins of violence, Rich's figures are "lovers caught in the crossfire / of terrorists of the mind." A commitment to openness in a violent world risks confusion and despair, deprivation as well as physical attack. And many bear these kinds of violence without making any commitment. Sustaining relationships amid an escalating sense of the stakes becomes more necessary and more difficult at the same time.

In "Twenty-One Love Poems," moments after feeling "both light and heavy" with her lover's erotic presence, Rich finds herself caged by discourses of separation and violence. In ways that echo the final lines of "The Burning of Paper," she writes: "And my incurable anger, my unmendable wounds / break open further with tears, I am crying helplessly, / and they still control the world, and you are not in my arms." The new, relational solitude also extends to ambiguities of poetry itself. In moments, Rich's speaker recoils. Maybe, in the end, writing by definition amounts to assimilation, to surrender, even to self-imprisonment: "What kind of beast would turn its life into words?" Maybe writing itself is a lethal kind of shelter, a withdrawal from the sustaining energies of mutual action. Answering the challenge, she finds that there are words, and then there are *words*: "yet, writing words like these, I'm also living." No matter the medium, she senses the lingering danger of the self-inflicted wound, "the failure to want our freedom passionately enough." And, in relational space, even to despair can be to "break open further."

Rich's speaker pushes on through the sequence as the connective tissue of the relationship frays and fails. All of it can be used. Like voices, she finds that silences can be no longer personal as well; silences can (maybe must) be shared. As part of relational solitude, silences are no more private property than words; they are not passive and benign at all, and they may be aggressive and mutually destructive. And, of course, not all silences emanate from men. Facing her lover, a woman, the speaker says, "Your silence today is a pond where drowned things live." In relational space, silences are mutual: "Whatever's lost there is needed by both of us—." It's as if she is addressing the needs of a therapist turned lover and, in turn, addressing the turned tables of responsibility: "show me what I can do / for you, who have often made the unnameable / nameable for others, even for me." With or without a willing or capable partner in the search for a common language, she has learned, again, that the relational force is located in the body because "voices of the psyche drive through the flesh / further than the dense brain could have foretold." The mutual energies of survival are shared in speech, in silence as well as in difference. And sharing can create new meanings *from* difference:

> and our bodies, so alike, are yet so different
> and the past echoing through our bloodstreams
> is freighted with different language, different meanings—
> though in any chronicle of the world we share
> it could be written with new meaning
> we were two lovers of one gender,
> we were two women of one generation.

The erotic relational presence of women with each other can confront the language of power with an emergent grammar of mutual force, as in "Phantasia for Elvira Shatayev," "*forces so taken up and shared / and given back.*" These forces are means of survival.

As in speech and silence and the furthering encounters with embodied truths, "Twenty-One Love Poems" charts the unknown as a place of new possibility, a terrain shared by women's relational quests. In

"Unsounded" from *A Change of World*, forays into unknown territory are solitary, "These are latitudes revealed / Separate to each." In "Trying to Talk with a Man," Rich's speaker has company, but she would be better off alone: "out here I feel more helpless / with you than without you." It doesn't have to be that way. Different as they are as persons, the couple in "Twenty-One Love Poems" become a presence of blurring, furthering, and clarity, "The rules break like a thermometer, / quicksilver spills across the charted systems, / we're out in a country that has no language". The two are off the grid, in a region of "pure invention" where "the maps they gave us were out of date / by years . . ." Nonetheless, "the music on the radio comes clear— . . . / a woman's voice singing old songs / with new words, with a quiet bass, a flute / plucked and fingered by women outside the law."

The final sections of the sequence make it clear that Rich's notion of relational process and collective ethics involves all phases of experience, as much when relationships end or change as when they are beginning. The key is to remain open to what has happened, what is happening, and what comes next. The stakes are real, the potentials are powerful, necessary, and the dangers are too serious for romance: "No one's fated or doomed to love anyone." Turning away from the practical work of mutuality, her lover says, *the more I live the more I think / two people together is a miracle.* Rich's speaker waves off the virtues of the mystical: "Am I speaking coldly when I tell you in a dream / or in this poem, *There are no miracles?*" As her diver learned, Rich knows that living outside the law does not imply a total loss of control. New methods and maps must be *made.* The necessary elements exist between people in their everyday worlds, in their bodies, in their speech and in their silences, all with the potential to be meaningfully shared: "(I told you from the first I wanted daily life, / this island of Manhattan was island enough for me.)" Not a vacation or a miracle,

> two women together is a work
> nothing in civilization has made simple,
> two people together is a work
> heroic in its ordinariness,

The most serious danger is not wanting to survive passionately enough. Living relationships are work, are not virtuous in themselves, can be dangerous "where the fiercest attention becomes routine." And the dangers and casualties of people's mutual lives are not always talked about, but at times they are hardly hidden. All we need to do is "look at the faces of those who have chosen it."

In opened, relational life, the flow between the personal and the beyond personal goes both ways. At the end of "Twenty-One Love Poems," Rich's speaker imagines her lost lover, a talented woman who failed to want their freedom passionately enough. Echoing the husband's failure to make the relational leap in "Ghost of a Chance" (1962), Rich writes:

> I discern a woman
> I loved, drowning in secrets, fear wound round her throat
> and choking her like hair. And this is she
> with whom I tried to speak, whose hurt, expressive head
> turning aside from pain, is dragged down deeper
> where it cannot hear me,

Opening, however, also means that the world resides in the self. Rich realizes that, in mutual terrain, in love, conversations with the beloved are also conversations with oneself. The lover drowning in silence is a shadow twin: "and soon I shall know I was talking to my own soul." An opened woman in the relational world of her life, alive to herself and to the mutual rhythms around her, Rich has learned, can cast "back to where her solitude, / shared, could be chosen without loneliness." Relational solitude is not a destined or fated tunnel or cage, it is "a cleft of light" (and shadow) one chooses to encounter, to engage. Rich ends the sequence in the open space of that choice:

> I choose to be a figure in that light,
> half-blotted by darkness, something moving
> across that space, the color of stone
> greeting the moon, yet more than stone
> a woman. I choose to walk here. And to draw this circle.

Section III of *The Dream of a Common Language* examines relationships of various kinds between women and establishes a new space for open questions. Where are the borders and boundaries in a counter-tradition of crossed boundaries? What are the necessities and capacities of separation in the furtherance of a women-centered mutual reclamation of the past and vision for the future? How can women learn to speak for themselves and to each other when patriarchal laws (separation, individuation, competition) no longer determine what is normal and what is natural? In a reconstituted reality, what would be the shape and nature of women-centered forms? The poems weave a net of images that take up these questions set and reset at shifting angles to each other.

Emanating from the near-sonnets in "Twenty-One Love Poems," the scattered, unpunctuated verses of "Not Somewhere Else, but Here" (1974) search for the strength to wring truth from failed relationships between women:

> To have enough courage   The life that must be lived
> in terrible October
> Sudden immersion in yellows   streaked blood   The fast rain
> Faces   Inscriptions   Trying to teach
> unlearnable lessons   October   This one love
> Repetitions   from other lives   the deaths
> that must be lived   Denials   Blank walls
> Our quick stride side by side   Her fugue

In a world not defined by patriarchal division and silence, what can be learned from relationships that fail but don't necessarily end? Indeed, what does the "failure" of a relationship between women mean? Possibly failure means an impediment to necessary change or growth? Possibly a relationship fails when it restricts relation necessary to survival? The poet is not sure. But against the patriarchal false witness—that "it does not pay to feel"—the poem insists on openness, inveighs against the fear that would numb and silence the truth-sense of the emotional body:

> Her face   The fast rain tearing   Courage
> to feel this   To tell of this   to be alive
> Trying to learn   unteachable lessons

In this space lessons are embodied, truth is a living presence, and divisions may be very real, but they are not absolute:

Spilt love   seeking its level   flooding other
lives   that must be lived   not somewhere else
but here   seeing through blood   nothing is lost

In "Upper Broadway" (1975), in the painful shadow of the images above, Rich notes the destructive persistence of power hierarchies in failing relationships between women: "I have written so many words / wanting to live inside you / to be of use to you." In light of this reality, there is still a role for creative autonomy even as a function of an ultimately relational truth: "Now I must write for myself for this blind / woman scratching the pavement." If women's relationships are to be more than havens from—and can become mirrors of—patriarchal norms, textures must be woven to bear the full range of women's experience. Arriving at middle age, nearing midcareer, Rich surveys the scene and reckons she's about halfway there:

I look at my hands and see   they are still unfinished
I look at the vine and see the leafbud
inching towards life
I look at my face in the glass and see
a halfborn woman

In "Paula Becker to Clara Westhoff" (1975–76), Rich reimagines two women as proto-lovers, collaborators, whose partnership was torn apart by obligatory marriages, whose friendship failed (but maybe didn't end) when Becker died giving birth to a child she really did not want to have. Set against history and the present, "Nights and Days" (1976) poses the key questions women have to ask and answer for themselves and with each other:

and I ask myself and you, which of our visions will claim us
which will we claim
how will we go on living
how will we touch, what will we know
what will we say to each other.

If women do not pursue such questions, they—like the women in the poems "Sibling Mysteries" (1976) and "A Woman Dead in Her Forties"

(1974–77)—will go on wondering about what has held them back from each other and to what extent those same forces (masculine myths such as the "fact of being separate" accepted as reality) alienate each from herself. One basis for fathoming these crucial questions exists in women's emotional bodies. In "A Woman Dead in Her Forties," the speaker rehearses the still-unlearned lesson, *everything you feel is true.* Amid layers of madness in a world men have forced to betray itself in their (falsified) image, women's emotional bodies become an irreplaceable political compass: "how the body tells the truth in its rush of cells." The political boundaries established by patriarchal norms have defended themselves most powerfully via enforced silences at the borders. Conversations between women, based on the world they sense within and around them in the body's "rush of cells," amount to an invaluable form of dissent from an imposed so-called tradition in which "Most of our love took the form / of mute loyalty."

In the extended sequence "Natural Resources" (1977), Rich switches out the climbers and the diver and imagines a miner's foray into the mineral wealth of an alternate form of vision, strength, and creative purpose. If women were to devote their creative energies not to purifying destructive elements (as in "Power") or to attempting to refashion men's isolate quests for rarified heights ("Phantasia for Elvira Shatayev"), what would be the key attributes and structure of the endeavor? In the effort "to extend herself," Rich informs that her "miner is no metaphor," nor is she an exception to the rule: she "goes / into the cage like the rest." She is subject to natural forces like everyone else, "is flung // downward by gravity" and "must change / her body like the rest." The range of relational action is not extreme save in subtlety, the skill that "turns a doorknob . . . so quietly, that no one wakes," a hand that "ascertains / how they sleep, who needs her touch." Subject to natural laws, yes, but these are hard-won skills, not innate or mythic gifts: "It is only she who sees; who was trained to see." Understood as an alternate tradition, these at times invisible skills reveal their valences of strength. This is ordinary—not exceptional—strength. When it does appear, this kind of strength can be mistaken for weakness. Gentleness, for instance,

But gentleness is active
gentleness swabs the crusted stump

invents more merciful instruments
to touch the wound beyond the wound

At times strength is a skill for recognizing the unrecognized, a consciousness that becomes adept at the use of peripheral or marginal images as mirrors of refracted and empowered self-regard, a patience that encodes a hidden passion of purpose:

This is what I am: watching the spider
rebuild—"patiently", they say,

but I recognize in her
impatience—my own—

the passion to make and make again
where such unmaking reigns

the refusal to be a victim

This relational force is vested not in monuments—or in counter-monuments—but in the ordinary "enormity of the simplest things," articulated in the immediate and discontinuous quality of time Rich found herself trapped in during her first years as a mother: "the fibers of actual life / as we live it, now." It is an aesthetic of everyday use rather than one of refined perfection:

this fraying blanket with its ancient stains
we pull across the sick child's shoulder

or wrap around the senseless legs
of the hero trained to kill

this weaving, ragged because incomplete
we turn our hands to, interrupted

over and over, handed down
unfinished, found in the drawer

Like the spider with its passionate patience, a contemporary practitioner learns to use her ancestors as sources of strength, their "vanished pride and care // still urging us on, urging on / our works."

Just as women's patience and gentleness can be mistaken for apathy and passivity, the mundane, often-demeaned labor of survival might include slyly cloaked and expertly calibrated intensities of social transformation. According to the discernments of an alternate tradition of power, of *relational force,* heroines are not an Olympian few who play king of the hill in icy extremities. In "Transcendental Etude" (1977), the first of many poems dedicated to her life partner, Jamaican-born novelist and scholar Michelle Cliff, Rich contrasts what she is finding under the tips of her fingers with the competitive extremities of virtuosi and the "theatricality, the false glamour cast / by performance." She writes: "there are no prodigies / in this realm, only a half-blind, stubborn / cleaving to the timbre, the tones of what we are." The relational fabric employs materials gained through creative acts of active gentleness and passionate patience: "the truths we are salvaging from / the splitting-open of our lives." The net of women's relational force encodes a complexity woven into the "fibers of actual life" and is far more widely cast and pervasive than a heroic individual, or even an exceptional few, could possibly vouch for. So then, in "Natural Resources," Rich concludes with another key moment:

> I have to cast my lot with those
> who age after age, perversely,
>
> with no extraordinary power,
> reconstitute the world.

Building on the image of relational survival at the beginning of *The Dream of a Common Language,* this key image of recalibration echoes through the rest of Rich's career. We will come back to it as another touchstone as we chart the course outward.

Earlier in "Natural Resources," a smug male interviewer inquires about the possibilities—ones he considers ridiculous—of separate worlds for men and women: "*Can you imagine // a world where women are absent . . . // If so, then, / a world where men are absent?*" Rich writes: "(He believed / he was joking.) Yet I have to imagine // at one and the same moment, both." The line breaks pit a woman's subtle necessity to *imagine* against a man's self-satisfied license to merely *believe* and to joke about things he has never had to imagine. Rich signals a furthered and deepened exploration of presence and absence that turns upon much more than the "fact" of physically showing up or taking off. This exploration would not be a diver's (or miner's) errand in depth and shadow, however. This quest would take place in the open, in public and private defiance of the laws of historical light, the rules of patriarchal power.

"Natural Resources" was written during the same period when Rich—most certainly pushed along by her relationship with Cliff—was writing and publishing essays exploring historically constituted racial, ethnic, and sexual identity, such as "Disloyal to Civilization" (1978), "Split at the Root" (1982), and "Compulsory Heterosexuality" (1980). During the decade to come, Rich would increasingly explore questions of relational presence from her standpoint as a white Jewish lesbian. The next stage of her historical emergence (from depths, from shadows) was being prepared in "Natural Resources":

> There are words I cannot choose again:
> *humanism   androgyny*
>
> Such words have no shame in them, no diffidence
> before the raging stoic grandmothers:
>
> their glint is too shallow, like a dye
> that does not permeate
>
> the fibers of actual life
> as we live it, now:

Rich's dawning insistence on identity, historical contingency, and (intersectional) particularity draws upon and extends the kind of sight she described in "From the Prison House": "it sees // detail not on TV . . . // it sees / the violence / embedded in silence." At that time, such categorical identities were indeed "embedded in silence," rigorously enforced, rarely addressed and rarely questioned. In her next book, *A Wild Patience Has Taken Me This Far*, Rich begins to engage those silences and, at times, to challenge the categories they guard. In "Frame" (1980), she positions herself as witness to a Black woman's experience of being racially profiled, falsely arrested, and abused while incarcerated. Riffing on Walt Whitman, Rich's speaker adopts the historical (racial) marker and defies its (meaning her) assigned role: *What I am telling*

*you / is told by a white woman who they will say / was never there. I say
I am there.*" In "Mother-in-Law" (1980), after years of half statements
and isolating silences, Rich imagines a new, more direct honesty with
her in-laws: "Your son is dead / ten years, I am a lesbian, / my children
are themselves." Rich's emergence into relational presence came about
in an intensely gendered period. At this moment, for her, all relational
presence involved women. It was part of the arc of her life, the development of her vision, that at this point she wrote "my children" instead of
"my sons."

As we have seen above, Rich meant to cast her lot with those who,
"with no extraordinary power / reconstitute the world." Most immediately thereafter, in *A Wild Patience Has Taken Me This Far,* those would
be women. Insofar as it was possible—and maybe consciously bent
in ways beyond what was possible—*A Wild Patience* would be Rich's
separatist book. It is a search for openings made possible by a focus on
how women, despite having "no extraordinary power," formulate their
considerable—possibly revolutionary—force in the world; to a large extent, it is a world where actual men are absent, replaced by a clarified,
abstracted patriarchal principle.

"The Images" (1976–78) opens the book in a space that had been
largely erased from history, the embodied, intimate space between women:
"Close to your body, in the / pain of the city." What is known in this
space builds on tactile and erotic foundations, "touch knows you before
language / names in the brain." Outside the frame of women's—really,
lesbian—relational body-knowledge, "a howl, police sirens, emergency,"
faceless men and the masculine world of attackers and attacked exist
abstracted, "registering pure force" and "ripping the sheath of sleep."
Building on the active gentleness of healers and the passionate patience
of spiders, and "drawn against fear and woman-loathing," Rich affirms:
"We are trying to live / in a clearheaded tenderness—." Conscious that
the relational space of body-knowing is not a haven, that "no-man's-land
does not exist," she guards herself: "I can never romanticize language
again / never deny its power for disguise for mystification." At the crux,
where their world is actually reconstituted, words that misunderstand
their speakers, codes of the oppressor's language, even the scripts offered
by terrorists of the mind, are not to blame. Or that blame is not enough.
For Rich, a more proximate danger lies in how women "continually fail

to ask are they true for us." Here Rich imagines a space where women's mutual labor can claim agency and accept responsibility.

Rich's couple of lover-warriors are surrounded. "Two women sleeping / together have more than their sleep to defend." The question—"are they true for us"—presents women with the key paradigm of defense. Because "no-man's-land does not exist," the lovers must make their way through the streets, in which seeing means much more than a personal choice. Rich describes how her figures

> see our bodies strung
> in bondage and crucifixion across the exhausted air
>   when did we choose
>   to be lynched on the queasy electric signs
> of midtown when did we choose
>   to become the masturbator's fix
>   emblem of rape in Riverside Park   the campground

The speaker returns home from the language gauntlet "a woman starving for images" of

>   all the lost
>   crumbled   burnt   smashed   shattered   defaced
>   overpainted   concealed and falsely named
> faces of every past we have searched together

In the face of violent historical and contemporary silencing, disfigurement, and erasure of women's mutuality, Rich imagines that the lost images "could rise reassemble re-collect re-member / themselves as I recollected myself in that presence." The images of a reconstituted women's world are intellectual, historical, aesthetic, and erotic; above all, they are *relational*. Survival is a mutual task:

>   as every night close to your body
>   in the pain of the city, turning
> I am remembered by you, remember you
>   even as we are dismembered

By the late 1970s, the relational and reciprocal process that spelled the difference between the masculine "yourself" and the women's "ourselves" in "Phantasia for Elvira Shatayev" is no longer on a suicide mission to frozen altitudes. Reconstituting a mirror of masculine power is not the point; alternate means must be explored, refined, and enacted.

What about the individual in a relational world? Rich's conception of the feminist self is plural, dialectical, even in solitude. In "Integrity" (1978) she seems to take her stand, alone:

> I recognize: the stand of pines
> violet-black really, green in the old postcard
> but really I have nothing but myself
> to go by; nothing
> stands in the realm of pure necessity
> except what my hands can hold.

But even an imposed solitude does not cease the relational motion. Rich's realization echoes the shadow twin from "The Alleged Murderess Walking in Her Cell"; in "Integrity," she writes: *Nothing but myself? . . . My selves.* / After so long, this answer. / As if I had always known." Situated among the re-membered presences of women's experience—in feminist relational solitude—a woman can realign the energies of her selves. In "The Stranger," Rich had described the clarity of anger as a means to mercy: "my visionary anger cleansing my sight / and the detailed perceptions of mercy / flowering from that anger." As a feminist tradition is reassembled, women can fathom alternate chemistries, alchemies of new ethical metabolisms. In "Integrity," returning to the passionate patience of the spider, she realizes this relational, interior freedom:

> Anger and tenderness: my selves.
> And now I can believe they breathe in me
> as angels, not polarities.
> Anger and tenderness: the spider's genius
> to spin and weave in the same action
> from her own body, anywhere—
> even from a broken web.

Rich's refashioned hands assume control of forces both creative and destructive; accrued in their relational expertise, indeed, is the decision about which is which. Rich describes "these two hands":

> and they have caught the baby leaping
> from between trembling legs
> and they have worked the vacuum aspirator
> and stroked the sweated temples

Here Rich breaks from the false/factual oppositions of masculine power and its patterns of competition and revenge in the logic of violence. *A Wild Patience* reassembles lost valences of a radical, feminist, anti-racist, at times lesbian tradition of mutual action among women. In place of the oppressor's language—a masculine mythology of individuation, competition, and isolation—women would be able to use angles and refractions in this recovered tradition as mirrors for redemptive labor. The facts are relational. Assimilation into the masculine mythology is suicidal. In "The Spirit of Place" (1980), Rich gazes skyward as (her former "fierce half-brother" from "Orion" in 1965) "Orion plunges like a drunken hunter / over the Mohawk Trail." Orion is far from the only threat: "All the figures up there look violent to me / as a pogrom on Christmas Eve in some old country." But even nature offers alternate options, mirrors of fierce protection, healthy rebellion, and mutual survival. In "Images," she finds a mirror of protective intimacy for the lovers: "We are the thorn-leaf guarding the purple-tongued flower / each to each." In "Culture and Anarchy" (1978), Rich situates her wide survey of nineteenth-century women's creation and rebellion in the mirror of the "Daylilies" that "run wild, 'escaped' the botanists call it / from dooryard to meadow to roadside." Throughout the poem, over several pages, she quotes from letters and journals, assembling alternate constellations of women's love and action as if they are shadows cast by the daylily's "headlong, loved, escaping life."

As she had forecast in her 1971 essay "When We Dead Awaken," in her life with Michelle Cliff, Rich realized an experience in which "the energy of creation and the energy of relation" *were* brought together. "Culture and Anarchy" contains early images of that transformation:

Upstairs, long silence, then
again, the sudden torrent of your typing

Rough drafts we share, each reading
her own page over the other's shoulder
trying to see afresh

Perhaps slightly in disbelief, the poet remarks the novelty of this working together: "An energy I cannot even yet / take for granted." In the
mirror of relational creative process, Rich cites Susan B. Anthony's
description of her trip to Haworth, *the home of the Brontë sisters. . . .*"
For Anthony, the scene of the sisters' (and, presumably, their brother's)
"short and ill-environed lives" made for *"a most sad day."* Embedded in
the tragic story, however, Rich finds a resonant refraction of the relational creative tradition: *"the sisters walked up and down / with their arms
around each other / and planned their novels. . . ."* Anthony wonders how
"much the world of literature has lost" due to such outrageous circumstances. Rich shares Anthony's outrage. But at the same time, Rich's images of creation and relation pose the question as to whether the fugitive
brilliance of *Jane Eyre* and *Wuthering Heights* could have been created in
the isolated, competitive masculine mode. Like those of her climbers in
"Phantasia for Elvira Shatayev," Rich's images here pose questions about
whether the Brontës' work survives because the sisters did not live "to
settle for less."

Sifting together the socially pragmatic, abolitionist, and feminist energies of dozens of nineteenth-century women artists and activists, Rich
constructs a radical and versatile vision of feminist activist consciousness
that refuses to accept any of its assigned roles or the divisions between
them. All is not peaceful in that sky either. Conflict between women has
its history too. In ways that echo precisely how she described to me her
own falling out with Denise Levertov over the necessity of connections
between the Black liberation movement and the movement against the
Vietnam War, Rich quotes Elizabeth Barrett to Anna Jameson:

. . . and is it possible you think
a woman has no business with questions
like the question of slavery?

Then she had better use a pen no more.
She had better subside into slavery
and concubinage herself, I think, . . .
and take no rank among thinkers and speakers.

At times the radical feminist tradition operates as the back side of history's monumental mirror. Rich likens women's insurgent, creative energies to "leaflets / dissolving within hours, / spun of necessity and / leaving no trace." She contrasts them with the official record, cast in the false universals of her own adolescence: "The heavy volumes, calf, with titles in smooth / leather, red and black, gilt letters spelling: / THE HISTORY OF HUMAN SUFFERING." In effect, Rich turns the mirror around: "I brush my hand across my eyes /—this is a dream, I think—and read: / THE HISTORY OF WOMAN SUFFRAGE." With her reconstituted constellations of women's action etched into place, she can turn the mirror back around, women's erased labor on the other side now showing through:

THE HISTORY OF HUMAN SUFFERING
like bound back issues of a periodical
stretching for miles

With both sides of the historical mirror in view, Rich sees, again, that even universals have gender roles:

OF HUMAN SUFFERING: borne,
tended, soothed, cauterized,
stanched, cleansed, absorbed, endured
by women

In "Waking in the Dark" (1971), such fluidly erotic, insurgent, and relational energy is "the saying of a dream." The speaker wishes "there were somewhere / actual we could stand." Seven years later, "Culture and Anarchy" closes with Rich's speaker actually standing there—in the image of (in this case lesbian-feminist) relational process reconstituting the formerly isolated feminist consciousness: "How you have given back to me / my dream of a common language / my solitude of self." The change registers in acts at various levels of experience, especially in the labor of daily tasks—the constantly undone work of women's work—

that links the intimate and erotic needs of consciousness to the feminine forms of the natural world:

> I slice the beetroots to the core,
> each one contains a different landscape
> of bloodlight filaments, distinct rose-purple
> striations like the oldest
> strata of a Southwestern canyon
> an undiscovered planet laid open in the lens

In "For Memory" (1979), insurgent reauthoring of sky and earth as mirrors of places for women to inhabit and reinforce their own and each other's means and needs occurs in the nonlinear rhythmic paradigm of women's work, undone as it is done. As if to say, so be it, feeling her way with the wild and passionate patience of the spider, the speaker closes the poem:

> Freedom. It isn't once, to walk out
> under the Milky Way, feeling the rivers
> of light, the fields of dark—
> freedom is daily, prose-bound, routine
> remembering. Putting together, inch by inch
> the starry worlds. From all the lost collections.

These visions are not the stuff of fancy and fantasy. They are not echoes of thunder, they do not sound like male power in reverse. However, they still resound—as in "From the Prison House," with its call for a politically attuned visionary vision—in the need to see "detail not on TV / the fingers of the policewoman / searching the cunt of the young prostitute." In "The Spirit of Place," in the face of "male dominion, gangrape, lynching, pogrom," Rich asks, "will we do better?"

A Wild Patience Has Taken Me This Far explores a world of women reconstituted in preparation for engagement with

> The world as it is: not as her users boast
> damaged beyond reclamation by their using
> Ourselves as we are   in these painful motions
>
> of staying cognizant:

With its complex reassembling of fragments and ruins, of lost histories
and alternate pantheons, *A Wild Patience* bears its modernist moorings.
But Rich closes the final sequence of the book, "Turning the Wheel"
(1981), by veering away from the ultimate, ineffable goals of T. S. Eliot
or the abstract political answers of Ezra Pound, and also away from the
secluded countermodernisms of Marianne Moore and Virginia Woolf.
Instead, she turns back to the social, to the relational as heroically ordinary, erotic process. Like a wheel turning inside a turning wheel,
"8. Turning the Wheel," the final section of the sequence, appears to be
headed to a woman-centered modernist's unifying symbolic end:

> The road to the great canyon always feels
> like that road and no other
> the highway to a fissure   to the female core
> of a continent

The speaker continues:

> I am traveling to the edge   to meet the face
> of annihilating and impersonal time
> stained in the colors of a woman's genitals
> outlasting every transient violation
> a face that is strangely intimate to me

But instead of aiming at the kind of ultimate encounter that helped
land the male modernist tradition in its postmodern cul-de-sac of isolation, Rich's speaker veers back to the process-driven rhythms of relational solitude, back to contemporary encounters with the aim to live in
(and to change) the world as it is, "not as her users boast." The second
stage of Rich's career concludes with her refusing the ultimate symbolic
road, even if it leads to "the female core / of a continent." "Turning the
Wheel" ends with the poet headed back to the mutual world reconstituted by relational possibility—she turns her car around and goes back
to the woman she loves:

> Today I turned the wheel   refused that journey
> I was feeling too alone on the open plateau
> of piñon juniper   world beyond time

of rockflank spread around me   too alone
and too filled with you   with whom I talked for hours
driving up from the desert   though you were far away
as I talk to you all day   whatever day

No longer a stand-in for masculine isolation and its abstracted goals, relational solitude leads Rich's speaker back to real people. Many were surprised at where that turnabout led next.

"solitude of no absence"
The Fugitive Condition of Social Solitude, 1981–1991

"a struggle at the roots of the mind"
Searchings beyond Feminism

In no way is it a clear break, but a marked shift initiates the second half of Adrienne Rich's career. Rich's approach to poems was never stable, but even so, it is necessary to note the tectonic-scale changes in the last three decades of her work. In her 1993 foreword to *Collected Early Poems: 1950–1970,* Rich stressed that her poetic quest led beyond "neighborhoods already familiar." In the early 1980s, her departing from the by-then familiar terrain involved many facets (ideological, formal, geographical) of her life and work. Owing to her aim to document a historically engaged process in her work, these changes register in her poems image by image, book by book. After exploring and clarifying certain core feminist principles in the 1970s, Rich never exactly left those principles behind, but in poems written after the publication of *A Wild Patience Has Taken Me This Far* (1981), she did venture beyond various restrictions and orthodoxies that feminist ideologies and methods had, she felt, come to accept and encode.

Pushed ahead by her life with Michelle Cliff and her associations with Black feminist poets such as Audre Lorde, Cheryl Clarke, and June Jordan, Rich began to explore her own multidimensional sense of social identity as a white, upper-middle-class Jewish lesbian. Her poems traverse the shared territory and the boundaries associated with the many facets of her identity and those of the people around her. Easily the single biggest ideological shift came from Rich's encounters with Marxist philosophies and the philosophies of other anticolonialist aesthetic movements. While Rich was never a participant in any one of these movements to the extent she had been a feminist in the 1970s, her poems sifted together valences and switched out (and combined) the lenses they offered.

Up until the early 1980s, Rich had lived her life mostly between Boston and Baltimore. As her battles with rheumatoid arthritis intensified, she found it necessary to avoid the harsh winters of the Northeast. In 1983 she and Cliff moved to Santa Cruz, California, where they would live the rest of their life together. Rich was no pastoral poet, but she interacted intensely with the social and natural environments surrounding her. While she returned to Vermont and to New York City often, moving her life to California profoundly altered the tableaux of her poems. The natural and social settings of the West Coast and Southwest were more than backdrops. The deserts, farmland, and coastline became living participants in the poetic errand Rich felt herself compelled to execute.

During our conversations and in our correspondence from 2000 to 2012, Rich revisited Raymond Williams's *Marxism and Literature* (1977) many times, especially the last chapter, titled "Creative Practice." Williams's emphasis on specific historical events and changes over undifferentiated transcendental or metaphysical accounts of creative and social action was a particularly powerful factor in Rich's expanding social and artistic vision. She returned to the final paragraphs of that chapter again and again, including the following passage:

> Creative practice is thus of many kinds. It is already, and actively, our practical consciousness. When it becomes struggle—the active struggle for new consciousness through new relationships that is the ineradicable emphasis of the Marxist sense of self-creation—it can take many forms. It can be the long and difficult remaking of an inherited (determined) practical consciousness: a process often described as development but in practice a struggle at the roots of the mind—not casting off an ideology, or learning phrases about it, but confronting a hegemony in the fibres of the self and in the hard practical substance of effective and continuing relationships.

Readers of the present study can already easily recognize how Rich's career in poems resembles what Williams describes as "the active struggle for new consciousness." The relevance of this passage to Rich only in-creased over time. She recognized herself in this statement. Her poems move back and forth across crucial issues and venues of experience. She mined her dreams and peripheral perceptions for cues to the ongoing "struggle at the roots of the mind," her mind and the minds of people she encountered. And, in keeping with her commitment to relational knowing and being, most of all, she invested time and energy in the "practical substance of effective and continuing relationships." Maybe better than any other single source, Williams's statement above serves as a lens through which we can see the fibers that Rich wove together across the last three decades of her work and life. In the discussion that follows, I will refer frequently to phrases from this passage, along with a few others already acknowledged, as refrains to frame Rich's goals and mark her progress across the second half of her career in poems. Williams's words bear repetition, given their clarity and their direct rele-vance to Rich's work.

In her poetry of the 1970s, Rich had clarified crucial gendered and sexual terms of conflict and formulated practical methods for resisting the power dynamics encountered by women under patriarchal surveil-lance and coercion. That clarity required a tactical narrowing and ab-stracting of vision. She had marshaled her senses as filters to engage the world around her and to mark the widespread violence enacted by indi-viduated, isolated, and competitive patriarchal structures and the meta-phors of mastery, achievement, and power that went along with them. This work had been absolutely necessary. Through it, Rich discovered and developed her sense that survival is a mutual endeavor, that many of the facts of liberated experience are relational. But once she had gained this vision, she did not intend to make it a stable method of living and working. Patriarchy did not operate only in familiar neighborhoods, nor did responses to it. And it didn't operate by itself.

In the series "Sources" (August 1981–August 1982), from *Your Native Land, Your Life* (1986), Rich takes account of her experience as a woman, as a daughter, wife, and mother, but also as an assimilated Jew, an American with southern roots, a northeastern American living on sto-len land, and a white woman in the remnants of a slave economy. In a direct address to her father, she affirms her feminist critique of his iso-lated, American "private castle in air," an approach to family that puts

daughters in jeopardy, in "that most dangerous place, the family home."
Rich then identifies how the terms of feminist critique reduce the complexity of her father's historical position: "All this in a castle of air, the
floating world of the assimilated who know and deny they will always be
aliens." She continues:

> After your death I met you again as the face of patriarchy, could name
> at last precisely the principle you embodied, there was an ideology at
> last which let me dispose of you, identify the suffering you caused,
> hate you righteously as part of a system, the kingdom of the fathers.

All this was true enough. But it was *not* enough because Rich sensed
how refusing the contradictory historical complexity of other people's
lives becomes another kind of dangerous place, a shelter for hidden and
denied aspects of oneself. Functioning partially in that way cripples a
person's attempts to contribute to the "practical substance of effective
and continuing relationships." So the area must be traversed again, and
again, tactical (in this case feminist) insights not denied but not left in
stable frames, either. Rich continues, speaking to her father, and widening the lens:

> . . . I saw the power and arrogance of the male as your true watermark;
> I did not see beneath it the suffering of the Jew, the alien stamp you
> bore, because you had deliberately arranged that it should be invisible
> to me.   It is only now, under a powerful, womanly lens, that I can
> decipher your suffering and deny no part of my own.

Throughout the rest of her life, Rich's shifting lens would be "powerful, womanly" to be sure, but it would continue to cast its nets of relational feeling and finding in new configurations. In "North American
Time" (1983), she marks the warning sign of stabilized vision: "When my
dreams showed signs / of becoming / politically correct / no unruly images
/ escaping beyond borders." In "One Kind of Terror: A Love Poem" (1983),
she notes her resistance to a socially or ideologically trained vision:

> Well, I am studying a different book
> taking notes wherever I go

the movement of the wrist does not change
but the pen plows deeper

my handwriting flows into words
I have not yet spoken

As much to herself as to the reader, or would-be follower, or even her enemies, she announces:

prepare to meet the unplanned

the ignored   the unforeseen   that which breaks
despair   which has always travelled

underground   or in the spaces
between the fixed stars.

In her work from the 1980s, Rich expanded her creative practice of
relational solitude into a wider lens of historical and political vision.
Rich's dialectical lyrics would continue to use the tensions between cold
clarity, burning shadows, and blurred borders. Increasingly, rather than
being engaged at the level of perception (phenomenological) or in diver's
(psychoanalytical) terms, those tensions would be articulated socially
and politically. As I noted in the Introduction to this study, in her brief
review of *Later Poems* (the most concisely insightful writing about Rich's
later work that I have found), Cynthia R. Wallace notes "a certain air
of *populatedness* in the book . . . the negotiations of relationships, the
responsibility implicit in dialogues both intimate and public." Wallace is
exactly right. Rich would aim images at the struggle between the limits
imposed by one's historical or social situation and the Marxist-inspired
capacity for human self-making and realization. In "North American Time," she counters the delusional American insistence on lyrical
transcendence:

try pretending
your time does not exist
that you are simply you
that the imagination simply strays
like a great moth, unintentional

In contrast, Rich contends that the lyric imagination must engage the ways it is coerced by the currents of history that live in the present. In "Sources," she begins with a sense of historical origins that are not of one's choosing:

> There is a *whom,* a *where*
> that is not chosen   that is given   and sometimes falsely given
>
> in the beginning we grasp whatever we can
> to survive

Here Rich initiates a search for relation (as survival) of another, more broadly social order. People cannot be neatly fixed in or simply freed from this given sense of a "*whom, a where.*" But she is not about to be shackled to anyone's sense that those first, fundamental questions should have the last word or determine the path. In "Delta" (1987), from *Time's Power,* her handwriting flows into a manifesto, a declaration that engaging one's social situation does not close (but, in fact, initiates a radical opening of) the shutters of possibility. The rest of the poem, "Delta," quoted here in full, announces the molten core of the third phase of Rich's career:

> If you have taken this rubble for my past
> raking through it for fragments you could sell
> know that I long ago moved on
> deeper into the heart of the matter
>
> If you think you can grasp me, think again:
> my story flows in more than one direction
> a delta springing from the riverbed
> with its five fingers spread.

I will deal with the radical, expansive, and elusive second half of Rich's career as a tale of four solitudes, all relational in their unique, overlapping ways: *social* solitude, in which figures explore American experience in relationships astraddle divisions between historical American identities; *fugitive* solitude, in which people's experience or pursuit of social solitude puts them at odds with and on the run from standard American social structures; *dissident* solitude, in which fugitives from American social alienation band together in organized action against mainstream (anti) social structures and institutions; and *radical* solitude, in which people seek relationships to themselves and each other that are impossible to account for in any available political or social discourse of identity.

All of these shifting structures of solitude stem from and develop relational patterns established in Rich's earlier career. The phases do develop in a general succession, but they also develop in association, combining and, at times, conflicting with each other. In general, Rich's exploration of social solitude—with certain fugitive elements—spans her books from the 1980s and early 1990s: *Your Native Land, Your Life* (1981–85), *Time's Power* (1985–88), and *An Atlas of the Difficult World* (1988–91). Fugitive solitude develops—with a few radical elements—into dissident solitude across works from the 1990s and into the twenty-first century: *Dark Fields of the Republic* (1991–95), *Midnight Salvage* (1995–98), and *Fox* (1998–2000). Dissident solitude verges into radical solitude in *The School among the Ruins* (2000–2004). Rich's explorations in radical solitude inform her final two collections, *Telephone Ringing in the Labyrinth* (2004–6) and *Tonight No Poetry Will Serve* (2007–10). After that, as she puts it in "Endpapers" (2011), a brief section of uncollected poems pursues the radical vitality of her journey "out beyond / the numerology of vital signs / into predictless space."

"where the pattern . . . becomes a different pattern"
Initial Crossings in Social Solitude

In *Your Native Land, Your Life,* Rich frames a newly engaged kind of creative solitude. She expands the feminist relational solitude of the 1970s that became possible, as in "Splittings" (1974), between women who "refuse these givens" and bridge "the splitting / between love and action." I will call this expansion in Rich's creative vision "social solitude." Social solitude involves experiences that place the subject beyond socially and historically inherited and/or imposed home turf, beyond initial questions of "a *whom,* a *where*" that take place in "neighborhoods already familiar." As she would write in 1993, her poetic errand "lies outside those neighborhoods." Social solitude engages Rich's work in an emergent American multitude. A traditional *lyric solitude* such as Wordsworth's offered the questing consciousness a romantic interstice in reigning social constraints, a freedom Rich found, in practice, often reduced to modern isolation by racial exclusion, masculine myths, and patriarchal powers. Rich's feminist *relational solitude* enlisted mutual patterns and practices in experience in ways that enabled connections between women in resistance against these constraints. *Social solitude* calls the subject into a web of new relations among formerly unacknowledged connections within and across the boundaries of class, gender, sex, race, and region. In the process, Rich enacts the call-and-response, interactive patterns of survival she initially discovered in "Phantasia for Elvira Shatayev" and drew into focus in *The Dream of a Common Language* and *A Wild Patience Has Taken Me This Far*. But beginning in *Your Native Land, Your Life*, she casts these patterns in dimensions that radiate far beyond her strictly feminist frames of the late 1970s.

Situating the speaker as well as the notion of poetic travel and knowing in newly social and historical terms, Rich's two longest poetic sequences bookend *Your Native Land, Your Life*. The opening sequence, "Sources," pursues two questions: "*With whom do you believe your lot is cast? / From where does your strength come?*" Rich knows that racial and ethnic identities, as well as her life as a woman, play profound roles in the history and present of these questions. Empowered by what Williams calls "the Marxist sense of self-creation," Rich also knows that the determinisms cannot be the final answers. She is critical of her father's "rootless ideology // his private castle in air," but she also knows that, for a Western poet, if the term *Western* means anything, questions of identity cannot be pursued strictly in Old World terms. Her identity is modern, American, and she is not to be limited to narrow questions of Old World ethnic and racial singularities, any more than she accepted the patriarchal codes in the 1970s. Her consciousness had also been formed as part of an American multitude. As an American Jew born in 1929, she had been a teenager when the nightmare of European ethnic rivalry had resulted in genocide in World War II. For her, and by implication and extension for any modern person, to claim identity strictly in Old World terms of ethnicity was to embrace ghosts made of smoke:

The Jews I've felt rooted among
are those who were turned to smoke

Reading of the chimneys against the blear air
I think I have seen them myself

the fog of northern Europe licking its way
along the railroad tracks

to the place where all tracks end

The narrative of ethnic rivalry had reached "the place where all tracks end," had found its catastrophic conclusion in one line of modern history. Even so, Rich knew that story had continued in alternate terms elsewhere. Historically imposed conclusions, no matter their specific claims to finality and totality, were *never* the whole story:

The place where all tracks end
is the place where history was meant to stop
but does not stop   where thinking
was meant to stop but does not stop
where the pattern was meant to give way at last
                                but only
becomes a different pattern
                          terrible, threadbare
strained   familiar   on-going

Resolved that her poetic vision is not free-floating—transcendental—nor is it absolutely bound to nineteenth-century identity markers of any kind, in "Sources," Rich identifies changed patterns of association in New World terms. This poetic work that makes present-tense connections across historical borders of difference takes place in social solitude.

From where might one derive the sources of strength for living an American life, and with whom might an American poet cast her lot? On the jacket of *Your Native Land, Your Life,* Rich declares solidarity with oppositional traditions in North America. Her strength comes "from imaginations that have dwelt here, at risk, unfree, assaulted, erased . . . from the traditions of all of those who, with every reason to despair, have refused to do so." In "Sources," Rich searches for patterns and images to connect among the lives and histories of people "who are not my people by any definition." By that Rich meant not by any *existing,* historical definition; she knew that those patterns had moved on and that an American poet had to move with and help further them even

if it meant that her vision destroyed certain stabilities on which the
world thought it depended. As she writes in "Sources," she meant to
keep on even if her "look becomes the bomb that rips / the family home
apart." Radicalized by motherhood in the 1950s, Rich contributed to
movements in the 1960s and 1970s that mobilized women's energies in
ways that altered the gendered and sexual dynamics of family and cultural structures. She knew it would not stop there. In "Sources," she
resolves, "I can't stop seeing like this // more and more I see like this
everywhere."

This was a "powerful, womanly" poetic vision built from a force that
"rips / the family home apart." But more than disruption, this vision
(as in "Natural Resources," 1977, dedicated to working with those who,
"with no extraordinary power, / reconstitute the world") bore the task
of identifying the "practical substance" of emergent relationships. As
a result, "Sources" makes several key connections in reconstituting an
American consciousness that cannot be contained within Old World
definitions or identities. With both branches of her family rooted in
the Deep South, and having herself journeyed from Baltimore to New
England in the late 1940s, Rich was, as she put it, "following a track of
freedom." From that point of view, she considered the region's historical
resources. Focusing on historical "imaginations that have dwelt" in New
England, she writes:

If I try to conjure their lives
—who are not my people by any definition—

Yankee Puritans, Québec Catholics
mingled within sight of the Northern Lights

I am forced to conjure a passion
like the tropism in certain plants

bred of a natural region's
repetitive events

beyond the numb of poverty
christian hypocrisy, isolation

—a passion so unexpected
there is no name for it

so quick, fierce, unconditional
short growing season is no explanation.

In her essay "The Tensions of Anne Bradstreet" (1966), Rich medi-
tates on the lives of Puritans and French Calvinists of the early colonial
period in New England and marvels at the fearful and "intense light of
significance under which these lives were lived out." She also remarks
on how stringent circumstances gave rise to a "vitality of pure conviction." She concludes that simply "to find room in that life for any men-
tal activity which did not directly serve certain spiritual ends, was an
act of great self-assertion and vitality." So one facet of an American inheritance matched an environmental severity to the mind's declaration
of freedom from predetermined certainties. In "Sources," she allows
that, yes,

> These upland farms are the farms
> of invaders, these villages
>
> white with rectitude and death
> are built on stolen ground

There's no running from that. Nonetheless, Rich recognized an uprooted
rootedness in the passion, conviction, and vitality encoded into the consciousness, "the endless / purifications of self" of the region's settler-
invaders. This was itself a radical act at the time. "There being," she
writes, "no distance, no space around / to experiment with life."

But the cultural history of New England was not derived simply
from invaders who had been persecuted in Europe. Considering the cul-
tures native to the region, Rich asks, "has any of this to do with how /
Mohawk or Wampanoag knew" the land and themselves? Expanding
her contemplation of American vitality, she wonders if "the passion I
connect with in this air" is a "trace of the original // existences that knew
this place." Standing in the New England terrain, she asks:

> is the region still trying to speak with them
>
> is this light a language
> the shudder of this aspen-grove a way

of sending messages
the white mind barely intercepts

Reading here I pause at the ambiguous or dual sense of the word "intercepts." One the one hand, to "intercept" a message could mean to hear and receive a coded meaning. According to its social and historical situation, however, a white mind, as it "intercepts," even in danger and seeking resources to survive, even seeking solidarity, nonetheless may also exert police functions of capture and arrest. The convergence of those senses and the resulting sense of danger contributes to the complex textures and to the overarching, embattled mission for growth and cross-cultural connection in this era of Rich's career. For decades, Rich's poems encoded nuances through an open nearness to the rhythms and textures of the world around her in rural Vermont and Massachusetts. As in the work of any modernist-influenced poet, often those images grounded her poems in perceptual/sensory acts that could liberate her from an "ego" framed in abstracted, detached, and modern terms. In social solitude, she wonders about this intimate proximity in social and historical—rather than strictly perceptual—terms. Here she reads an alternate source, a *sense* of American morality:

are signals also coming back
from the vast diaspora

of the people who kept their promises
as a way of life?

In "Sources" Rich identifies her childhood sense that, "through the immense silence / of the Holocaust," and while living in her father's "private castle in air," she had "some special destiny." It was a way of coping with "growing up safe, American" while, like other Jews, if she had been in Europe she might have been "living in a bombed-out house / or cellar hiding out with rats." Or worse. On the other hand, there were many people struggling with destroyed housing and basement rats in Rich's native, segregated Baltimore as well. Later in the poem, she returns to her sense of destiny: "an oldfashioned, an outrageous thing . . . //—a thought often peculiar to those / who possess privilege." Was it racial and class privilege that, as a child, she had transformed in her mind into a sense of destined purpose? Possibly. In part, certainly. But what about the other parts? Sensing nonetheless other energies in the American vitality she has inherited, she writes:

> but there is something else: the faith
> of those despised and endangered
>
> that they are not merely the sum
> of damages done to them:

A Jewish child living in Poland or in a more traditional community in, say, Brooklyn, might have encountered that "something else: the faith" in Jewish tradition. But this dislodged American comes across it along another trajectory, in the tradition of a people who

> have kept beyond violence the knowledge
> arranged in patterns like kente-cloth
>
> unexpected as in batik
> recurrent as bitter herbs and unleavened bread
>
> of being a connective link
> in a long, continuous way
>
> of ordering hunger, weather, death, desire
> and the nearness of chaos.

In "The Spirit of Place" (1980), from *A Wild Patience Has Taken Me This Far,* she notes African diasporic patterns connecting women's arts, "the Alabama quilt / the Botswana basket." She echoes those connections in the lines above from "Sources." Along with the sense that her journey north "was following a track of freedom," Rich's youthful sense of purpose recognized something of itself in the African American tradition, in which many of the spirituals, often narrating—and/or masking— the quest for freedom, were themselves patterned on the Old Testament. Rich had first studied the Black literary tradition while preparing her SEEK classes. She had also been an important voice—and a keen listener—in the nascent conversations about racial and class divisions within the feminist movements of the 1970s. In "Sources," Rich made initial connections to resources coded in an American woman's sense of vitality based in a multiracial inheritance. Relation in these terms, too, and no less than the feminist sense of relation from the 1970s, was what it meant *"to survive."*

So it was that "the eldest daughter raised as a son" in a "castle of air" designed for assimilation grew into a Jewish American lesbian-feminist poet, inheritor of a complex tradition, facets of which were divided from (at times in conflict with) each other: the Puritan passion of New England that flickered from the poems and accounts of women from the colonial era; half-intercepted messages emanating from the landscape intended for indigenous people who were by then elsewhere in the diaspora; and a sense of freedom and destiny that owed part of its patterns to the fugitive and subversive means of Black survival in North America. In her foreword to *Arts of the Possible* (2001), looking back on her position astraddle these historical divisions, Rich notes, "Sometimes I felt ideas that attracted me mutually repelling each other." In what I am calling social solitude, Rich's poems sought means by which an American creative practice could take responsibility for and take advantage of the power and conflicted complexity of its multiracial inheritance.

In "Sources," imprinted by these patterns in ways that had no name in Old World identities, a dutiful, rule-following daughter, the

> faithful drudging child
> the child at the oak desk whose penmanship,
> hard work, style will win her prizes
> becomes the woman with a mission, not to win prizes
> but to change the laws of history.

That American intersectional alchemy would draw on a multicultural, New World pattern of "passion so unexpected / there is no name for it." It would, as Rich wrote, burst formal "boundaries of perfection" and take her into regions of experience far from "neighborhoods already familiar."

That passion would begin in terms familiar enough, but its errand would not be accountable in the terms the world would associate with Rich's own ethnic origins. Through what Raymond Williams calls "a struggle at the roots of the mind," Rich would fathom a way to nudge and steer her destiny in relation to an as-yet unnamed and emergent sense of environs:

> Say that she grew up in a house
> with talk of books, ideal societies—
> she is gripped by a blue, a foreign air,
> a desert absolute: dragged by the roots of her own will
> into another scene of choices.

The men in her life had forsworn elements of themselves and their worlds, "had memorized the formula . . . of the assimilated" and "ended isolate." Her father claimed to be "bound by no tribe or clan / yet dying [he] followed the Six Day War," mapping Israel's conquest and seizure of territory in the Middle East. Addressing her late ex-husband, and recalling a "formula you had found, to stand between you and pain," she notes the attempt to avoid engaging the full complexity of one's historical and personal situation. In the end, he "drove to Vermont in a rented car at dawn and shot himself." For herself, for her sons, for women and oppressed people globally, and also for the memory of the men she had loved, Rich committed to forge a wider set of possibilities. She set out to explore an expansive and relational presence, a social solitude, because, she felt, "no person, trying to take responsibility for her or his identity, should have to be so alone."

In order to "change the laws of history," one must certainly first make a fluid and truthful inventory of the familiar. But this errand, as Rich wrote in the foreword to *Collected Early Poems,* ultimately lay outside "neighborhoods already familiar." Concluding "Sources," one of her most important sequences of poems, a series for her unprecedented in its form, scope of inquiry, and address, she writes:

> I have wished I could rest among the beautiful and common weeds I
> cán name, both here and in other tracts of the globe.   But there is no
> finite knowing, no such rest. Innocent birds, deserts, morning-
> glories, point to choices. leading away from the familiar. When I
> speak of an end to suffering I don't mean anesthesia. I mean knowing
> the world, and my place in it, not in order to stare with bitterness or
> detachment, but as a powerful and womanly series of choices: and

here I write the words, in their fullness:
powerful;   womanly.

Moving within the multiracial inheritance of an American person
would not be easy given the violently divided and conflicted past and
present of the social landscape. In section II of *Your Native Land, Your
Life,* Rich accounts for how white inheritors of cultural power and class
privilege struggle to find their place in the living textures of the world
around them. One problem is white people's obliviousness to the dual-
edge reality of being racially advantaged in a multiracial story. In "North
American Time," she notes how the need to conserve assumptions about
white racial innocence makes the United States a place "where the context is never given." With a subtle eye on class privilege, in "In the Wake
of Home" (1983), she opens:

> You sleep in a room with bluegreen curtains
> posters   a pile of animals on the bed
> A woman and a man who love you
> and each other   slip the door ajar
> you are almost asleep   they crouch in turn
> to stroke your hair   you never wake
>
> This happens every night for years.
> This never happened.

In this way an invisible kind of capital—privilege, a key asset in a fraudulent system—is either silently built into a person's life or not. Against
the great American myth of the self-made life (then being mobilized
with a vengeance by Reagan-era conservatives), this poem images web
after web of supportive and constraining fibers in "the family coil so
twisted, tight and loose." Rich asserts the ubiquity of the web against
the myth of self-reliance:

> You who did and had to do
> so much for yourself   this was done for you
> by someone who did what they could
> when others left for good

This is a set of connections that support and constrain, a fabric erased in the history of autonomous individuals according to a myth "where the context is never given." To acknowledge and explore the never-given context is to reconsider and historicize the American self, to interrogate and historicize the myth of the American family:

> What if I told you your home
> is this continent of the homeless
> of children sold   taken by force
> driven from their mothers' land
> killed by their mothers to save from capture
> —this continent of changed names and mixed-up blood
> of languages tabooed
> diasporas unrecorded
> undocumented refugees
> underground railroads   trails of tears

Understanding that, in these American narratives, many families bear their own perilous cartographies of silence, she asks: "What if I tell you, you are not different / it's the family albums that lie." Social solitude calls us to historicize and reconsider our place in a wider, more diverse conception of American responsibility and vitality. As Rich writes in "Sources," this is relational work, or it can be, because "no person, trying to take responsibility for her or his identity, should have to be so alone."

All families bear their silences. But for Rich, whiteness amounts to a noiseless and dangerously remote chamber, a silence of another order, a system. In "Virginia 1906" (1983), she likens a white woman's consciousness to a passenger "held in a DC-10 above the purity / of a thick cloud ceiling in a vault of purest blue." The nature of the woman's remove and the myths with which she is "dreaming of innocence" put her beyond historical reach, out of social touch. The American myth insists that such removal *is* security; Rich figures its perils. She notes that if "no one can reach her / she is drawing on unnamed, unaccountable power." Like everyone in some way, in ways more than some and less than others, the woman in the poem has been subject to abuse. Rich asks, "what if forever after, in every record / she wants her name inscribed as *innocent*." What if she

does not want to hear of any violation
like or unlike her own, as if the victim
can be innocent only in isolation
as if the victim dare not be intelligent

Riding in her ahistorical vehicle of innocence and isolation, Rich writes, "This woman I have been and recognize / must know that beneath the quilt of whiteness lies / a hated nation, hers." But the safety of being out of reach precludes engaging what she knows, or could know, of her world. Here whiteness presents itself as an ultimate kind of autonomy, another lethal shelter. The innocence of being out of touch—beyond reach—prevents her from connecting to what she knows of herself. Without those connections, what *is* intelligence? What if intelligence as chartered by the system becomes the skill of *avoiding* those connections? In that state, Rich finds, one is incapable of moving in the American inheritance. That dangerous dance necessitates a selective and destructive unwillingness to see: "Because I have sometimes been her, because I am of her, / I watch her with eyes that blink away like a flash / cruelly, when she does what I don't want to see."

Rejecting this self-imposed reliance on "unnamed, unaccountable power," a reliance rooted in ignorance, Rich writes: "I am tired of innocence and its uselessness." She asks, for "what protections / has she traded her wildness and the lives of others?" In the place of unreachable innocence, we need to pierce "the quilt of whiteness" and describe how actual lives "contort and twist / making their own shapes, wild." Rich ends "Virginia 1906" asking how a white woman can "stop dreaming the dream / of protection, how does she follow her own wildness / shedding the innocence, the childish power?" In gendered terms, Rich had learned such "wildness" was not owned. Instead, she knew, it was collectively generated and actively shared. In the end, vital wildness was rooted in mutuality.

In the 1970s, Rich had built a feminist-identified relational solitude, a way that women who were committed to the connection between "love and action" could join in mutual work of reconstituting the world. Those women could be alone in their work, in their imaginations, but in no ways isolated like those whose presence, in the end, depended on an "unnamed, unaccountable power" (white power, patriarchal power). For women like those in "Twenty-One Love Poems," who "grasp [their] lives inseparable," this was a crucial stage in the reconnection between "the energy of creation and the energy of relation" Rich called for in her essay "When We Dead Awaken" (1971). But what happens to the notion of relation and solidarity when broadened beyond feminism and into a multiracial multitude of working people? What *are* socially imposed identities in solitude?

"Yom Kippur" (1984–85) opens with the question "What is a Jew in solitude?" And what is solitude recast as an investment in and exploration of relationships across Old World identities and American social divisions? The emergent American multitude of the late twentieth century is rife with conflict and violence. In "Virginia 1906," piercing "the quilt of whiteness" reveals "rough earth," a "hated nation." As pioneers such as the freedom riders and sit-in students of the early 1960s came to know all too well, social solitude entails a voyage for the intrepid. In "Yom Kippur," Rich wonders openly about who has access to these locations of experience. She asks:

> To love the Stranger, to love solitude—am I writing merely about
> privilege
> about drifting from the center, drawn to edges,
> a privilege we can't afford in the world that is,

Among people hated for their sexuality, gender, race, or religion, what constitutes access to this kind of border-crossing social solitude? In the face of those dangers, how can one overcome the historical isolation of an inherited and enforced group identity? And if that is all there is to it, then why are the privileged so intensely isolated themselves? Why is the shelter lethal? There has to be something else at work. Fingering the antisocial grain in the American psyche, Rich writes: "Close to the center, safety; toward the edges, danger." She continues: "Solitude, O taboo, endangered species / on the mist-struck spur of the mountain, I want a gun to defend / you."

The socially engaged solitude Rich has in mind cannot be defended by antisocial means (such as guns), nor can it be bought, privatized, and hidden away in so-called safety. The task in social solitude is to create what Williams calls "new consciousness through new relationships." Clearly this is not a kind of private property; social solitude cannot be one's *own*—cannot be *owned*—in those terms. Rich writes:

The glassy, concrete octagon suspended from the cliffs
with its electric gate, its perfected privacy
is not what I mean
the pick-up with a gun parked at a turn-out in Utah or the Golan
        Heights
is not what I mean
the poet's tower facing the western ocean, acres of forest planted to
        the east, the woman reading in the cabin, her
        attack dog suddenly risen
is not what I mean

True to its relational roots in her earlier career, social solitude must be
shared. Newly moved to California, "Three thousand miles from what
I once called home," Rich seeks relations framed beyond the borders
of any neighborhood she had called familiar. Singling out Robinson
Jeffers's (note the image of Tor House, "the poet's tower," above) con-
tempt for the supposedly socially dissociated "multitude," Rich casts her
impulse to blur and connect through a social solitude into a vision of
cross-border natural formation *and* social connection:

Robinson Jeffers, multitude
is the blur flung by distinct forms against these landward valleys
and the farms that run down to the sea; the lupines
are multitude, and the torched poppies, the grey Pacific unrolling
        its scrolls of surf,
and the separate persons, stooped
over sewing machines in denim dust, bent under the shattering
        skies of harvest
who sleep by shifts in never-empty beds have their various dreams
Hands that pick, pack, steam, stitch, strip, stuff, shell, scrape
        scour, belong to a brain like no other

Viewed through this lens, the singularities and strangeness coveted as
authentic by the isolated lyricist exist aplenty in the multitude. Is the
lyrical taste for empirical precision and particular strangeness really incompatible with a socially engaged approach? Can that lyrical lens focus
only in "neighborhoods already familiar"? Rich asks, "Must I argue the

love of multitude in the blur or defend / a solitude of barbed-wire and searchlights, the survivalist's final / solution, have I a choice?"

Given the false choice among socially determined identity, isolation, and lyrical (transcendental) process, Rich holds out for an approach that could figure the border-crossing vitality of the multitude in the lyrical lens of the imagination. Such a passion could touch its strangeness as part *of* (instead of apart *from*) the unruly multiracial social terrain of an unfamiliar (but *not* foreign) world. Yes, the self contains multitudes, and no American multitude can be accounted for in terms of Old World identities, terms that in the 1980s erased and entrapped American lives by truncating and falsifying Americans' image of themselves, each other, and their world. From this imperative, Rich scripts a lyrical method, a four-line manifesto for social solitude:

> Find someone like yourself.   Find others.
> Agree you will never desert each other.
> Understand that any rift among you
> means power to those who want to do you in.

It is worthwhile to pause here. If by "Find someone like yourself.   Find others" Rich means assemble in company exclusively made of persons like yourself, then the above is an ironic commentary on the suffocating insularity of community and the dangers of unanimity. If, on the other hand, she means what the line says—in effect, assemble in company like and unlike yourself and defend that solidarity—then we can take these lines as the call to social solitude that I read them to be. Does "Find others" mean "others like yourself" or "historical strangers"? I think the sweep of Rich's work supports the latter, and the reading I offer here. In any case, both readings of the passage amount to the same thing, conveyed either ironically or directly: survival requires relations astraddle historically imposed borders. The errand of poetry lies outside "neighborhoods already familiar." The errand of relational survival has expanded.

Rich certainly believed that people—people like and unlike each other—who combine "the energy of creation and the energy of rela-tion" in these ways will upend the traditional understandings and gen-erate new experiences of social *and* solitary spaces. As a result, in social solitude we can expand our relational capacity, fulfilling its role by exploring new possibilities in a uniquely American social and political life. Rich writes:

> when we who refuse to be women and men as women and men are
> chartered, tell our stories of solitude spent in
> multitude
> in that world as it may be, newborn and haunted, what will
> solitude mean?

In one way after another, Rich would pursue this question throughout the rest of her career in poems. She would live that question for the rest of her life. As it shifted through the decades, taking on its fugitive, dissident, and finally radical patterns and textures, social solitude would come to mean the connection between "the energy of creation and the energy of relation," an emergent social presence, the quest to further what Raymond Williams calls the "practical substance of effective and continuing relationships." That practical substance would extend beyond the borders of anyone's historically partitioned, inherited home turf: identity. In the lives of the multitude it was already—had long *been*—happening.

As discussed in depth in the second chapter of this book, Rich had worked for most of the 1970s against the patriarchal structures that framed the supposed "fact of our separateness." In poems such as "Twenty-One Love Poems," she had marveled at the social and political power found in erotic connections between women. Collaborations between women provided texture and rhythms out of which she had woven her images of relational solitude. In "Phantasia for Elvira Shatayev" (1974), she recorded her discovery of relational energy: *I have never seen / my own forces so taken up and shared / and given back.* A decade later, in "Yom Kippur," she adds another piece to the puzzle:

> Close to the center, safety; toward the edges, danger.
> But I have a nightmare to tell: I am trying to say
> that to be with my people is my dearest wish
> but that I also love strangers
> that I crave separateness

Rich understands very well how this will sound to exactly those readers who had been reading her most closely over the past decade and more; it sounds strange enough to herself. She continues:

I hear myself stuttering these words
to my worst friends and my best enemies
who watch for my mistakes in grammar
my mistakes in love.

The continuity police in the age of deconstruction would sound the alarm, she knew. She went on. It's no accident that *Your Native Land, Your Life* concludes with an extended sequence titled "Contradictions: Tracking Poems" (1983–85).

As the conservative backlash consolidated its mainstream power in the early 1980s, resistance became a matter of subcultures pushed underground and largely factionalized. Identities. Difference. Meanwhile, Rich followed her expanded quest for relation and its nightmare love of separateness and strangers into a new poetics of social solitude. The central question from "Sources" echoed: "Did anyone ever know who we were / if *we* means more than a handful?" How free can an American lyrical imagination be if, in the end, it remains trapped in the Old World definitions of who and what a person is? If it can operate only on its tiny plot of inherited and familiar turf? Much of American life was lived beyond these definitions, so how could poetry and the imagination stay within them? As she embarked on this intuitive, contradictory direction, Rich knew a few things: she was a woman now in her fifties; American political power was leaning back toward its mythic nationalist, white supremacist, and patriarchal foundations; she was technically still "at home" in the United States but living thousands of miles from her familiar territory; and she was facing increased pressures from rheumatoid arthritis, which afflicted her body with pain and limited her mobility.

Rich concludes *Your Native Land, Your Life* with a dynamic, dialectical series. Various forms of confinement serve as the thesis. Early in "Contradictions: Tracking Poems," she images women imprisoned after striking back at abusive husbands and partners. One explains: "*I stopped letting him do it / so I'm in for life.*" Another woman faces being declared insane and committed by her "*brother-in-law,*" who is "*a shrink / with the State.*" She confides: "*I have to watch my step. / If I stay just within bounds they can't come and get me.*" Identifying with a paradigm of resistance and danger, Rich writes: "I'm afraid of prison. Have been all these years." But the most immediate connection isn't law and its patriarchal institutions, it's Rich's body, whose disease threatens to incarcerate her: "I have my fears."

> Unable one day to get up and walk
> to do what must be done
> Prison as idea   it fills me
> with fear   this exposure to my own weakness
> at someone else's whim

As it is with the multiracial and transhistorical resources Rich's speaker connects with in "Sources" at the opening of the book, these are partial, at times contradictory connections. After a medical procedure, still somewhat sedated, Rich realizes:

> I came out of the hospital like a woman
> who'd watched a massacre
> not knowing how to tell
> my adhesions   the lingering infections
> from the pain on the streets.

Discourses of identity and difference are in place to account for these distinctions. Rich understands this but responds to a kind of undertow moving across those dimensions of experience:

>   from the center of my body
> a voice bursts   against these methods
> (wherever you made a mistake
> batter with radiation   defoliate   cut away)

She is searching for a place within an unfamiliarity, a place in a "*we*" that "means more than a handful." As a response to "Violence as purification: the one idea," the singular identity, the identity made up only of familiarity, she holds: "Trapped in one idea, you can't have your feelings; / feelings are always about more than one thing." She is aware that such connections and contradictions don't make for prize-winning rule followers such as the woman and poet she was raised to be. She doesn't care. Echoing her insistence on experience as process, with its associated oversteps and mistakes, sketched in poems such as "Tear Gas" (1969) and "Transcendental Etude" (1977), Rich continues:

> If to feel is to be unreliable
> don't listen to us
> if to be in pain is to be predictable
> embittered   bullying
> then don't listen to us
> If we're in danger of mistaking
> our personal trouble for the pain on the streets
> don't listen to us

If the keepers of orders and borders mean to discredit unruly voices forged in social solitude, so be it. If you think connections and relations between people across historical divisions are errors, go ahead. We will listen to each other and survive by means disallowed by bureaucracies and the identities they administer.

But the differences/borders cannot be ignored. They must be addressed, changed. Fingering the key grain of difference in her sense of social solitude, Rich makes it clear that an imagination never floats free of history. Here we can hear an echo of Rich's neighbor from "The Burning of Paper Instead of Children" (1968), who mistakes kids burning math textbooks for an image of Nazi Germany. Accenting the importance of historical distinction over emotive connections, the poem's speaker coldly refuses her neighbor's association: the "burning of a book arouses no sensation in me."

But poetry is not there merely to adorn structures set in place by historians, demographers, and sociologists. As it is in "Sources," the point of poetry is not to obey rules and "win prizes / but to change the laws of history." If mistakes are metaphors created by orthodox (often bureaucratic and/or market-driven) assumptions employed by a system to quell its dissidents, then maybe the mistakes are worth it. Maybe they're not even mistakes. According to what are these moves judged mistaken or not? Twinning her afflicted self with the social body in search of the other side of the coin of difference, Rich writes:

The problem, unstated till now, is how
to live in a damaged body
in a world where pain is meant to be gagged
uncured   un-grieved-over   The problem is
to connect, without hysteria, the pain
of any one's body with the pain of the body's world

As with the hysteria-prone neighbor in "The Burning of Paper Instead of Children," Rich cautions against overdoing it. But she knows that American experience is not reducible to (is not possible within) the containers she had been given to understand it in. The social divisions are real; at times they are lethal, even genocidal. True. But Rich sensed within and around her an American multitude of interaction and interdependence going on between at least *some* people, maybe linking aspects—fluent but submerged dimensions—of *every* person. Rich ends *Your Native Land, Your Life* in search of social solitude, in search of contours of presence in a submerged (possibly emergent) American multitude. She plays both sides of the contradiction (dialectic?) between connection and distinction:

You for whom I write this
in the night hours when the wrecked cartilage
sifts round the mystical jointure of the bones
when the insect of detritus crawls
from shoulder to elbow to wristbone
remember: the body's pain and the pain on the streets
are not the same   but you can learn
from the edges that blur   O you who love clear edges
more than anything   watch the edges that blur

Writing of the great jazz guitarist Charlie Christian, Ralph Ellison asserted that "because jazz finds its very life in endless improvisation on traditional materials . . . the jazzman must lose his identity even as he finds it." In her next book, *Time's Power: 1985–1988* (1989), in poems that depart from meaning even as they arrive to it, Rich's speaker makes her initial forays into the social solitude charted in *Your Native Land, Your Life.* Ellison's figure of the jazzman is not graspable in stable terms of understanding and identity; jazz players riff on the certainties around them, on the tradition. Members of a group might pass those riffs among them, but no one stays on the trodden path, exposed to the light of certainty (what Rich calls "the sickening light of the precinct") for long. Paradoxically, Rich's poems in *Time's Power* show that a new consciousness informed by social solitude effectively makes one a fugitive from the actual society ("a hated nation") comprising the American multitude. The hated nation is also a self-hating nation. Still, Rich forged ahead with lyrics exploring a shifting and expanding sense of social relation. In "Delta" she writes: "If you think you can grasp me, think again: / my story flows in more than one direction."

"forbidden face-to-face"
Social Solitude Up Close

For a decade in the 1960s, Rich had struggled toward a relational orientation to her world, one she sought to depict in her poems. She worked toward the sense that the nature of experience at its most meaningful was actively negotiated among people. In *The Dream of a Common Language* and *A Wild Patience Has Taken Me This Far,* Rich largely realized these goals. Politically, her work was in an immediate conversation with women's movements across the country. Privately, via an explicitly feminist (and then lesbian-feminist) *relational solitude,* as in "Twenty-One Love Poems" and "Transcendental Etude," her poems and daily life challenged and reinforced each other in vibrant and illuminating ways. The force generated in relational solitude was real and crucial to her life and work, and to the women's movement. But by the early 1980s, Rich felt its scope was too limited. As she wrote in the foreword to *Arts of the Possible,* Rich found that her "thinking was unable to fulfill itself with feminism alone."

Following with *Your Native Land, Your Life,* Rich had explored her identity in terms "powerful;   womanly," including but going beyond gender and sexuality, and in ways that included her ethnic/racial identity but, crucially, went beyond it as well. As many have noted, echoing her essay "Split at the Root: An Essay on Jewish Identity" (1982), she addressed her identity as an American Jew in her family and with her in-laws. But, in a way rarely if ever remarked, as I have described above, these poems also traced several cross-racial connections and pursued their importance to Rich's life and to her *possible* identities as a North

American woman and as a poet. To use a phrase that has become a refrain in this study, Rich knew that her poetic career could not be restricted to "neighborhoods already familiar."

Rich began to explore *social solitude* by situating her poetry in a historically and geographically grounded American sense of divided diversity, a riven social plurality of enforced differences and blurred edges. In "Yom Kippur" she wonders:

> when we who refuse to be women and men as women and men are
>   chartered, tell our stories of solitude spent in
>   multitude
> in that world as it may be, newborn and haunted, what will
>   solitude mean?

The social charter of North American identity is complex, multileveled, intersectional. In part to guard against the ways that the women's "*movement* was being parochialized into 'women's culture,'" Rich was called by her sense of social solitude to operate across or astraddle the borders that framed her historical home turf. The American multitude is violently divided from and in denial of its complexity, in denial of both its divisions and its blurred edges. So poems that operate athwart or astraddle the borders almost immediately take on *fugitive* quality. If you don't play by the rules of division, you will be cast out. Rich's poems from the 1980s bear out these dynamics with daring and visionary precision as they pursue the tandem implications of social solitude and its fugitive nature.

Early in *Time's Power,* Rich scripts moments of social solitude that echo the connections made in *Your Native Land, Your Life.* She weaves an expansive American sense of vitality, a sense of (as she writes in section 25 of "Contradictions: Tracking Poems") "who we were / if *we* means more than a handful." In the opening poem of *Time's Power,* "Solfeggietto" (1985–88), the speaker remembers her mother, a classically trained pianist, through the music of her childhood. In "Sources," Rich signals the place of the African American tradition in her own imaginings of a destiny for herself, a sense of purpose and possibility distinct from the Anglo-American epic of Manifest Destiny. The speaker in "Solfeggietto" recalls that she didn't "wonder / what that keyboard meant to" her mother, "the hours of solitude" spent practicing for "prize-recitals." In the following section, she asks: "Freedom: what could that mean, for you or me?" She continues:

what I remember isn't lessons
not Bach or Brahms or Mozart
but the rented upright in the summer rental
One Hundred Best-Loved Songs on the piano rack

As with her destiny in "Sources," Rich's sense of "Freedom" is not phrased in the languages and traditions of Europe. Nor is it owned. It is not practiced in search of prizes in conservatory-like isolation. The meaning of the word comes alive in social solitude amid distinctly American resonances and contradictions. As suggested by the titles of the songs in the popular songbook—two of which are among the most famous spirituals in the African American tradition—"Freedom," as an American word, is powerfully inflected by Black people's historical quests. Addressing her mother, the speaker goes on:

And so you played, evenings and so we sang
"Steal Away" and "Swanee River,"
"Swing Low," and most of all
"Mine Eyes Have Seen the Glory of the Coming of the Lord"

A closer look into the origins of these songs reveals a tangled thicket of racial and national ambiguities, a laboratory of social solitude. In "Solfeggietto," Rich draws on a deeply complex genealogy for the sound of American freedom as she encountered and internalized it in childhood. As is fairly well known, "Steal Away" and "Swing Low" are among the spirituals popularized in the late nineteenth and early twentieth centuries by the Fisk Jubilee Singers. Performing these songs in choral arrangements across the United States and in Europe, this singing group, made up of Fisk University students, came to represent what W. E. B. Du Bois famously called "the articulate message of the slave to the world." In *The Souls of Black Folk,* Du Bois added that these songs "tell of death and suffering and unvoiced longing toward a truer world, of misty wanderings and hidden ways." Although "Steal Away" and "Swing Low" are commonly understood to be of anonymous or communal authorship, some sources stress the importance of the versions of these songs credited to Wallace and Minerva Willis. This narrative deepens the complexity of the history encoded in the music. With origins in Mississippi, the Willises were Black slaves of a Choctaw owner (Brit Willis) who rented their labor to Spencer Academy for Choctaw Boys near Doaksville, Oklahoma. According to this version of the story, the Reverend Alexander Reid, superintendent of Spencer Academy, forwarded the songs to the Fisk Jubilee Singers, who made them famous. So the genealogy of freedom encodes a complex history of cross-racial connection and conflict.

The other songs Rich credits among the sources of what freedom meant to her are likewise complex. Famed American composer Stephen Foster wrote "Swanee River" (also known as "Old Folks at Home") while he was living in Cincinnati in 1851. Du Bois described "Swanee River," which was part of the minstrel tradition of racial (often racist) masquerade and parody, as one "of the songs of white America [that] have been distinctly influenced by the slave songs or have incorporated whole phrases of Negro melody." The lyrics to "Mine Eyes Have Seen the Glory of the Coming of the Lord," otherwise known as "The Battle Hymn of the Republic," were written by Boston-based abolitionist Julia Ward Howe in 1861; the song's music was based on performances of "John Brown's Body," a song sung by Union troops during the Civil War. Howe's husband, Samuel Gridley Howe, was a member of the Secret Six, a group of men who funded John Brown's antislavery activities. So in the opening poem of *Time's Power,* Rich's character recalls the origins of what words such as "freedom" meant to her, origins that bristle with the cross-racial vexations and possibilities at the core of what social solitude is all about. So central are these words and melodies to the American view of freedom that it is no accident that "Mine eyes have seen the glory of the coming of the Lord" were the final words Martin Luther King Jr. uttered from a public podium.

In "The Desert as Garden of Paradise" (1987–88), Rich wonders about uniquely situated American points of view, about traditions of thought and action with particular origins in North America. In "Sources," Rich notes how her sense of destiny was inflected by "the faith" of those who refused to be "merely the sum / of damages done to them." In "The Desert as Garden of Paradise," she retraces that vein in the tradition of historically situated—as opposed to transcendental—American thought:

What would it mean to think
you were born in chains and only time,
nothing you can do
could redeem the slavery
you were born into?

In effect, in these images, Rich conjures a cross-racial American pragma-
tism counter to both continental idealist and American transcendental
thought. On behalf of a historically situated North American consciousness, she asks: "What would it mean to think"? Developing further,
she considers native traditions in the Southwest, of the desert "where
drought is the epic," of people

who persist, not by species-betrayal
but by changing themselves

minutely, by a constant study
of the price of continuity
a steady bargain with the way things are

In ways that distinguish *Time's Power* sharply from *Your Native Land,
Your Life,* however, the complexities of difference and connection that
accompany social solitude in the later book are intimate. They mostly
play out in the domestic and interior lives of Rich's figures. At times
these dynamics directly challenge the relational practices Rich established in the 1970s. In "Culture and Anarchy" (1978), from *A Wild
Patience Has Taken Me This Far,* Rich framed realized connections between "the energy of creation and the energy of relation" she forecast
in "When We Dead Awaken." As we saw in the second chapter of this
study, this poem was written during the first years of Rich's relationship
with Jamaican-born writer Michelle Cliff. In it, Rich images women living and working together:

Upstairs, long silence, then
again, the sudden torrent of your typing

Rough drafts we share, each reading
her own page over the other's shoulder
trying to see afresh

An energy I cannot even yet
take for granted: . . .

Near the end of the poem, against the backdrop of nineteenth-century
women's voices found mostly in letters to each other, Rich addresses
her beloved, finding herself fully immersed in newly assembled call-
and-response rhythms of a feminist relational solitude: "How you have
given back to me / my dream of a common language / my solitude of
self." The poem closes quoting a letter from Elizabeth Cady Stanton to
Susan B. Anthony. The quote presents the unity of creation and relation,
relational solitude realized: "*Yes, our work is one, / we are one in aim and
sympathy / and we should be together. . . .*"

In *Time's Power,* exposed to persons' distinct historical and social
identities, as well as to unique personal metabolisms and chemistries,
the collaboration between women worker-lovers grapples with experiences of difference. The feminist unity of love and action is not so easy.
Refracted through lenses of social and historical difference, the partner-
workers are no longer so neatly one. In fact, those tidy unities are not
the goal at all. In "The Desert as Garden of Paradise," Rich accents the
sense of difference across which relation must extend:

our blood is mixed in, borderland magenta
and vermilion, never to become one
yet what we're singing, dying in, that color

two-worlded, never one

In "Love Poem" (1986), through such partial but crucial connections
across difference, Rich's speaker addresses her partner-lover's "dark blood
under gold skin / testing, testing the world / the word." She continues:
"to your mud-river flashing / over rocks your delicate / coffee-bushes."
Even, possibly especially, in this intimacy across difference, Rich discov-
ers that there's "more I cannot know / and some I labor with." Where
in *A Wild Patience* the contemporary couple cooperates seamlessly, in
Time's Power, Rich's sense of "labor with" includes open struggles between, and veiled struggles within, the women. In "The Novel" (1986),
the speaker watches her lover hiding from work and life (and maybe
from the speaker herself): "All winter you went to bed early, drugging

yourself on *War and / Peace*." Accusing her partner of pretending to be at work, she goes on: "All winter you asked nothing / of that book though it lay heavy on your knees." She warns that all avoidance is temporary:

> you felt the pages thickening to the left and on the right-
> hand growing few, you knew the end was coming
> you knew beyond the ending lay
> your own, unwritten life

In "Sleepwalking Next to Death" (1987), one of Rich's most striking and subtle sequences, the speaker confirms her commitment in no uncertain terms:

> For I mean to meet you
> in any land   in any language
> This is my promise:
> I will be there
> if you are there

But maintaining the integrity of the "energy of relation" requires that differences be acknowledged—living connections are not always (maybe seldom are) direct. Maybe they are never complete. Even in the face of sworn allegiance such as that made by the biblical Ruth to her mother-in-law, Naomi, the needs are intense:

> If you wrote me, *I sat next to Naomi*
> I would read that, *someone who felt like Ruth*
> I would begin reading you like a dream
> That's how extreme it feels
> > that's what I have to do.

At times, as if under a compulsion she doesn't fully understand, one partner insists on, even instigates, differences she feels might free living, neglected creative energy from its rut in routine and certainty:

> Every stone around your neck you know the reason for
> at this time in your life   Relentlessly
> you tell me their names and furiously I

forget their names   Forgetting the names of the stones
you love, you lover of stones
what is it I do?

Whether the source is difference, avoidance, or too-stable certainties, as they straddle historical and social divisions, the relational solitudes from the 1970s are no longer as perfectly mutual as they once were. Rich follows with an image of collaboration bearing precise but very different echoes of the unity of creation-relation imaged in "Culture and Anarchy." Rich confirms that difference is a two-way street. She describes her lover who in "The Novel" uses Tolstoy to avoid her "own, unwritten life":

Calmly you look over my shoulder   at this page   and say
It's all about you   None of this
tells my story

The borders between members of the multitude play out in intimate (relational) *and* public (social) experience. In *Time's Power,* Rich approaches the one as if it is the shadow of the other. Immediately following the *"None of this / tells my story"* lines of intimate division, Rich's speaker stands at the U.S.–Mexico border as "many waited to cross over / from the Juarez barrio / to El Paso del Norte." In contrast to the divided lover-workers above, she sees "women, in pairs, strolling / across the border / as if taking a simple walk." Then, almost quoting the African American spiritual, "Many thousands go," she confides the intimate, relational textures of what freedom means to her: "I stood by the river and thought of you."

Rich stresses the practical nature of cross-border, relational labor across differences in social solitude. The next line in "Sleepwalking Next to Death" precisely echoes the syntax from the famous final stanza of "Images for Godard" (1970). In 1970, against formalist perfection/abstraction, Rich wrote: "the notes for the poem are the only poem," "the mind of the poet is the only poem," "the moment of change is the only poem." In 1987, writing against abstract identity politics and imagining herself in the role of a nurse who attends women injured and suffering in attempts to negotiate the border between them, she writes: "The practical nurse is the only nurse." She continues:

                    it will be a long day
a long labor
                    the midwife will be glad to see her
it will be a long night

Assuming her imagined duties attending to injuries at the social (national/
racial) border, Rich emphasizes the intimate dimensions of historical divisions: "Will you let her touch you / Will you tell her you're fine?" Imag-
ing the intimate struggles with difference when social (public, historical)
and relational (feminist, private) solitudes collide, Rich writes:

I'm afraid of the border patrol
                                   Not those men
of La Migra who could have run us
into the irrigation canal with their van
                                   I'm afraid
of the patrollers
the sleepwalker in me
                    the loner in you

As with the lovers in "Twenty-One Love Poems," serious danger looms
in "the failure to want our freedom passionately enough," when we police and "border patrol" ourselves and each other.

    At this point we notice for the first time an important new reso-
nance that accompanies images at the crossroads of relational and social
solitude. Whether dreamers or loners, pioneers of social solitude often
feel like *fugitives,* even in intimate experiences. Because the pressure of
historical differences laces private space with silence and distrust, Rich's
speaker seeks a runaway intimacy, an on-the-run renewal of the lover-
worker's capacity for relation:

I want five hours with you
in a train running south
                              maybe ten hours
in a Greyhound bound for the border
the two seats side-by-side that become a home
an island of light in the continental dark
the time that takes the place of a lifetime

In that fugitive space, "an island of light in the continental dark," Rich's speaker frames a new commitment to realigning the energies of relational solitude in acknowledgment of differences exposed by her figures' historical identities. Intimacy also has a history. It floats no freer than does the imagination. To believe that it does amounts to a romance that real relationships cannot afford. In these terms, Rich frames the relational necessity between fugitive members of the new multitude:

> I promise I won't fall asleep when the lights go down
> I will not be lulled
> Promise you won't jump the train
> vanish into the bus depot at three a.m.
> that you won't defect

As characters seek intimate connections across social differences, or in public spaces organized around historically defined identities, a new dimension of creative space appears in Rich's poems: *fugitive solitude.* Images of social connections made across differences and, as it were, on the run will not be found in frames sanctioned by the institutions that structure the social world. Also, in this fugitive space we come across Rich's first explicit acknowledgment that she is working, in effect, beyond feminism. She is reaching beyond relationships as institutional and professional practice. In "For an Album" (1987), Rich writes: "our story is not about women / victoriously perched on the one / sunny day of the conference." Rather, social connections made by fugitives will appear in

> moments
> when even slow motion moved too fast
> for the shutter of the camera:
> words that blew our lives apart, like so,
> eyes that cut and caught each other,
> mime of the operating room
> where gas and knives quote each other

Rich would never disavow feminism as such. But, especially as it took institutional and professional form, she meant to work and live toward connections beyond those frames of reference as well. Her search remained syncopated. She was not going to "perch on the one." In this she felt her life and work drawing her beyond terms even oppositional professional discourses would sanction, or could fathom. This intensified the fugitive quality of her expanding practice of solitude.

As if lit by "candle-stumps" left "on ledges by fugitives," the connective and subversive energies of social solitude flicker into view and collect in "Harper's Ferry" (1988). A young white woman has set out alone, fleeing abuses in her family. She arrives injured at a house on the outskirts of town where John Brown and his men plan their insurrection. Echoing questions (in "Sources" and "Solfeggietto") she has posed about her personal sense of freedom and destiny, and also addressing the floating safety of the white woman in "Virginia 1906," Rich asks:

> Whatever gave the girl the idea you could run away
> from a family quarrel? Displace yourself, when nothing else
> would change? It wasn't books:
>
> it was half-overheard, a wisp of talk:
> *escape   flight   free soil*
> softing past her shoulder

As an instance of the American self in social solitude, and because "this girl is expert in overhearing," Black discourses about destiny and freedom directly inform the young white woman's sense of her world and her place in it. In the 1960s, Rich's pursuit of truth in poems changed from a solitary sheltered endeavor into a mobile, cooperative process toward collective understandings, a *movement*. Likewise, in "Harper's Ferry" Rich's solitary fugitive listens to talk about "a strategy of mass flight." She overhears *"No more   Many thousand go,"* fragments from the spiritual "No More Auction Block," with its refrain, "Many thousands gone." From those eavesdropped lyrics, Rich's fugitive learns what to do when

> the cotton swells in its boll and you feel yourself engorged,
>   unnameable
> you yourself feel encased and picked-open, you feel yourself
>   unenvisaged

But the story and the strategy the girl has overheard are about more than herself. The implications are collective. The patterns are mutual. There is a way to be "ready for more than solitary defiance."

Images of social solitude and the fugitives who seek it and reckon with its implications constitute the spine of *Time's Power.* Through them Rich suggests that subversive connections must elude and resist the confines of social structure and the powers that operate behind them. Those moments can create new identities, new kinds of principled kinship:

> The men are dark and sometimes pale
> like her, their eyes pouched or blank or squinting, all by now
> are queer, outside, and out of bounds and have no membership
> in any brotherhood but this: where power is handed from
> the ones who can get it to the ones
> who have been refused.

An unprecedented collection of fugitives has taken shape in social solitude. As if conscious of her Black partner looking over her shoulder, Rich recognizes how she projected her image into the historical origins of social solitude. She writes: "This would be my scenario of course: that the white girl understands / what I understand and more." The slightly salty, self-mocking irony is not a retraction. Differences are real. So is the border-crossing, relational work of what it means "*to survive*" beyond the brackets of feminist relational solitude. In social solitude, Rich's fugitives engage both with and beyond "a *whom,* a *where* / that is not chosen   that is given   and sometimes falsely given," as part of finding and at times creating "who we were / if *we* means more than a handful."

At this point, the stakes are clear enough. The task is defined. Rich's fugitives in social solitude must refine their forces and imagine them transmuted in the hands of a new multitude of political vitality and private renewal. Methods will involve what Williams calls "the hard practical substance of effective and continuing relationships." This is not the work of catharsis, conversion, and epiphany. Still less is it the work of isolated, antisocial geniuses. As Williams writes, "the active struggle for new consciousness" is not about "casting off an ideology or learning phrases about it, but confronting a hegemony in the fibres of the self." In "Turning" (1988), the closing sequence in *Time's Power,* Rich asks, "What would you bring along on a trek like this? / What is bringing you along?" As with Williams's description, there are no simple answers, no existing models. The work takes place in the face of active and passive obstacles, "where swimming against the current will become / no metaphor: this is how you land, unpurified, / winded, shivering, on the further shore."

In their lyric and angular peripheries, in the moments when change actually takes place, what Williams calls the "hard practical substance" of relation might not appear hard or practical at all. Instead, in "Turning," Rich holds that much will depend on "the prickle of memory." Needed connections might entail "This eyeflash, / this touch, handling the drenched flyers, / these glances back at history—." The question before the imagination in social solitude is "how to break a mold of discourse." Absent epiphanies, one has to trust "how little by little minds change / but that they do change." In ways she engaged across her career, Rich knew that the forces of isolation present a formidable obstruction. Identifying the danger, Rich's speaker in "Turning" addresses her intimate. Here as elsewhere throughout *Time's Power,* it is tempting and likely accurate to imagine her speaking directly to Michelle Cliff, but it is also necessary to respect the general nature of the address. Rich's voice echoes back through the difficult crosscurrents where relational and social solitude converge, the complex private patterns of *Time's Power*:

> our changes of mind have come
> with the stir of hairs, the sound of a cracked phrase:
> we have depended on something.
> What then?   Sex isn't enough, merely to trust
> each other's inarticulate sounds,
> —what then?   call it mutual recognition.

The final section of the series closes the book by switching the address from the intimate to the public but retaining a sense of radical openness, of expanded and deepened mutual recognition and possibility. The reader becomes part of a fugitive community in the approaching future, a future that only a certain kind of time-between-fugitives can bring about. Social solitude depends on possibilities of relation that are not at home, not welcome, some outlawed, by the world as it is. She ends the book with a call to fugitive relation in social solitude, "solitude of no absence, / forbidden face-to-face":

so I have thought of you,
whatever you are—a mindfulness—
whatever you are: the place beyond all places,

beyond boundaries, green lines,
wire-netted walls
the place beyond documents.

Unnameable by choice.
So why am I out here, trying
to read your name in the illegible air?

—vowel washed from a stone,
solitude of no absence,
forbidden face-to-face

—trying to hang these wraiths
of syllables, breath
without echo, why?

After gathering fugitive social elements, testing them in the most private reaches of relational experience, the final lines in *Time's Power* establish the paradigm of social solitude and script its fugitive condition as it straddles history, "solitude of no absence, / forbidden face-to-face." In that space, embodied and imagined relationships can, as Rich writes in "The Desert as Garden of Paradise," "go where no song has ever gone." Many of us go there every day in our lives, or need to. Any American life requires it, all depend on it. We, if we are to be "more than a handful," must achieve it. The next book would deploy that paradigm in the most socially extensive and mutually ambitious poetic sequence of Rich's career.

"take the mirrors and turn them outward"
Social Solitude Realized

An Atlas of the Difficult World: Poems 1988–1991 (1991) breaks Rich's practice of arranging poems into books chronologically. The rather scattered-seeming poems of the second half of the book were actually written first, leading up to the title sequence, in which Rich moves to "take the mirrors and turn them outward," enacting the practice of social solitude more expansively than anywhere else in her career. As she acknowledged in her foreword to *The Fact of a Doorframe: Poems Selected and New* (1984), and by means we have examined closely in *Your Native Land, Your Life,* Rich had labored to understand her position as "neither unique nor universal, but a person in history, a woman and not a man, a white and also Jewish inheritor of a particular Western consciousness, from the making of which most women have been excluded." Even while that was taking place, Rich knew clearly that the exploration of her *own* identities was not the end and aim of her work and life. "Increasingly," she continued, writing poems "has meant hearing and listening to others, taking into myself the language of experiences different from my own—whether in written words, or the rush and ebb of broken but stubborn conversations."

In *An Atlas of the Difficult World,* the poems leading up to the collection's title poem resemble those in *Time's Power.* Echoing "Delta," Rich's first-person manifesto of poetic freedom and growth, poems such as "Marghanita" (1989), "Olivia" (1988), and "For a Friend in Travail" (1990) portray would-be victims, women who save their own lives by thwarting impositions and expectations that surround them. Marghanita is "the artist" in her family; we are told, "she got away." The fugitive figure in "She" (1988) also escapes capture: "Clogged, the fine nets bulge / and she is not there." After decades in the crucibles of relational and social solitude, however, Rich knows that freedom cannot be measured by mobility alone, and certainly not by detachment. Fugitives in social solitude mostly seek connections. In "Olivia," Rich cautions: "I know the power you thought you had— // [. . .] you—paid by them, to move / at some pure point of mastery." Coded complexly in the poems of preceding decades, one thing is for sure: isolation disguised as solitude is not the answer. Survival entails an expanding sense of mutuality.

Depicted in terms of social solitude, fugitives in the early poems of *An Atlas of the Difficult World* are not alienated from people. Instead, they are often in flight from people's alienation. As we have seen above, freedom is measured in connections, deep in "the fibres of the self" as well as in what Williams calls the "practical substance of effective and continuing relationships." So, like the borderland nurse in "Sleepwalking Next to Death," Marghanita returns to deal with practical matters. She attends what's left after her brother's death: "hating and loving come down / to a few columns of figures, / an aching stomach, a care taken: something done." In "That Mouth" (1988), Rich reaches beyond the familiar—"This is not the father's kiss / the mother's"—to signal her need for a much wider sense of connection, the "unsweetened taste / of the whole ocean, its fathoms." These are preliminary images, the first signals of an emerging structure. When it does emerge, the lens will be diversely social, not psychoanalytical or metaphysical, and more political than strictly perceptual. Early in the book's title poem, Rich emphasizes her concentration on social—instead of metaphoric or metaphysical—locations: "the sweep of the great ocean / eluding me, even the curve of the bay, because as always / I fix on the land.   I am stuck to earth. What I love here."

These poems emphasize the dangers and struggles at the core of what social solitude has always been about. In "Eastern War Time" (1989–90), a "woman of sixty" lies awake at night, "eyes open," envisioning the most resonant ancestors and pioneers of social solitude, the brave and embattled border crossers:

> the young who do not wander in the moonlight
> as in a poem   faces seen
> for thirty years   under the fire-hoses
> walking through mobs to school
> dragged singing from the buses

Protesters, sit-in students, freedom riders were intrepid voyagers, fugitives from and activists against division and alienation (in this case racial segregation). They provided Rich with models for how to work beyond "neighborhoods already familiar." Of course, these pioneers were more often endangered than congratulated as they sought forbidden social relation as survival. They were stalked and threatened with reprisals, violence, and murder. But these voyages continued; there is no other way for American experience to cease repudiating what it has already become. There is no other way for Americans to "refuse . . . the splitting / between love and action" so that their actual lives can take place. The effort puts them—which means us—at odds with the society as it says it is.

This history of social solitude asserts itself against dangers such as those faced by protesters and freedom riders. Contemporary targets exist as well. Rich refuses to airbrush these images into nostalgia "left for another generation's / restoration and framing." In "Eastern War Time," Rich speaks in the voice of social solitude's living memory: "I'm nothing if I'm just a roll of film / stills from a vanished world." She continues:

> I can't be restored or framed
> I can't be still   I'm here
> in your mirror   pressed leg to leg beside you
> intrusive inappropriate bitter flashing
> with what makes me unkillable though killed

The life-and-death stakes echo those faced by the feminist pioneers of relational solitude in "Phantasia for Elvira Shatayev," who challenged definitions premised on the competitive individuality of patriarchy. Resisting the assumption that survival requires assimilation into that system, in fact arguing the opposite, near the poem's end Rich asks: "*what does it mean 'to survive'*"? She completes the image: "*burning together in the snow We will not live / to settle for less.*" As we have seen above, to survive circa 1974 for Rich meant achieving a relational solitude in which one's "*own forces*" could be "*so taken up and shared / and given back.*" In social solitude and its fugitive extensions, Rich widens the scope of relation across historical differences.

Connections in social solitude intensify and expand Rich's question of what it means to survive, of the difference between the "*victim*" and the "*survivor.*" In "Through Corralitos under Rolls of Cloud" (1989–90), her character comes through a bout of the flu. She feels as if sickness split the self in two: "it's as if part of you had died in the house / [. . .] and now this other's left to wash the corpse." Rich pursues the question: "what do you know / of the survivor when you know her / only in opposition to the lost?" What if survival meant—as it did for the freedom riders and protesters "dragged singing from the buses"—expanded social presence more than personal safety? Echoing—even down to the italics—the concluding moments of "Phantasia for Elvira Shatayev," in "Through Corralitos under Rolls of Cloud," Rich asks:

> What does it mean to say *I have survived*
> until you take the mirrors and turn them outward
> and read your own face in their outraged light?

Rich follows with this: "That light of outrage is the light of history."
Turning the mirrors out is then to see oneself and others as people "in
history." In relational solitude, women measured survival in "*forces so
taken up and shared / and given back.*" This took place in new kinds of
conversations and erotic connections between women. In social solitude, we "take the mirrors and turn them outward," measure freedom
in social reflections and refractions, in images of ourselves cast beyond
"neighborhoods already familiar." What image does one have in the
multitude? What "if *we* means more than a handful?" And what image
does that multitude have in one's own imagination? Does one's *own* self-
image survive in that world, in those worlds, and vice versa? Can it do
that and still be one's own? Can any of this be owned? What are the
intimate borders in one's social relations? What are the social borders in
our intimate relations? Can we survive within them? As Rich did in her
life, her questing persona answers no.

     In "Through Corralitos under Rolls of Cloud," Rich finds that un-
conscious borders exist even in the most banal thoughts, such as the
wish "that those we love / be well." In these terms, even the idea of
wellness needs to be questioned: "whatever that means, to be well." The
lens of social solitude reveals the borders in our oppositional thought,
borders that we must cross or destroy in order "to say *I have survived*"
in the social sense: "Outrage: who dare claim protection for their own /
amid such unprotection? What kind of prayer / is that? To what kind of
god? What kind of wish?" According to the expansive relational geography of social solitude, "solitude of no absence, / forbidden face-to-face,"
elsewhere and otherness are never as far away as we have been told they
are. In effect, social solitude asks: What if to be a "*victim*" meant a life
lived inside historical borders, in terms (as Rich writes in "Sources") of
a "*whom,* a *where* / that is not chosen that is given and sometimes falsely
given"? What if being a "*survivor*" meant that one's "*own forces*" could be
"*so taken up and shared / and given back*" in ways unscripted by historical
divisions, in locations beyond "neighborhoods already familiar"? By the
logic of social solitude, we are all freer in cross-border dynamics than we
are inside our—*any* of our—enclosed bunkers of self- (and similar) regard. Ownership itself is part—maybe the foundation?—of the system
of division.

     Indeed, to go beyond desires and fears rehearsed along history's partitions and oppositions warps the terrain upon which distinctions such as those between survivors and victims are made. For instance, how many in the mobs attacking freedom riders could be said not to have survived that experience? What about those who stood idly by or looked away? How many in the mobs—or among those watching them—were already walking victims of the history that entrapped them? Speaking as one of the endangered freedom fighters and embattled protesters, in the 1960s, James Baldwin used to taunt, "I am *not* the victim here, I know one thing from another." As Baldwin's assertion intimates, how many of the so-called victims, the targets of those fire hoses and bombs and mobs on the way to school, how many even of the killed, had already freed themselves, or had begun to, and had set about freeing others, or had sought to, and would never therefore *be* victims? By which social mechanisms had who been entrapped? And by what? And by exactly what historical practices had who been freed? And from what? These are questions of social rupture and repair far more than ones about quivering lyrical equivocations. Social solitude incubates a force that, as Rich writes in "Final Notations" (1991), "will occupy your thought / as a city is occupied, as a bed is occupied / it will take all your flesh, it will not be simple." This kind of renewal requires that social borders be crossed in ways that will feel to many like a violation: "You are coming into us who cannot withstand you / you are coming into us who never wanted to withstand you." Social solitude calls to the transformative stranger in us all.

What if this so-called threat is not really danger? What if it is the only hope there is? What if it is both a real danger and the only hope? Turning mirrors outward is a metaphor for disruptive and interactive social travel: "you are taking parts of us into places never planned / you are going far away with pieces of our lives." However fearful and challenging, these are the liberating forces of Rich's accumulating sense of poetic vision, of poetic purpose. Many in her audience of feminists as well as her other audiences were not ready for this. She knew that. Others, distant from her work in the 1970s, maybe some not yet born, were already living these risks. She knew that, too. After testing social solitude in *Time's Power* and theorizing it in the early poems of *An Atlas of the Difficult World,* she decided it was time to "turn [the mirrors] outward" and try out the expansive vision that social solitude makes possible in "outraged light," in "the light of history."

"fathoming what it means / to love my country"
Social Solitude Deployed

"An Atlas of the Difficult World" (1990–91) casts the widest and most intricate net of innovative presence Rich had ever attempted in poems. The long lines become a living lattice of connections and differences that—with the possible exceptions of calculated and deliberate cruelty and warfare—refuse stable trenches of otherness. The vision from social solitude presents nonresolving tableaux of existing and possible relations between diverse and widespread actions of human, natural, industrial, agricultural, and political energies. With an obvious debt to Walt Whitman and echoing Muriel Rukeyser and Hart Crane, among others, and arguing against antisocial elements of West Coast modernism provided by Robinson Jeffers, "An Atlas of the Difficult World" charts nonsystematic vistas of social connectedness.

The poem sketches and explores how human, technological, natural, and agricultural terrains of midcoast and inland California run together. The opening images of the sequence present ambiguous communions. Human and mechanical voices merge: "A dark woman, head bent, listening for something /—a woman's voice, a man's voice or / voice of the freeway." As had the railroads, roadways follow riverine paths, "night after night, metal streaming downcoast." The world's body connects to the bodies of its inhabitants, "the haunted river flowing from brow to groin." Workers commune with the land and the machines and chemicals used to exploit it and them:

> past eucalyptus, cypress, agribusiness empires
> THE SALAD BOWL OF THE WORLD, gurr of small planes
> dusting the strawberries, each berry picked by a hand
> in close communion, strawberry blood on the wrist,
> Malathion in the throat, communion,

Out of this living and lethal vascular network, anonymous voices sound their sense of separateness, of disconnection. Rich's imagination in social solitude weaves them together. In probing the nature of ethnic identity and diaspora in "Yom Kippur," Rich asks, "What is a Jew in solitude?" In "An Atlas" she approaches the question of solitude from the situation of (maybe class) mobility from relative vulnerability to relative security. Is this the voice of the American Dream?

One says: "I never knew from one day to the next
where it was coming from: I had to make my life happen
from day to day.   Every day an emergency.
Now I have a house, a job from year to year.
What does that make me?"

As one danger replaces the former, we move on to the next. The questions are beyond the personal, but the networks of connection are wide (social) rather than deep (psychoanalytical) such as in "Diving into the Wreck" (1972) or "Meditations for a Savage Child" (a rare undated poem that closes *Diving into the Wreck,* 1973). "I fix on the land," she writes. "I am stuck to earth." The need to turn the mirrors outward and widen the social lens of the lyric cannot be reduced to personal desire. Over and over we are told: "I don't want to hear." But Rich's figure still listens. We are told, "I don't want to think." But she considers anyway. Rich's speaker confides, "I don't want to know." But she seeks to find out, nonetheless, what she can, despite "wreckage, dreck, and waste," because "these are the materials." Signaling the presence of overlooked resources, she extends the empirical catalog of materials:

and so are the slow lift of the moon's belly
over wreckage, dreck, and waste, wild treefrogs calling in
another season, light and music still pouring over
our fissured, cracked terrain.

The visionary vision in social solitude is not a passive collecting, not an objective pose or even a committed and empathetic witnessing. The stakes in the identification are deeper and more complexly twisted than that. In "Dreamwood" (1987), from *Time's Power,* Rich describes "a woman dreaming when she should be typing" as she creates "a map of variations" so that "the material and the dream can join." Relational solitude made for means of survival by connecting love and action. In social solitude, the sense of reality and the sense of the possible flow together. The scripts of social solitude constitute a vision, composed *and* recorded, empirical *and* visionary. The borders between are unstable. Or maybe we are trained to mistake the vitality in the borderlands of social solitude for instability. Rather than unstable, maybe the borders would be better viewed as vibrant, alive, surviving. In "An

Atlas," Rich emphasizes the relational nature of the form, a partially formalized conversation:

> I promised to show you a map you say but this is a mural
> then yes let it be   these are small distinctions
> where do we see it from is the question.

Rich's point of view emanates from the mobile mural of social solitude;
the connections argue against isolation, essential silences, and disloca-
tions. Differences are negotiated. The mural depicts what Williams calls
the "practical substance of effective and continuing relationships."

"Where do we see it from is the question." Assessing her own path
in the mirror turned outward of "An Atlas," Rich looks back on the era
of *A Wild Patience Has Taken Me This Far*. In "Culture and Anarchy"
(1978), she had reconsidered Susan B. Anthony's vision of the Brontë sisters' impoverished methods ("*with their arms around each other*") of com-
position in their "*short and ill-environed lives*." As we have seen above,
Rich reads these images as embattled instances of relational solitude.
Looking back in "An Atlas," she notes the failing of her own privileged,
intellectual position among the ill-environed lives immediately surrounding her as she worked in rural Vermont:

> One hot afternoon I sat there reading Gaskell's *Life of Charlotte*
>   *Brontë*—the remote
> upland village where snow lay long and late, the deep-rutted
>   roads, the dun and grey moorland

Despite Rich's privilege and the connections between the physical settings of her subject and herself, she traces the limits of the previous (relational) stage in her shifting version of creative (now social) solitude.
Identifying the limitations of relational solitude that she failed to see,
she remembers herself as she sat:

> —trying to enfigure such a life, how genius
> unfurled in the shortlit days, the meagre means of that house. I
>   never thought
> of lives at that moment around me, what girl dreamed

and was extinguished in the remote back-country I had come to
      love,
reader reading under a summer tree in the landscape
of the rural working poor.

Having glimpsed through the "intrusive inappropriate bitter flashing" memory of social solitude what she had missed in her past work
and life, Rich extends her social vision to glimpses of what she does not
see in the present. Returning to a familiar image (the spider as source
of passionate patience in labor—women's work—that goes unnoticed
and/or gets undone as it happens), Rich notices a spider completing her
web in the vacation house she is about to close and leave vacant for the
winter:

nothing comes without labor, she is working so
      hard and I know
nothing all winter can enter this house or this web, not all labor
      ends in sweetness.

But maybe the house empty of people is still in no way vacant. Then the
lens of social solitude opens into differences—and possibilities—it cannot
fathom. The next image echoes back over decades to "The Roofwalker"
(1961): "Was it worth while to lay—/ with infinite exertion—/ a roof I
can't live under?" Allowing for a world with multiple realities beyond her
understanding, possibilities her *own* immediate needs do not bear a sense
of, Rich completes the image in "An Atlas":

But how do I know what she needs?   Maybe simply
to spin herself a house within a house, on her own terms
in cold, in silence.

In the mirrors turned outward of social solitude, the image of invisible
private necessity resonates in larger terms. Rich follows with a section
recounting the pressure and peril faced by whole spectrums of workers against the further squandering of sorely lacking and badly needed
social labor. She images a multitude at work, or that could be at work,
attending to—and enlarging our idea of—practical needs:

Waste. Waste.   The watcher's eye put out, hands of the
                    builder severed, brain of the maker starved
those who could bind, join, reweave, cohere, replenish
now at risk in this segregate republic
locked away out of sight and hearing, out of mind, shunted aside
those needed to teach, advise, persuade, weigh arguments
those urgently needed for the work of perception
work of the poet, the astronomer, the historian, the architect of
                    new streets
work of the speaker who also listens
meticulous delicate work of reaching the heart of the desperate
                    woman, the desperate man
—never-to-be-finished, still unbegun work of repair—it cannot
                    be done without them
and where are they now?

Moving up and down the coast near where she lived in Santa Cruz, Rich's mural-atlas of difficulty and possibility sifts together the locations of work that reconstitutes the world, or that *could* do that. From images of San Quentin and Angel Island to the inland farms under corporatized clouds, diasporas from Europe, Africa, and Asia collide and sift into the indigenous territory of Mexican and Indian peoples, all of it within "views of the Palace of Fine Arts, / TransAmerica / when sunset bathes the three bridges" of the Bay Area.

"An Atlas of the Difficult World" deepens the questions and expands the spaces that historicize personal identity. It also introduces the role of difference that resocializes and deparochializes relational process. In "Sources," Rich poses the initial questions of social solitude:

With whom do you believe your lot is cast?
From where does your strength come?

Her answers in that poem invoke sources from a multiracial American multitude. In "An Atlas," Rich addresses the need for collective answers that apply to more than a handful. Beyond personal, the questions become mutual ones. The needs are connective, the questions are enjambed:

Where are we moored?   What
are the bindings?   What behooves us?

As with the ill-treatment of the practical labor and laborers dedicated to
the social fabric, Rich finds that neglect, even hostility, greets questions
about collectives. We do not, however, confront the situation empty-
handed, unarmed. Natural, intimate, and erotic energies remain within
our grasp, if we are willing to reach out:

> but this is not a bad dream of mine   these are the materials
> and so are the smell of wild mint and coursing water remembered
> and the sweet salt darkred tissue I lay my face
> upon, my tongue within.

Just as intensely as did the relational work in the 1970s, social solitude
relies on an erotics of language, love, and action.

Cities may be crumbling and segregated, but they still resonate with
the incomparable energies of human interinvolvement capable of bridg-
ing divisions:

> It was New York, the dream-site
> the lost city the city of dreadful light
> where once as the sacks of garbage rose
> like barricades around us we
> stood listening to riffs from Pharaoh Sanders' window
> on the brownstone steps

The collective voice blown from windows also runs together in underground tunnels: "bodies young and ordinary . . . / pressed against other
bodies." Rich continues:

> as darkly we felt our own blood
> streaming   a living city overhead
> coherently webbed and knotted   bristling
> we and all the others
>   known and unknown
> living its life

Social solitude throbs with a living pulse, the connective beat of what it means to survive expansively in a world designed to divide and isolate. But that vibrant world does not resound with images of safe spaces. Women have learned to empower themselves, to love each other and the world. All their poetic arguments are not with themselves, or even with each other. And yet still they are endangered:

> A crosshair against the pupil of an eye
> could blow my life from hers
> a cell dividing without maps, sliver of ice beneath a wheel
> could do the job.   Faithfulness isn't the problem.

Hatred, violence, disease, and innumerable unmotivated dangers threaten even the most sophisticated and realized relational solitude. Survival means moving outward in an expanding radius of relation.

Rich concludes "An Atlas of the Difficult World" with expansive visions of American suffering and the labor of creation and relation that must radiate into the twenty-first century. She sketches a portrait of a pervasive, masculine loneliness in private and public, "with your best friend, his wife, and your wife," "in the prairie classroom with all the students who love / you." She wonders if this loneliness "is a white man's madness." Rich acknowledges the reality of this suffering among (white?) men, and proceeds: "I honor your truth and refuse to leave it at that." Rich contends that it is still poetry, even if the most important arguments are not with ourselves.

She then turns and addresses another kind of isolation, "*Soledad,*" among a burgeoning, disproportionately working-class and nonwhite American prison population. She quotes extensively from George Jackson's prison notebooks published under the title *Soledad Brother.* In a spectacular turn, she lets Jackson (circa 1970) diagnose the isolated "white man's madness" of late twentieth-century masculinity. Through relational echoes from "Phantasia for Elvira Shatayev," "*I have never seen / my own forces so taken up and shared / and given back,*" out of which the rhythms of social solitude grew, we can hear Jackson describe his encounter with relational solitude in a very different kind of extremity:

> *But the significant feature of the desperate man reveals itself*
> *when he meets other desperate men, directly or vicariously;*

and he experiences his first kindness, someone to strain with him,
to strain to see him as he strains to see himself,
someone to understand, someone to accept the regard,
the love, that desperation forces into hiding.
Those feelings that find no expression in desperate times
store themselves up in great abundance, ripen, strengthen,
and strain the walls of their repository to the utmost;
where the kindred spirit touches this wall it crumbles—
no one responds to kindness, no one is more sensitive to it
than the desperate man.

There is obviously no safety here. But this area of Rich's mural-atlas suggests that acting in that space of connected and articulated desperation might be the only hope masculinity has to transform isolation into a solitude capable of relation.

Over decades Rich taught herself the redemptive possibilities of radical—if not desperate—gestures and built in poems a way to measure the mistakes and excesses that can come with quests beyond "neighborhoods already familiar." Nearing the end of her most expansive articulation of social solitude, in the first weeks of a new war (Operation Desert Storm, August 2, 1990–February 28, 1991), she looks out on a twisted vista:

—power and powerlessness run amuck, a tape reeling backward
          in jeering, screeching syllables—
some for whom war is new, others for whom it merely continues
          the old paroxysms of time
some marching for peace who for twenty years did not march for
          justice
some for whom peace is a white man's word and a white man's
          privilege

And as the revolving cosmology of social solitude finds a tenuous, gyroscope-like balance, she turns the gaze and narrows the lens, focusing once again on the labor of reconstituting the world, on social spiders of passionate patience who do the often invisible, often undone, always ongoing practical labor in the social fabric:

> some who have learned to handle and contemplate the shapes of
>   powerlessness and power
> as the nurse learns hip and thigh and weight of the body he has
>   to lift and sponge, day upon day
> as she blows with her every skill on the spirit's embers still burn-
>   ing by their own laws in the bed of death.

Again and again, these are the obscured and endangered redemptive energies, the acts that show up on Rich's screen of social solitude like body
heat on an infrared scope. No saviors, no gurus. But widespread skeins
of practical skill and care, resources for resistance and survival. Rich's relational solitude of the 1970s was built on scaffolds that "refuse . . . the splitting / between love and action." Her social solitude from the 1980s and
1990s constituted "a beauty built to last / from inside out, executing the
blueprints of resistance and mercy." In section XII, dedicated "(for M.),"
which I read as Michelle, the fugitive lovers drive in New Mexico, "clouds
an arm's reach away." The clouds are beautiful but Rich turns instead
to watch her beloved watch. The result is a portrait of relational space
bloomed into social solitude. Reimagining the connection between fugitive lovers living against alienation, an opposition worked out in "outraged light," in "practical substance," Rich describes a Black woman's eyes

>   drinking the spaces
> of crimson, indigo, Indian distance, Indian presence,
> your spirit's gaze informing your body, impatient to mark what's
>   possible, impatient to mark
> what's lost, deliberately destroyed, can never any way be
>   returned,
> your back arched against all icons, simulations, dead letters
> your woman's hands turning the wheel or working with shears,
>   torque wrench, knives with salt pork, onions, ink
>   and fire
> your providing sensate hands, your hands of oak and silk, of
>   blackberry juice and drums
> —I speak of them now.

Echoing the final lines of "Turning" that end *Time's Power,* Rich
closes "An Atlas" with an address to the social situation of her readers in

their solitude as they search for resources to focus their deepest dilemmas and for means to turn their own mirrors outward, toward each other. In social solitude we reflect each other. Among the many in the multitude, Rich addresses another anonymous fugitive from alienation:

> I know you are reading this poem
> as the underground train loses momentum and before running
> up the stairs
> toward a new kind of love
> your life has never allowed.

Driven by whatever dangers, fugitives in social solitude flee toward each other. In Rich's work that followed, during the rest of the twentieth century and into the twenty-first, her fugitives would probe for understanding of their condition—a transformative social fugitivity—and then attempt to find and mobilize resources, first each other, to create patterns linking alienated fugitives into collectives. In this way, across Rich's next books, a dissident solitude arises as fugitives work together in a mobile guerrilla struggle against emboldened and expanding forces of isolation, alienation, division, and social desiccation.

"So we are thrown together"
Fugitive and Dissident Solitude Mobilized, 1991–2006

"dissimilar / yet unseparate   that's beauty"
Fugitive Solitude

In "Notes toward a Politics of Location" (1984), Rich described the needs that led her to script social solitude as she did in the 1980s. "I need to understand how a place on the map is also a place in history," she stated. To replace the abstract geography with an engaged sense of place and experience, she needed to account for her position "as a woman, a Jew, a lesbian, a feminist" who is "created" by a history and who is also "trying to create" within it, often against it. In the preceding chapter, we have seen how Rich's social solitude brought together complex and contested relationships between persons positioned by history in North America. As Rich moved beyond her strict focus on women's experience from the 1970s, her vision of social solitude culminated in the broadly diverse and particularized American vistas of "An Atlas of the Difficult World" (1990–91). But as we have also seen, images of private and personal struggles (plausibly the poet's own as well as many clearly beyond her own life), experiences always at an angle to identities imposed by history, had been important all along as well.

Rich discussed her needs to account for herself and the world in explicitly North American terms, focused on the kinds of connections peculiar to the history of territories claimed by the United States. This sense of history was necessary, she wrote, "even if nation-states are now just pretexts used by multinational conglomerates to serve their interests." Informed by her study of Karl Marx as "a great geographer of the human condition," Rich sensed that national identities and the subidentities (gender, race, sexuality) scripted into conflict by them intensified forces of alienation/isolation against which her morphing sense of solitude struggled. She obviously understood the importance of those identities. But she sensed she would have to explore them indirectly and in ever-shifting combinations. Maybe, as with the version of feminism she helped forge in the 1970s, she would have to move beyond but not leave behind the focus on identities as chartered by the history that shaped them.

As the discourse for (as distinct from the experience of) identities—like everything else—became subject to the pressures of late capitalism, Rich worried that these features of our lives could become (maybe in part already had become) commodities, brand names in a "banal iconography" of a marketplace ruled by billionaires. In her essay "Arts of the Possible" (1997), she wrote:

> In a society in such extreme pain, I think these are any writer's, any artist's, concerns: the unnamed harm to human relationships, the blockage of inquiry, the oblique contempt with which we are depicted to ourselves and to others, in prevailing image making; a malnourishment that extends from the body to the imagination itself. Capital vulgarizes and reduces complex relations to a banal iconography. There is hate speech, but there is also a more generally accepted language of contempt and self-contempt—the term *baby boomers,* for instance, infantilizes and demeans an entire generation. In the interests of marketing, distinctions fade and subtleties vanish.

Of course, the marketplace can just as easily sell the reinforcement of distinctions (again in vulgar terms that lack subtlety) as it can make them fade. Also in search of the "practical substance" that Raymond Williams figures in "continuing relationships," Rich's poems in the 1990s and into the twenty-first century worked against the vulgarization and degradation of our images of ourselves and each other. Eluding and resisting commodification of ourselves and our relationships would become a key feature of Rich's vision of survival during the last decades of her work.

The fugitive condition—being on the run, astraddle borders, conspicuous and exposed—of Rich's figures in social solitude appeared in the periphery of poems in *Your Native Land, Your Life* (1986), *Time's Power* (1989), and *An Atlas of the Difficult World* (1991). As her poems became more expansively public, exposing the alienation of this public space from itself, the way it created and policed borders that served the owners of the structure, her fugitive figures sought ways to connect in the margins. Absent the brightly lit and socially expansive sense of possibility that Rich sought in the 1980s, a sinuous and shadowy fugitivity becomes the unmistakable focus in *Dark Fields of the Republic* (1995). With the darkness of the field comes a sense of menaced possibility. But the dark also aids a fugitive mobility. If "An Atlas of the Difficult World" was lit for the grand stage of history, the poems of *Dark Fields of the Republic* often act behind the curtain and in shadowed corners. In her speech to the 1979 graduating class at Smith College, titled "What Does a Woman Need to Know?," Rich noted the crucial importance of oppositional learning, "flashes of insight that came through the eye of the outsider." During the 1970s, feminist discourses had stabilized her vision, she felt. As in "Amends" (1992), the poems in fugitive solitude recall the flashes and rhythms in the "eye of the outsider"; they move like

moonlight picking at small stones

as it picks at greater stones, as it rises with the surf
laying its cheek for moments on the sand
as it licks the broken ledge, as it flows up the cliffs,
as it flicks across the tracks

as it unavailing pours into the gash
of the sand-and-gravel quarry
as it leans across the hangared fuselage
of the crop-dusting plane

as it soaks through cracks into the trailers
tremulous with sleep
as it dwells upon the eyelids of the sleepers
as if to make amends

If there was a grand epic to aspire to, by the 1990s, Rich knew it would not be scored in national terms, nor would its connective vocabulary depend on owned identity markers (race/ethnicity, gender, sexuality), which had become, at least from her Marxist-inflected point of view, brand names in the national marketplace of literary culture, each identity for sale in its owned shopwindow. The force of this new, fugitive solitude moved rather like the verbs used to describe the movement of moonlight in "Amends": pick, rise, lick, pour, lean, soak, dwell.

For twelve years Presidents Ronald Reagan and George H. W. Bush and their administrations had preached the racially divisive and firmly patriarchal gospel of privatized wealth on behalf of the American god of profit. Bill Clinton had risen to power in 1992 largely by accommodating whatever left-leaning national discourse there had been—whatever vestige of progressive political energy had remained from the 1970s—to the conservative assault on a publicly expansive, racially inclusive, and cooperative American sense of itself. Pockets and methods of resistance were almost as divided as the mainstream, as Rich looked on in "And Now" (1994). Referring to *An Atlas of the Difficult World* in all but its title, she writes:

> I tried to listen to
> the public voice of our time
> tried to survey our public space
> as best I could

Attending the widespread, motivated foreclosure of the connections across the dividing lines of gender, class, and race that she had imagined in social solitude, Rich sensed

> precisely how the air moved
> and where the clock's hands stood
> and who was in charge of definitions
> and who stood by receiving them
> when the name of compassion
> was changed to the name of guilt
> when to feel with a human stranger
> was declared obsolete.

The public space for the new multitude of citizens she had been envisioning was being seized and transformed into a depopulated ether traversed by fast-developing networks conveying phenomena (information) most relevant to an unprecedented accumulation of private and corporate wealth. Neoliberalism established its reign. Under the pressure of these new, global powers, the poems in *Dark Fields of the Republic* push ahead. The connections Rich had hoped to make in public leaned instead into the shadows. Thereafter, Rich reimagined the surviving connections of social solitude—looking for ways to "to feel with a human stranger"—in ever more self-consciously and tactically fugitive terms.

Departing from a distinctly North American social solitude, early poems in *Dark Fields of the Republic* enlist sources and envision conversations in explicitly international terms. Bertolt Brecht, Osip Mandelstam, and Rosa Luxemburg convey the possibilities and dangers of Marxist and internationalist opposition to nationalistic and totalitarian forces in twentieth-century European history. Opening the collection, Rich locates her speaker in the United States, but the conflict is not strictly national. In "What Kind of Times Are These" (1991), she writes: "this is not somewhere else but here, / our country moving closer to its own truth and dread." She reminds that even though "this isn't a Russian poem," her country has "its own ways of making people disappear." Global dangers are no longer strictly a matter of Cold War–era operatives vying for national interests. The forces of disappearance are global and commercial. As a fugitive must, Rich conceals her exact position as well as that of the land she describes: "I know already who wants to buy it, sell it, make it disappear."

The sense of fugitivity in *Dark Fields of the Republic,* indeed, has everything to do with the politics of location. In "Notes toward a Politics of Location," Rich had described her search for historical position in her body, "that living human individual whom the young Marx called 'the first premise of all human history.'" As a feminist, she had assumed the role of "the empirical witch . . . trusting her senses . . . against the anti-material, anti-sensuous, anti-empirical" power of institutional patriarchy. By the 1990s Rich had come to understand the facets and markers of identity themselves, and the individual possibly above all, as brand names in the commercial conquest of public space for private interests. In ways of which she was becoming increasingly aware, trusting the senses, especially one's *own,* becomes dangerous when, as she quotes from Marx (1844), "all physical and intellectual senses [are] replaced by the simple alienation of all these senses, the sense of having." In "What Kind of Times Are These," *locating* the tract of land makes it vulnerable to those who would "buy it, sell it, make it disappear."

Like a tract of land in danger of being developed, a person becomes threatened when located in terms suited to ownership. These terms also make a person suitable for being sold. In "In Those Years" (1991), the self undergoes a similar politics of location: "we found ourselves / reduced to *I*." Once located, or "found," in this way, the self itself can be reduced to property, to the "sense of having." In the resulting marketplace, and under the pressures of capital mapped by Marx but operating at speeds and scales unimaginable in nineteenth-century terms, Rich writes, "we lost track / of the meaning of *we*, of *you*." The processes of alienation are also the processes of individuation. Instead of treating the "I" as "the first premise of all human history" that Marx held it to be, Rich's poems in *Dark Fields of the Republic* handle it more like the initial conundrum—or delusion—of North American (possibly of Western) identity. Relational pretty much from the start, in poems at least since the early 1980s, Rich had consciously sensed her way toward an alternate mooring for the self, for herself, in history. As she wrote in "Contradictions: Tracking Poems" (1983–85), she had sought a sense of connection as "if *we* means more than a handful." In *Dark Fields of the Republic*, Rich engages—often enough as if in the dark—creative practice as a search for a real basis on which such connections could contribute to what Williams calls the "practical substance of effective and continuing relationships." Many of the terms available via the map of American identities had already, she sensed, been bought, sold, and made to disappear.

By the logic of her fugitives from alienation, Rich's figures and their associated pronouns could elude the brutality of the market—avoid being reduced to brands to be bought and sold, to be *owned* as private property—only by her refusal to label them in ways the market recognizes. These poems resist those (identity) politics of location that operated in ways that the market—the pressures of capital—could assimilate without changing its structures much, if at all. For the rest of Rich's career, her figures as well as her readers would have to recognize and locate subjects in her poems and therefore in themselves and each other according to other—fugitive—senses. The sense of relation at the core of all of Rich's developing solitudes was the most important among the fugitive senses for persons pressured into having individual lives, lives they were told they could *own*. But lives owned by whom? Located and identified in these ways, those lives entered the global marketplace for someone—most likely "someone" on behalf of globalized financial interests—to *buy.* Rich's later poems cultivate a sense of relational presence that *cannot* be owned, that the market cannot locate, that people bent on buying and selling cannot recognize.

In *Dark Fields of the Republic,* fugitive solitude marks a space in which the relationship between creation and relation becomes a conversation at once more elusive, more intimate, and more open than previously possible in Rich's poems. We can trace the development very clearly in echoes between precise images of collaboration across the decades. We recall the image of relational solitude where energies of creation and relation come together as women work in close proximity, reading over one another's shoulders, in "Culture and Anarchy" (1978) from *A Wild Patience Has Taken Me This Far:*

> Upstairs, long silence, then
> again, the sudden torrent of your typing
>
> Rough drafts we share, each reading
> her own page over the other's shoulder
> trying to see afresh

In her essay "When We Dead Awaken" (1971), Rich called for the energies of creation and relation to "be united." At the end of "Culture and Anarchy," in quotes from letters between nineteenth-century women activists, we find exactly that:

> *Yes, our work is one,*
> *we are one in aim and sympathy*

In the late 1980s, when social difference came home to roost in *Time's Power,* Rich questioned the unity between women and signaled the need to acknowledge and explore differences imposed by history. In her foreword to *Blood, Bread, and Poetry* (1986), she recalled the "passionate factuality" of "Black feminists" who insisted to their white counterparts, *"But you don't know us!"* Echoing this crucial call to recognize social difference in "Sleepwalking Next to Death" (1987), Rich implicates herself—at least her first-person speaker—in the practice of paternalism and appropriation that results from this ignorance:

Calmly you look over my shoulder   at this page   and say
It's all about you   None of this
tells my story

Having composed her mural of social solitudes in attempts to accom-
modate and connect across intimate and social differences in "An Atlas
of the Difficult World," Rich next imagined an intimate collaboration in
which social differences were in no way denied. While not denying difference, she realized, her people could not play out differences between
each other in ways determined by social and historical forces, either. As
a result, as a scaffold of angular—fugitive—connections, *Dark Fields of
the Republic* scripts a shadowy and shifting play of collaboration under
siege. Relationships encounter forces that have made commodities out
of the once-oppositional terms of identity. Those social identities—and
especially their relationships to each other—had been made part of the
commodification system, had been taken to market. So, pursuing terms
of fugitive relation—terms of connection that cannot be bought—Rich
holds the "sense of having" a self to *own* and strict historical codes of
difference to the side. In "To the Days" (1991), she returns to her image
of creation—relation "wheeling" under a "steadily rising" sense of siege
with a new, wide-open sense of possibility:

A typewriter's torrent, suddenly still.
Blue soaking through fog, two dragonflies wheeling.
Acceptable levels of cruelty, steadily rising.
Whatever you bring in your hands, I need to see it.

Rich's fugitives from alienation in the 1990s understand the intimate
and political need to look harder at each other and further in themselves,
and harder at themselves and further in each other. Like "[b]lue soaking through fog," a new sense of survival comes into focus, one more
powerful—at once more and less personal—than anything the identity
vocabulary of dread commerce could locate, name, and make disappear.
    "Calle Visión" (1992–93) presents Rich's first self-conscious itinerary
in (or toward) fugitive solitude. Where does this "vision street" exist?
What territory does it traverse? Owing to the politics of fugitive location
explained above, Rich does not specify. With "scrub oak and cactus in

the yard," we would imagine a stretch of desert. Is it in the mind, in a dream? We don't know. But by now we do know *why* we don't know. As if noting that capital has made commodity-property of our thoughts as well as our social identities, Rich begins the series with the warning that this street is "Not what you thought: just a turn-off / leading downhill not up." After describing the room awaiting the fugitive, she affirms that the road leads to a deeply personal (possibly deeper than personal) space:

> this is your room
> in Calle Visión
>
> if you took the turn-off
> it was for you

But what about you made you turn off? Who is this you? Rich does not specify. As the dwelling morphs from house to hotel to hospital, the injuries are historical, personal, and perceptual: "Calle Visión   wounded knee / wounded spine   wounded eye." But in this space, "your heart beats on unbroken . . . your heart is still whole." Rich repeats her surprise: "how is this possible // since what can be   will be taken / when not offered in trust and faith." Possibly that is *exactly* how. In fugitive solitude, sharing is owning, is work against breaking. Maybe something shared cannot be broken; maybe something unbroken in that way cannot be bought and sold. In these terms, things shared in noncommercial ways, "in trust and faith," cannot be located, owned, made to disappear.

In contrast, when located or identified in terms recognized by capital, "what can be   will be taken." So fugitive solitude is a newly subtle and sinuous search for connections to honor in "trust and faith," for the possibilities of shared experience, shared in terms that do not accept or deny, but rather emulsify and recombine, history's vocabularies of identity and difference. In her foreword to *Blood, Bread, and Poetry,* Rich argues that emulsifying and recombining the terms of identity/difference becomes necessary when we are fighting a "simultaneity of oppressions" that cannot be reduced to one dimension. In fugitive solitude, Rich deals tactically with the reality that our complexity cannot be reduced to simple arithmetic (double- or triple-jeopardy) equations either. The demands and the needs are more various and complex than that. The resources used to answer those needs are often counterintuitive.

By the time Rich was writing "Calle Visión," her method of fugitive connection had been in the works for more than a decade. In "Contradictions: Tracking Poems" Rich had asked the key questions as her feminist relational solitude expanded out of "neighborhoods already familiar" and into wider social relevance: "O sister of nausea   of broken ribs   of isolation / what is this freedom I protect   how is it mine." She had inched ahead toward a sense of freedom—one of sharing, not owning—athwart the rules of division, isolation, and private property: "The problem, unstated till now, is how / to live in a damaged body." Sensing the situation was beyond self-diagnosis, was widely dispersed and political, she continued: "The problem is / to connect, without hysteria, the pain / of any one's body with the pain of the body's world."

But as she looked out on the violently divided world that history was busy delivering to her awareness, and to her senses "damaged" by the "sense of having," she did not see the connection. At this point, difference still ruled, imposing its isolation: "remember: the body's pain and the pain on the streets / are not the same." On guard against "hysteria," her word for illegitimate connection, she accepted the reality of difference that social solitude accepts as part of its expansive sense of presence. Nonetheless, she also allowed that that was not the whole story. The codes of social solitude also contend with difference: "but you can learn / from the edges that blur   O you who love clear edges / more than anything   watch the edges that blur." But how, exactly, do edges blur? And the fugitive's dilemma: how to locate blurred edges without converting them into brand names (POC, women's culture, Oprah's Book Club) for private owning, for public showing and auction? This is what it is. As Rich wrote in 2007, "Poetry, like silk or coffee or oil or human flesh, has had its trade routes." After all, how does a writer tell her agent that she has created *nothing* to sell? Still, there are ways to resist locating art as means to sales. In fugitive solitude, finding these ways is what it has become "*to survive.*"

In "To the Days," we see how fugitive solitude calls on a radically open-ended relation and creation: "Whatever you bring in your hands, I need to see it." Going beyond the "edges that blur," despite differences, in "Calle Visión," Rich asserts an unmitigated sense of fugitive connection between body and world:

Calle Visión   never forget
the body's pain

never divide it

If once-oppositional identity markers now operate as brand names in the language of the marketplace of division and disappearance, then the stakes are too high for fugitives to equivocate with the terms of social difference. Focusing on the pain when "the edges that blur" the body and the street appear, and refusing to "divide it," Rich connects her pain to "the pain of the body's world."

Here the fact of labor itself becomes the basis for connections between bodies situated in different social locations. This pain is strewn throughout the labor force. It works under the newly pervasive and destructive pressures exerted via neoliberal operations of capital. In "Calle Visión" Rich continues: "the gasses that rise from urine and feces // in the pig confinement units known as nurseries / can eat a metal doorknob off in half a year." Quoting Corinthians by way of Studs Terkel, Rich holds that the connective tissue of blurred edges appears in the conditions of workers' labor:

And the fire shall try
every man's work   :Calle Visión:
and every woman's

if you took the turn-off
this is your revelation   this the source

In "Sources" (August 1981–August 1982), Rich asked: "*With whom do you believe your lot is cast? / From where does your strength come?*" In the preceding chapter we saw how Rich framed a New World, cross-racial, and "powerful;   womanly" answer to these questions in social solitude. Sources of strength and connections in North America could not be an Old World matter of ethnic origin and blood. Challenged by owners and marketeers of all kinds, these sources were created by multiracial, gendered historical processes. As Rich wrote in "Harper's Ferry" (1988), by now all the producers of subversive connections "are queer, outside, and out of bounds." In *Dark Fields of the Republic,* she reroutes those questions according to methods and conditions of labor under the new pressures of neoliberal capital.

Rather than the "edges that blur" in social solitude, in fugitive solitude Rich locates the source by feeling for the edges that *burn*. The next section of "Calle Visión" draws explicitly on labor as a source of connection. Rich links the burning pain in industrial labor with that of her debilitating arthritis: "repetitive motions of slaughtering / —fire in wrists   in elbows—" and "fire in the chicken factory fire / in the carpal tunnel." The pain of workers, never divide it. This is a radical gesture with ambiguous roots in Rich's sense of connection in previous eras. In "Phantasia for Elvira Shatayev" (1974), Rich scripted the initial fibers of relational solitude—"*fire ropes our bodies / burning together*"—among women climbers who "*will not live / to settle for less*." Extending across social divisions, Rich's fugitive sense of labor in "Calle Visión" connects her body's burning pain to that of workers killed in a blaze engulfing a factory, "some fleeing to the freezer some / found 'stuck in poses of escape.'" The connection is strikingly similar to that made by her neighbor in "The Burning of Paper Instead of Children" (1968)—the connection between Nazis and kids burning math books, which Rich refused. Focusing on the labor of workers and its situation enables her to connect (to "never divide") the pain between bodies, without hysteria.

In "Calle Visión," Rich connects to workers across divisions of class (and likely race) in ways her (and our) contemporary world of (commodity) identity would largely disallow or disavow. Viewed through the lens prepared by the pressures of capital, in which experience and identity are private properties, individual commodities to be owned, Rich's depiction of these burning edges would be called appropriation. In the late 1960s, Rich considered her neighbor's sense of connection illegitimate, hysterical. In "The Burning of Paper" she asserts, coldly: "The burning of a book arouses no sensation in me." In "Calle Visión," Rich nonetheless traces a fugitive, indeed a burning, line of connection joining all workers subject to the pressures of transnational capital in the final decade of the twentieth century. Her phrase from "Phantasia for Elvira Shatayev," "*fire ropes our bodies / burning together*," echoes precisely the images linking the writer to industrial laborers in "Calle Visión." The resonance between the images of connection and their contexts shows clearly the connection between Rich's relational solitude in the 1970s and where her quests led in later stages. The expansion across borders (class, race, gender) is likewise obvious. Rich affirms the connection that leads to the basic premise of fugitive solitude, a premise she sees as endangered all around her in the 1990s: "once we were dissimilar / yet unseparate   that's beauty." Workers became strangers to otherness.

For Rich the issue of being "dissimilar / yet unseparate" is one of tactical or practical creation rather than one of sentimental or romantic longing. In *Poetry and Commitment* (2007), Rich hones in on labor and its role in the basic matter of dissident poetic action, quoting from exiled anti-Apartheid poet and activist Dennis Brutus: "My verse works." She stresses, quoting James Scully, that such dissident work "would act as part of the world, not simply as a mirror of it." Solidarity and difference, connections and edges that blur or burn, are the only hope workers have of even incremental gains in functional control of their labor. Rich's "Calle Visión" scripts images of what Williams calls "creative practice . . . the active struggle for new consciousness." The vision road leads to a space in which fugitive solitude crystallizes into a distinct, conscious condition. As always, the most basic struggle is against isolation:

This place is alive with the dead and with the living
I have never been alone here

I wear my triple eye as I walk along the road
past, present, future all are at my side

In a way she would further explain in the final years of the twentieth century, the situation of labor in late capitalism provides the substructure for Rich's sense of how fugitive solitude makes it possible, as she wrote in "Contradictions: Tracking Poems," "to connect, without hysteria, the pain / of any one's body with the pain of the body's world."

If fugitive solitude makes connections between laborers possible, this clearly does not mean that appropriation and difference don't exist. In "Six Narratives" (1994), Rich figures stories of complex and intimate connection and difference. She echoes the sense of appropriation ("*It's all about you   None of this / tells my story*") in "Sleepwalking Next to Death" in clearly marked, gendered terms. Targeting a gathering that resembles the Great Mother Conference founded by Robert Bly, Rich writes:

You were telling a story about women to young men   It was
     not my story
it was not a story about women it was a story about men
Your hunger a spear gripped in hand a tale unspun in your
     rented campground
clothed in captured whale-songs tracked with synthesized
     Andes flutes
it was all about you

Later in "Six Narratives," intimate fugitives negotiate the politics of location in the inter-"active struggle for new consciousness." The first person addresses her intimate: "I was telling you a story about love / how even in war it goes on speaking its own language." "Yes," responds her partner, pushing back, "but the larynx is bloodied / the knife was well-aimed into the throat." Asserting the noncommercial, fugitive status of connections, the first answers, "Well I said love is hated   it has no price." "No," her partner responds, refocusing the threat to fugitive relations and asserting the changed nature of the threat: "you are talking about feelings / Have you ever felt nothing? that is what war is now." In an image disturbingly relevant to the twenty-first-century opioid crisis, and so much else, Rich clarifies the destructive stakes: it's a winner-feels-nothing game.

If the edges between fugitives burn together in the pain of their labor, it follows that the pressures of isolation under late capitalism would erase feeling—as well as labor—altogether. Conditioned to avoid feelings and opt out of labor to the extent possible, would-be fugitives become captive, foreclosing the possibilities of connective burning. Rich's speaker ends "Six Narratives" straining to describe the conflict between the sexualized marketing of isolation and the burning necessity of connection:

So we are thrown together   so we are racked apart
in a republic shivering on   its glassy lips
parted   as if the fundamental rift
had not been calculated from the first into the mighty scaffold.

"the light we stand under when we meet"
Fugitive Inscriptions

Rich closes *Dark Fields of the Republic* with her densest and most complex exploration of fugitive solitude, "Inscriptions" (1993–94). Casting across possibilities stolen back from looming forces of isolation and disappearance, the poem's six sections sculpt profiles and pressure points crucial to the existence of Rich's fugitives' presence in their shared worlds. In the first section, titled "Comrade," Rich aligns her figures with the paradigm of fugitive solitude—being "dissimilar / yet unseparate"—established in "Calle Visión." She begins:

> Little as I knew you I know you: little as you knew me you
>   know me
> —that's the light we stand under when we meet.

Fugitive truths and connections are not fully revealed, or necessarily stable; they do not conform to the evidentiary protocol of institutional procedure. There will be no boxes on the HR survey for fugitive (meaning surviving) elements of identity. Rich knows all that so-called certainty can be bought and sold on the open market.

Clearly reciprocal but far less unified than was the aim in relational solitude, as noted above, fugitive presence is at once more and less personal than is one's place in the cross-difference, mongrel multitude of social solitude. The dilemma has deepened, the stakes in what it means *"to survive"* have gone up as neoliberal power has intensified its assault on shared public space and discourse. In a sketch of how a mutual fugitivity (or fugitive mutuality) might elude the politics of market-driven location, Rich scripts an open circuit of connection wired between the personal and the impersonal:

> My testimony: yours: Trying to keep faith
> not with each other exactly yet it's the one known and unknown
> who stands for, imagines the other   with whom faith could
>   be kept.

These are fugitives from alienation. The methods are angular. Profiles shift as the light flickers, but the aim is to be part of an emergent, surviving

multitude. Personal identity is not the point. Detachment is not an op-
tion. In 2007, Rich described this newly radical search for surviving
location as one for "news of an awareness, a resistance, that totalizing
systems want to quell: art reaching into us for what's still passionate, still
unintimidated, still unquenched." Mirrors are still turned outward:

> The self unlocked to many selves.
> A mirror handed to one who just released
> from the locked ward from solitary from preventive detention
> sees in her thicket of hair her lost eyebrows
> whole populations.

Rich had seen oppositional political movements infiltrated and massa-
cred; others had been assimilated into the marketplace. She had observed
insidious dangers to participants who lost or forfeited themselves to social
or personal momentum, carried along in movements and relationships
that needed unique, surviving energy from *everyone*. With that danger
in mind, in the second section of "Inscriptions," titled "Movement," she
sketches fugitive solitude as a stream that cannot be joined like a movement. She imagines a connective condition that draws uniquely on the
full-dimensional range of fears and desires, strengths and weaknesses,
needed in each person's improvised confrontation with experience:

> Times of walking across a street   thinking
> not *I have joined a movement* but   *I am stepping in this deep current*
> *Part of my life washing behind me*   *terror I couldn't swim with*
> *part of my life waiting for me*   *a part I had no words for*

This charts the surviving substance of a person in fugitive solitude. If
the connective tissue among fugitives depends on the edges that *burn*
in their labor, there is nowhere to hide. The freedom of fugitive solitude
calls on people to engage fully, to work, and to grow. What is shared
by people so engaged cannot be easily located, arranged in pyramids of
privilege, and positioned for auction.

> When does a life bend toward freedom?   grasp its direction?
> How do you know you're not circling in pale dreams, nostalgia,

```
                stagnation
but entering that deep current     malachite, colorado
requiring all your strength wherever found
your patience and your labor
desire pitted against desire's inversion
all your mind's fortitude?
```

In ways possibly like teachers and students, fugitives must fully and complexly challenge and support each other like *"this deep current,"* like "that deep current," like the streams of their labor in fugitive solitude. Rich's teacher, "someone with facts with numbers / with poetry," addresses her students: "—Your journals Patricia: Douglas your poems." The challenging and supportive current goes both ways. The student faces the teacher:

> —And now she turns her face brightly on the new morning in
>   the new classroom
> new in her beauty her skin her lashes her lively body:
> *Race, class . . . all that . . . but isn't all that just history?*
> *Aren't people bored with it all?*

The point is not boredom so much as how *"all that"* can be made part of the precise and complex currents of fugitive solitude. Meanwhile, the labels morph into new brand names for auction. Rich images the conditions of working—of learning and teaching—under pressures of capital in ways that echo those in "Calle Visión" and elsewhere, "the repeti- / tive blows / on spines whose hope you were, on yours." As it is with fugitives everywhere, as it is with Rich's teacher, lethal toxins from the environment permeate the student who works both with and against her own chemistry and metabolism: "She's a mermaid / momentarily precipitated from a solution / which could stop her heart."

In the fifth section of "Inscriptions," titled "Voices," Rich finds fugitive edges that burn workers together in the pain and pressure of their repetitive labor. The poem's first section addresses the work of writing and learning under reigning methods and institutional definitions: "That year I began to understand the words *burden of proof* / —how the free market of ideas depended / on certain lives laboring under that burden." Sooner or later, creative and intellectual forms and constraints attain the weight of physical force; in sensing the burden, which is otherwise abstract, seemingly weightless, one also initiates the resistance:

> I started feeling in my body
> how that burden was bound to our backs
> keeping us cramped in old repetitive motions
> crouched in the same mineshaft year on year

Meanwhile, if the creative intellectual work, "the active struggle for new consciousness," becomes isolated within the repetitive mold or stilled in its *own* mirror, it can be denied, reduced to what the world says it is, and sold in those terms and in those terms only:

> and the talk goes on, the laws, the jokes, the deaths, the way of
>   life goes on
> as if you had proven nothing as if this burden were what
>   you are.

In a radical and spectral connection, as if turning her mirror outward across the fields of labor around her, Rich finds a reflection of her writing in fugitive solitude in a photograph of workers who (like poets) arrange their pain in rows, deciding their length, against the threat of blank whiteness:

> (Knotted crowns of asparagus lowered by human hands
> into long silver trenches fogblanched mornings
> the human spine translated into fog's
> almost unbearable rheumatic beauty flattering pain
> into a daze a mystic text of white and white's
> absolute faceless romance

As the fugitive images appear out of the developing solution, Rich experiences "the photographer's / darkroom thrill discerning" the disabled writer and the disenfranchised farmhand as fellow workers. Both figures are partially trapped, both are partially blind, both "laboring under that burden." She writes:

                    two phantoms caught
trenchside deep in the delicate power
of fog : : phantoms who nonetheless have to know
the length of the silvery trenches how many plants how long
this bending can go on and for what wage and what
that wage will buy in the Great Central Valley 1983.)

Lyrical connections between fugitive laborers provide a skein of hope as
the scales of past, present, and future disasters reveal themselves, emerging from their decades-old, Cold War–era form and seeking new guises
of terror and isolation that workers must resist.
    In the beginning years of the Clinton administration, so-called lib-
eral politicians demonstrated their allegiance to neoliberal economics,
which favored the interests of a global elite over U.S. citizenry and contributed to the degradation of labor universally. Without even nomi-
nally progressive voices in U.S. national politics, as she nears the end of
Dark Fields of the Republic, Rich positions the connections and vistas of
social solitude in a losing battle against high-tech propaganda serving
conservative and neoliberal policies alike. "In the heart of the capital of
Capital / . . . I found a faux-marble sarcophagus inscribed / HERE LIES
THE WILL OF THE PEOPLE," she writes. "I had been wondering why for so
long so little / had been heard from that quarter." "[W]andering among
white monuments," Rich imagines busts that figure the Reagan–Bush
regime's propaganda morphed into the faux-progressive messaging of
the Clinton era: "I found myself there by deepest accident / . . . looking
for the Museum of Lost Causes." The final image of this section sounds
the epitaph of social solitude, at least for the foreseeable future. The frozen tones of kitschy and chauvinistic patriotism foreclose on the promise
of widespread, cross-difference connections:

A strangely focused many-lumened glare
was swallowing alive the noon.
I saw the reviewing stand the podium draped and swagged
the huge screen all-enhancing and all-heightening
I heard the martial bands the choirs the speeches
amplified in the vacant plaza
swearing to the satellites it had been a natural death.

To be sure, sinister darkness descends at the end of *Dark Fields of the Republic*. The always-contested promise of social solitude goes to eclipse. Propaganda claims "it had been a natural death" when actually it was a targeted hit.

In the final section of "Inscriptions," titled "Edgelit," Rich opens with a roll call of faux fugitives, would-be comrades, otherwise desirable women who instead accept and manipulate occluded versions of relational presence:

> One keen as mica, glittering,
> full at the lips, absent at the core.
> One who flirted with danger
> had her escape route planned when others had none
> and disappeared.

No matter the attractive packaging, Rich swears off dealings with those who use the reigning duplicities as models for faux relation, who think a fortified isolation of their *own* means safety.

But, as with the flickering and shifting light in "Amends" at the outset of the book, the encroaching dark of *Dark Fields of the Republic* is a dialectical dark, partly an eclipse of social possibility and partly a veil for fugitive mobility and the unsanctioned, subversive, mutual work of relational survival. Instead of waiting for morning, Rich works with the shifting presence of fugitive possibility according to the materials at hand:

> The bright planet that plies her crescent shape
> in the western air   that through the screendoor gazes
> with her curved eye now speaks: *The beauty of darkness*
> *is how it lets you see.*

The shifting textures of darkness themselves become a relational presence that carries unmistakable echoes of the importance of social darkness, nonwhiteness, in what Rich has learned from feminist and other oppositional conversations. In the essay "North American Tunnel Vision" (1983), she had described how key features of the "spiritual and moral vision of the United States" most associated with fugitive solitude "have been explored, expanded on, given voice most articulately by

women of color." As in the essay, the images of dark presence and sight
are meant to "acknowledge a precious resource, along with an indebted-
ness, that we can all share." So in "Edgelit," Rich writes:

> You   who sees me   You   who calls me to see
> You   who has other errands far away in space and time
> You   in your fiery skin   acetylene
> scorching the claims of the false mystics
> You   who like the moon arrives in crescent
> changeable changer   speaking truth from darkness

The "edgelit" darkness allows Rich a flickering second sight. In her "sixty-
fifth year," she sketches herself in a portrait of vitality, one pulse among
many in the darkness, one difficult to track, a comrade in the fugitive
multitude:

> *these vivid stricken cells*
> *precarious living marrow*
> *this my labyrinthine filmic brain*
> *this my dreaded blood*
> *this my irreplaceable*
> *footprint vanishing from the air*

The final image of *Dark Fields of the Republic* embarks outward. There
will be no return to the public murals of social solitude. Rich understood herself as a fellow flash in the darkness, one spark looking for others, a fugitive opening outward, "edgelight from the high desert / where
shadows drip from tiniest stones / sunlight of bloody afterglow." Concluding the book, she writes:

> These are the extremes I stoke
> into the updraft of this life
> still roaring
>
>   into thinnest air

As the fugitives move outward they find each other in locations that capital cannot metabolize and list for sale. These connections make new patterns possible. A shared sense of extremity takes shape. The eyes adjust to

the task and the dark, a darkness mobilized within and against the dark. In the midst of what, in "Rusted Legacy" (1997), Rich will term "dark's velvet dialectic," fugitives come together and patterns coalesce, creating a new force: the shared, mobilized solitude of dissidents.

"we are not a little / cell, but we are like a little cell"
Dissident Solitude

"[T]hat was a mission, surely," writes Rich in "The Art of Translation" (1995), the opening poem of *Midnight Salvage: Poems 1995–1998* (1999). We do not know the exact details of the assignment. Her speaker addresses a "daunting and dauntless" fellow writer, possibly a translator, who lives abroad. The "mission" entailed meeting this colleague and bringing her work home. Readers recognize the pressures faced by Rich's fugitives, but there is an emerging clarity about the political stakes as well as the imperatives for resistance. The speaker describes her departure: "to lift toward home, mile upon mile / back where they'd barely heard your name /—neither as terrorist nor as genius would they detain you—." Nonetheless, traveling "back to [her] country," she feels conspicuous "bearing / [her colleague's] war-flecked protocols." Both women's work has been thoroughly politicized by the surveillance: "the translators stopped at passport control: / *Occupation: no such designation— / Journalist, maybe spy?*" Given the clash between the contents of her "art's pouch / crammed with" her colleague's work and the neoliberal politics behind the surveillance at home, the speaker accepts the politicized situation:

That the books are for personal use
only—could I swear it?
That not a word of them
is contraband—how could I prove it?

No, the innocence of dissident work cannot be proved to the authors of division and isolation. Also, people's resistance in fugitive and dissident solitude is never strictly personal. So if caught, stopped or detained, she writes, "Like a thief I would deny the words, deny they ever / existed, were spoken, or could be spoken, / like a thief I'd bury them and remember where."

Midnight Salvage gives Rich's fugitive solitude a sense of clandestine and affirmative mission. As they access and adapt to the cooperative terms of the mission, her fugitives take on the conscious role of dissidents. Fugitives run and hide while assessing the system of alienation and isolation surrounding them. Dissidents mobilize those fugitive positions in acts of resistance; the fugitive necessity becomes a tactical matter of what Williams calls "the active struggle for new consciousness." As we have seen above, that struggle builds upon and mobilizes "the hard practical substance of effective and continuing relationships." Relationships among dissidents are not to be judged by romantic standards, they are not magical. Fugitives keep faith "not with each other exactly" but with the "known and unknown" in each other. This angularity is necessary because, like all of us, even dissidents inevitably carry the ill-programming from the systems of isolation. For this reason, often, living connections themselves will appear broken. Meantime, broken and corrupt modes masquerade as life, liberty, and happiness. Continuing—let alone effective—relationships have to learn how to identify those threats, threats from colleagues and opponents alike, and contend with them. In "The Art of Translation," Rich writes:

> It's only a branch like any other
> green with the flare of life in it
> and if I hold this end, you the other
> that means it's broken
>
> broken between us, broken despite us
> broken and therefore dying
> broken by force, broken by lying
> green, with the flare of life in it

Midnight Salvage declares the dissident status of Rich's poetry and scaffolds her apprehension of how dissident solitude resists the advancing forces of division and isolation being mobilized at the close of the twentieth century. In "For an Anniversary" (1996), the image of an osprey in its "nest on Tomales Bay" thinly masks the threatened political allegiances of dissident solitude: "The left wing shouldered into protective / gesture the left wing we thought broken."

The title sequence in *Midnight Salvage* records Rich's explicit realization that there will be no heroic return to the public murals of social
solitude. She also understands that fugitive solitude is to become no romance, no end in itself. No one is born to run. So she declares the need
to continue the work of dissident action, "Midnight Salvage." As the
sequence opens, Rich charts how the politics of isolation and division
permeate her consciousness like a crime scene: "thought's blood ebb between life- and death-time / darkred behind darkblue / bad news puls-
ing back and forth of 'us' and 'them.'"

Then teaching at Stanford University, Rich felt likewise constrained
by the situation of her labor as a teacher. Even her academic freedom
encoded its silencing, as if a kind of soundproofing in the elite environment canceled the subversive waves in her voice: "Under the conditions of my hiring / I could profess or declare anything at all / since in
that place nothing would change." Rich was then similarly stalked by a
dread sense that writing could be institutionalized and professionalized
in the then-burgeoning academic field of "creative writing" in American
universities. As the forms of silencing piled up, she

> could not any more
>
> peruse young faces already straining for
> the production of slender testaments
> to swift reading and current thinking : : would not wait
> for the stroke of noon to declare all passions obsolete

To be sure, this was no lost innocence. By the late 1990s, Rich had been
working for decades on creating and re-creating solitudes that connected her to coworkers in a morphing struggle against isolation and division, against domination. Rich well knew that, in Williams's words to
which she returned so often, the "active struggle for new consciousness"
was not a matter of surfaces and vocabulary, was "not casting off an
ideology, or learning phrases about it." Still less was it a matter of "swift
reading and current thinking." More than conversions and epiphanies,
as Williams wrote, this work entailed "a process often described as development but in practice [it was] a struggle at the roots of the mind . . .
confronting a hegemony in the fibres of the self." Even understanding
that, in "Midnight Salvage" (1996) Rich signals a new apprehension of

the radical stakes at hand. She records her recalibration whereby her sense of a fugitive solitude in angular contact to a shared mural of blurring and burning edges shifts into its consciously dissident extension. I quote the section in full:

> Had never expected hope would form itself
> completely in my time : : was never so sanguine
> as to believe old injuries could transmute easily
> through any singular event or idea : : never
> so feckless as to ignore the managed contagion
> of ignorance the contrived discontinuities
> the felling of leaders and future leaders
> the pathetic erections of soothsayers
>
> But thought I was conspiring, breathing-along
> with history's systole-diastole
> twenty thousand leagues under the sea a mammal heartbeat
> sheltering another heartbeat
> plunging from the Farallons all the way to Baja
> sending up here or there a blowhole signal
> and sometimes beached
> making for warmer waters
> where the new would be delivered : : though I would not see it

In the face of "managed contagion" and "contrived discontinuities," Rich imagines at least a sporadic communication with the progression of history above the surface of her medium. She captures how she had kept a kind of faith in beautiful, maternal images of caring for the promise of a future beyond oneself, beyond one's life. Or so she thought.

Next she records her coming to the surface of a changed system of utterly broken and fraudulent social contracts with which no faith could be kept. I quote this section in full as well. This is Rich's declaration of dissident solitude in poetry:

> But neither was expecting in my time
> to witness this : : wasn't deep
> lucid or mindful you might say enough
> to look through history's bloodshot eyes

into this commerce this dreadnought wreck cut loose
from all vows, oaths, patents, compacts, promises : :
                                                To see

not O my Captain
fallen cold & dead by the assassin's hand

but cold alive & cringing : : drinking with the assassins
in suit of noir Hong Kong silk
pushing his daughter in her famine-
waisted flamingo gown
out on the dance floor with the traffickers
in nerve gas saying to them *Go for it*
and to the girl *Get with it*

This is remarkable for the depth of feeling and for the clarity of the ap-
praisal; also remarkably, the sections of "Midnight Salvage" carry that
clarity without "surfacing" into statements in prose that one could parse
or peruse. The clarity that proceeds from deep feeling and patient attending sounds in song. The year after Rich wrote "Midnight Salvage,"
history would address her personally testing the veracity of her dissident's conclusion. It seemed as if history asked her if she really meant
what she had written. Maybe it was just another sales pitch?

   In July 1997, one could say that the fugitive was beckoned home and
offered "citizen" status in the land of bad faith. Adrienne Rich was no-
tified that she had been chosen by Bill Clinton's administration to be
one of twelve recipients of the National Medal of Arts. It seems that the
White House interns had not read *Dark Fields of the Republic.* Declaring
her dissident position, Rich refused the honor in a letter addressed to the
administration. A few weeks later, discussing the reasoning behind her
decision, she told Amy Goodman:

   I am concerned about what it means when we have two parties which
   are so close together in their collaboration with the wealthiest interests in the country and who are so alike in their disregard for the
   majority of people in this country. And I feel as if the relative creative
   freedom of artists and intellectuals ultimately depends on the conditions everywhere and the conditions of human labor everywhere.
   We're all working. We're all trying to do our work. And the circum-

stances, the conditions under which working people exist in the society are not something that can be separated and left aside from the position of the artist. I just don't see how you can do that. . . . And I feel as if this effort to segregate art is extremely dangerous, and it's a kind of—it is an attempt to hold art hostage, to make it a captive, a carved radish rose on the dinner table, if you will.

In refusing official accommodation, the fugitive shifts her status. *Midnight Salvage* traces Rich's journey into the last stages of her career. In dissident solitude, fugitives find each other and take up efforts to preserve and advance textured connections, the surviving remnants of social solitude. The bonds of dissident solitude no longer depend on the identity categories of the 1980s. In her explanation, Rich insisted that she acted on behalf of workers, herself among them. Dissidents also make guerrilla sorties against the forces that desiccate and divide human lives and the world at large. Rich gathers her sense of a dissident collective in the final section of the volume's title poem:

Old walls the pride of architects   collapsing
find us in crazed niches   sleeping like foxes
we wanters we unwanted we
wanted for the crime of being ourselves

She follows images of the loosely collective purposes of dissidents banded together for the tasks of midnight salvage with "Char" (1996), a poem dedicated to René Char, a poet who was also a commander in the French Resistance against the Germans in World War II. As a general orientation to dissident labor and what dissidents are up against, and seeing through to the neoliberal core of the Clinton administration and beyond, Rich quotes at length from Char's journal from the occupation, *Hypnos*:

This war will prolong itself beyond any platonic armistice. The implanting of political concepts will go on amid upheavals and under cover of self-confident hypocrisy. Don't smile. Thrust aside both skepticism and resignation and prepare your soul to face an intramural confrontation with demons as cold-blooded as microbes.

As Char had forecast, Rich finds that the labor of dissidents in defense and furtherance of human survival bears risks within as well as outside the communities of dissent:

knowing the end of the war
would mean no end to the microbes frozen in each soul
the young freedom fighters
in love with the Resistance
fed by a thrill for violence
familiar as his own jaw under the razor

To René Char's example Rich adds others to the list of guides for dissident solitude: Brecht, Marx, the photographer Tina Modotti, Hart Crane, Miles Davis, Paul Goodman, and Puerto Rican poet Julia de Burgos. But the basic guide comes first from her reading and rereading of Char's career, which she reclaims:

Hermetic guide in resistance I've found you and lost you
several times in my life   You were never just
the poet appalled and transfixed by war you were the maker
of terrible delicate decisions and that did not smudge
your sense of limits   You saw squirrels crashing
from the tops of burning pines when the canister exploded
and worse and worse and you were in charge of every risk
the incendiary motives of others were in your charge
and the need for a courage wrapped in absolute tact

Along with the dangers, intense dissident pleasures guide Rich's search for means to relational survival. Furthering the connections and networks of social survival cannot be monotonous drudgery. In the opening sequence of *Dark Fields of the Republic,* "What Kind of Times Are These," Rich echoes Rosa Luxemburg from a 1919 letter in which she wrote that successful resistance requires that one stay human by "enjoying every bright day and every beautiful cloud." Part of dissident labor is to prevent despair from overtaking life's full spectrum of experience and emotion. In the poem, Rich paraphrases, "To be human, said Rosa—I can't teach you that." Rich sensed herself operating under a kind of occupation less immediate (for her) but also less finite and less bounded than the German occupation faced by Char and his comrades. In "Camino Real" (1997), one of Rich's most perfectly balanced and powerfully diffuse single-section poems of the 1990s, she and Michelle Cliff drive with great pleasure from Santa Cruz to Los Angeles to visit Adrienne's youngest son. Rich's images lie across the graffiti-scrawled contemporary pastoral of suffering dotted with the historical coexistence of (and at times cooperation between) prisons and universities for profit. Rich burns away the distinction between the abuse and the documentation of abuse:

> The difficulty of proving
> such things were done for no reason
> that every night
> "in those years"
> people invented reasons for torture

She steers between Charles Olson's notion of happiness as magical and George Oppen's deliberate thought to "measure happiness." Drawing on Rosa Luxemburg, she resolves that "happiness is not to be / mistrusted or wasted / though it ferment in grief," and, as always, resisting magic and miracles, she concludes by claiming such practicalities as she has found:

> at the end of a day
>   of great happiness if there be such a day
>
> drawn by love's unprovable pull
>
> I write this, sign it
>   Adrienne

In "Merced" (1972), Rich looked down on Manhattan from a plane and thought

>   that somewhere there
> a cold center, composed
> of pieces of human beings
> metabolized, restructured
> by a process they do not feel

is spreading in our midst
and taking over our minds

Twenty-five years later, in "Rusted Legacy," she returns to a treacherous
image of the spaces and terms afforded the multitude in their experiences of themselves and each other:

Imagine a city where nothing's
forgiven   your deed adheres
to you like a scar, a tattoo   but almost everything's
forgotten   deer flattened leaping a highway for food
the precise reason for the shaving of the confused girl's head
the small boys' punishing of the frogs
—a city memory-starved but intent on retributions
Imagine the architecture   the governance
the men and the women in power
—tell me if it is not true you still
          live in that city.

In a social terrain whose metabolism comprises forgotten events that
bear indelible consequences, Rich surmises, one's sense of self would
contain the city, and one's sense of the city would mirror one's self. Each
needs the other to read the scarified and amnesiac whole, the gathering
together of which, at the close of the twentieth century, is crucial dissident activity:

This *I*—must she, must she lie scabbed with rust
crammed with memory in a place
of little anecdotes   no one left
to go around gathering the full dissident story?
Rusting her hands and shoulders stone her lips
yet leaching down from her eyesockets tears
—for one self only? each encysts a city.

Rich sets the final sequence of *Midnight Salvage* on the occasion of
the 150th anniversary of the publication of *The Communist Manifesto.*
"A Long Conversation" (1997–98) serves as a mural of love and action

on a new scale made possible in dissident solitude. Written in lyric and prose, and spliced with italicized quotations from Marx, Ludwig Wittgenstein, Che Guevara, Mandelstam, Samuel Taylor Coleridge, Aijaz Ahmad, Juliette Greco, and others, the twenty-page collage features multiple speakers who address themselves, the reader, and each other. "A Long Conversation" is Rich's mural in graffiti, a dissident mirror of "An Atlas of the Difficult World." In "Harper's Ferry" Rich had imagined the "queer, outside, and out of bounds" ancestors of these contemporary dissidents.

Dissident identities are practical, often occupational. In "A Long Conversation," someone is there to take care of birds damaged in an oil spill, someone else possesses pills to fight an infection "that is ransacking this region"; there is an upper-class social dropout trained as a nurse, and someone in the role of teacher (or close to it) acts "as if we are a class, . . . but we are long out of school." As if in hiding from systems of surveillance and interrogation, Rich's dissident speakers and singers have assembled "Like a little cell. Let's not aggrandize ourselves; we are not a little / cell, but we are like a little cell."

There is Marxist discourse about revolutionized means of production forcing changes throughout the *whole relations of society,*" leading to (temporary, shifting) differentiations between the bourgeoisie and the proletariat, who "must *sell themselves piecemeal, are a commodity, like every other article of commerce, and are consequently exposed to all the vicissitudes of competition, to all the fluctuations of the market.*" By these means does capital metabolize human beings for sale at auction. One of the practically identified speakers seizes upon the relevance: "Someone:—Technology's changing the most ordinary forms of human contact—who can't see that, in their own life?" Someone else: "But technology is nothing but a means." Then Rich's speaker and her partner break in: "Someone, I say, makes a killing off war. You:—I've been telling you, that's the engine driving the free market. Not information, militarization. Arsenals spawning wealth."

"A Long Conversation" moves along like this, sifting quotes, its dissident players commenting on them until an aesthete in their midst objects: "Now someone gets up and leaves, cloud-faced:—I can't stand that / kind of language. I still care about poetry." At this, the dissident voice of the poem appears:

All kinds of language fly into poetry, like it or not, or even if you're
only
      as we were   trying
           to keep an eye
              on the weapons on the street
                and under the street

Keeping one eye "on the weapons," the overarching task in dissident
solitude circa 1998 appears in relation to Che Guevara's insistence that,
as he wrote, "*At the risk of appearing ridiculous*," love be a part of revolutionary methods. Guarding herself against romance and the cruelty that
follows sentimentality—and also searching for a means to, as Rich put
it in "Contradictions: Tracking Poems," a "*we* [that] means more than a
handful"—Rich's dissident speaker offers:

I can imagine a sentence that might someday end with the word, love.
Like the one written by that asthmatic young man, which begins, *At
the risk of appearing ridiculous. . . .* It would have to contain losses,
resiliencies, histories faced; it would have to contain a face—his yours
hers mine—by which I could do well, embracing it like water in my
hands, because by then we could be sure that "doing well" by one, or
some, was immiserating nobody. A true sentence then, for greeting
the newborn.

Midnight Salvage works toward a vision of human connection and
community arranged in terms as yet unspeakable, diversely inclusive in
ways that do not replicate the rigid grids of identity that had been (and
were being) used to, at once, quarantine human life and torture human
beings. At the same time, these same identities were being traded like
commodities in the culture market. Rich seeks dissident sentences active
and vigorous in ways that do not immiserate themselves and others and
abuse the world in their wake. The language becomes a dissident tonal
and rhythmic space and envisions glimpses of what it might be like to
be in that space, "we wanters we unwanted we / wanted for the crime of
being ourselves."

In *Fox: Poems 1998–2000* (2001) the new century pulls on the poems,
stretching them into a new era. In "If Your Name Is on the List" (1999),
Rich writes: "We want to be part of the future dragging in / what pure

futurity can't use." The poet, seeking company and counsel—at times from her twinned self—wonders about what to bring across, what to leave behind. Taken together, the poems attend the twentieth-century questions of identity reluctantly, and feminism instructs in remedial tones. In "Regardless" (1998–99), dedicated to her longtime friend Hayden Carruth, and in "Nora's Gaze" (1998), Rich registers her corrective points, but the stirring force of her dissident, lyrical presence is elsewhere.

These poems that straddle the millennium seek new forms of being, presences that draw and stir human energies in ways that confound the figures of twentieth-century identity and difference and that resist capital's market metabolism. In "Fox" (1998), addressing her totemic animal in ways that echo back to the mid-1960s in poems like "5:30 A.M." (1967), Rich calls to the spirit that partially resides in herself, one unburdened by restrictions in human terms:

> I needed fox   Badly I needed
> a vixen for the long time none had come near me
> I needed recognition from a
> triangulated face   burnt-yellow eyes

Appeals to connections across difference are out of fashion, which she knows—possibly this is why "none had come near"? She calls across species anyway: "For a human animal to call for help / on another animal / is the most riven the most revolted cry on earth." Echoing the phrases in "Meditations for a Savage Child" (1972), she reaches into a depth athwart surface and even species divisions: "Go back far enough it means tearing and torn endless / and sudden." Rich's sense of twenty-first-century futurity might leave behind worn-out gadgets of the contemporary world, but she remains connected to prehistorical resources, a sense of relation and connection unscripted by the world around her: "back far enough it blurts / into the birth-yell of the yet-to-be human child / pushed out of a female the yet-to-be woman."

In "Messages" (1999), a response to Blaise Pascal's terror at infinite openness in a world where "instruments of force are more credible than beauty" and "cameras / for the desouling project are being handed out," Rich aims her (is this still dissident?) attention at as-yet uncharted forms of gesture and connection. She offers a radical (and satirical) image of futuristic desire, part animal, part technological:

If you want to feel the true time of our universe
Put your hands over mine on the stainless pelvic rudder
No, here   (sometimes the most impassive ones will shudder)
The infinity of these spaces comforts me
Simple textures falling open like a sweater

Those surprising images of overlap and connection provide the emergent textures in which dissident solitude morphs into more radical, open-ended, unclassifiable designs. In *Fox,* it's as if those futuristic images are written in a different color ink. In "Inscriptions," Rich had asked:

When does a life bend toward freedom?   grasp its direction?
How do you know you're not circling in pale dreams, nostalgia,
          stagnation
but entering that deep current   malachite, colorado
requiring all your strength wherever found
your patience and your labor
desire pitted against desire's inversion
all your mind's fortitude?

Echoing that question, in "Terza Rima" (2000), the first of her poems dated in the new millennium, her dissident speaker is incarcerated in the either/or language: "My name is a prisoner / who will not name names." She refuses nonetheless to accept the bifurcation of self and spirit:

She says: When my life depended
on one of two
opposite terms

I dared mix beauty with courage
they were my lovers
together they were tortured

Driven by a sudden rain into a bookstore and "Sick of my own old poems," she finds "Pier Paolo [Pasolini] / speaking to Gramsci's ashes" in the idiom of dissident solitude, "that vernacular voice / intimately political." Seizing Pasolini's lines like "a bite of bitter chocolate in the subway / to pull on our senses" she feels again the distinction between "pale dreams"

and the "deep current" of real freedom from "Inscriptions." The key is
a shared action between bodies, the senses that can animate "a public
privacy . . . a public happiness." Because

> without them we're prey
> to the failed will
> its science of despair

With that stirring fullness alive in and around her, she faces off with the
terms of the twentieth century and their opposites:

> How I've hated speaking "as a woman"
> for mere continuation
> when the broken is what I saw
>
> As a woman   do I love
> and hate?   as a woman
> do I munch my bitter chocolate underground?
>
> Yes.   No.   You too
> sexed as you are.   hating
> this whole thing   you keep on   it remaking

As if having looked back to the mural-atlas of the difficult world in-
dexed in broken categories that spill their contents into each other, Rich
finishes the longest sequence in *Fox* looking ahead:

> our shadows   reindeer-huge
> slip onto the map
> of chance and purpose   figures
>
> on the broken crust
> exchanging places   bites to eat
> a glance

Possibly her most important sequence from the twenty-first century,
"Usonian Journals 2000," an essay-poem from *The School among the Ruins*
(2004), concludes with a "Mission Statement" from a formalized and
utopian dissident group: "*The Organization for the Abolition of Cruelty.*"

As if explaining the possible action to someone interested in dissident solitude, the piece concludes:

> *In response to your inquiry: this is a complex operation. We have a wide range of specializations and concerns. Some are especially calibrated toward language*
>
>> *because of its known and unknown powers*
>>> *to bind and to dissociate*
>>
>> *because of its capacity*
>>> *to ostracize the speechless*
>>
>> *because of its capacity*
>>> *to nourish self-deception*
>>
>> *because of its capacity*
>>> *for rebirth and subversion*
>>
>> *because of the history*
>>> *of torture*
>>>> *against human speech*

Having responded to this inquiry by openly describing the dissident project, Rich goes on to deploy solitude in ways that become even more sinuous and unidentifiable in categorical terms. Even broken categories cannot index her visions; she scripts relation in ways that capital cannot police into place and purpose. In her final books, *Telephone Ringing in the Labyrinth* (2007) and *Tonight No Poetry Will Serve* (2011), the practitioners of relational, social, fugitive, and dissident solitude disperse into the social fabric of contemporary history and report back as they keep track of surviving parts of themselves and each other. The modes of previous solitudes likewise collapse and flash into being in newly emergent combinations, creating slippery and iridescent patterns that provide the images and signal the purposes of radical solitude.

"Voices from open air"
Mutually Embodied in Radical Solitude, 2006–2012

"suffused / by what it works in"
Radical Solitude

In "The Blue Ghazals" (1968–69), Rich images the role of pain in the tactical enforcement of division: "Pain made her conservative. / Where the matches touched her flesh, she wears a scar." In "Contradictions: Tracking Poems" (1983–85), she figures pain as a dangerous but useful tool of connection:

> remember: the body's pain and the pain on the streets
> are not the same   but you can learn
> from the edges that blur   O you who love clear edges
> more than anything   watch the edges that blur

For Rich, connections across divisions were signals of health, of survival. As if avoiding a dangerous ambiguity, her poems evince a reluctance to position sickness and injuries as vehicles of relation. But as social solitude morphs into fugitive, then dissident, and finally radical solitude, her battles against pain as well as her tolerance for (maybe reliance on) ambiguity led to a clear revision, an expansion.

Rich quotes the lines above from "The Blue Ghazals" as an epigraph to the fourth section of the sequence of poems "Axel Avákar" (2007–8). In the first lines of "I Was There, Axel," Rich's speaker reflects in revision, almost in reversal. Instead of making her conservative as it had in 1969, here "Pain taught her the language / root of *radical*." In her lyrical essay "Permeable Membrane" (2006), Rich dissolves instead of answering the question as to whether or not poetry should be political. Poetry is political in exactly the same sense that the decisions of everyday life (which grocery store to shop at, how far to live from where one works, which school to send one's children to) are political. Like those decisions, the "poetic imagination," Rich holds, "is never merely unto itself, free-floating, or self-enclosed. It's radical, meaning root-tangled in the grit of human arrangements and relationships: *how we are with each other.*" These connections signal the fluid and boundary-defying textures of radical solitude.

The radical imagination is suffused with its materials. Suffused: a condition antithetical to what the vaunted autonomy of the modern lyric (and modern subject) is all about. In the final section of "Inscriptions" (1993–94), Rich describes her searching of notebooks for a way to end *Dark Fields of the Republic*: "head, heart, perforated / by raw disgust and fear / If I dredge up anything it's suffused / by what it works in, 'like the dyer's hand.'" In the notes to the book she relates that she had wondered about the source of the quote, and a friend informed her that it was Shakespeare's Sonnet 111: "Thence comes it that my name receives a brand / And almost thence my nature is subdued / To what it works in, like the dyer's hand." She had mistaken the line. More than that, she had replaced the sense of autonomy with its radical alternative. Explaining why she kept the mistaken quotation in the poem, Rich writes: "I have kept 'suffused' here because to feel *suffused* by the materials that one has perforce to work in is not necessarily to be *subdued,* though some might think so." In images of radical solitude, Rich demonstrates otherwise. To be suffused—in *radical* relation—becomes what it means "*to survive.*" Rich's images of radical solitude depict relational states of intersuffusion.

Images of radical solitude aim to undo discourses of separation and hierarchy that are key to the articulation and deployment of power in every arena of contemporary life. This approach provides an alternative that runs counter to structures deep in the core of liberal freedom premised on autonomy. So radical relation—*interspection*—becomes a kind of mutual suffusion between the world and the poet, between art and society. "There's a permeable membrane between art and society," Rich writes. "A continuous dialectical motion. Tides brining the estuary. River flowing into sea. A writer describes the landmass-'stained' current of the Congo River discernible three hundred miles out on the ocean. Likewise: the matter of art enters the bloodstream of social energy. Call and response." In "From Strata" (2010–11), published among the previously uncollected poems in *Collected Poems,* she writes: "Say a pen must write underground   underwater   so be it." No one can predict or police how the materials in radical solitude suffuse each other:

> Throw the handwritten scraps of paper
> into the toilet bowl
>
> to work their way spiraling down
> the open gullet of advanced barbarism
>
> So : if you thought no good came from any of this
> not the resistance nor its penalties
>
> not our younger moments nor the continuing on
> then, I say, trash the evidence
>
> So : a scrap of paper   a loved bitter scrawl
> swirls under into the confluence
>
> of bodily waste and wasted bodies :
> —a shred   absorbed, belonging

Radical suffusions. More radical work is done by an anonymous particle in the social mass than by a celebrated symbol enshrined on a pedestal. Radical solitude is musical and erotic work:

> My hands under your buttocks   your fingers numbering my ribs
> how a bow scrapes, a string holds the after-pluck
>
> astonishing variations   hours, bodies without boundaries

In "Letters Censored / Shredded / Returned to Sender / or Judged Unfit to Send" (2005), from *Telephone Ringing in the Labyrinth* (2007), the key is to find phrases for the action of radical solitude, for mutual suffusion: "*liquefaction* is a word I might use for how I would take you." As in "Draft #2006" (2006), these are methods of recuperation for citizens who face division and quarantine at every turn: "Tenant already of the disensoulment projects."

Beginning with the terrorist attacks of September 11, 2001, and the consequent notion of undeclared and continual warfare, of surveillance of everything except international networks of financial wealth, the young twenty-first century rained down cruelty in drone strikes and foreclosures, in coarse cultural grit and abrasives as fine as invisible soot. None escaped. Transcendence was not on the table. The pursuit and practice of liberal autonomy too often devolve into isolation, solipsism, and competition within the hierarchy pyramids of a nation at war. Most nations, by then, were at war with themselves as internal factions competed for favored status in deals with transnational capital. In spring of 2012, Adrienne Rich struggled with her own body, balancing medications (and sheer tolerance) for pain and faltering eyesight against what windows of vision and lucidity she could gain from the maneuvers. During an era in which, as she put it, "the idea of perpetual war has dropped whatever masks it ever wore," Rich worked on a libretto for Antonio Gramsci, "Fragments of an Opera." In images of Gramsci held immobile as a child for medical reasons and imprisoned as an adult for political ones, Rich conjured a mirror image in her subject. A subject seeking outward:

Historian's voice:

A kind of mind
That would address
Duress
Outward in larger terms

A mind inhaling exigency
From first breath
Knows poverty
Of Mind
As death

On March 3, 2012, Adrienne e-mailed me the last in a series of drafts I had seen of this poem, along with a brief note saying, among a few other things, "I think I've taken Antonio as far as I can. Here are a few revisions, please feel no pressure." That draft of the poem was dated 2010–12. Its title was "Fragment of a Libretto." The date and Adrienne's short note signaled to me that she thought it was the final draft of the poem. But those impressions were never really final; with Adrienne there was always the sense of furthering. In any case, revised within a few weeks of her death on March 27, 2012, the last version of the last of her poems that I saw ended like this, searching through her subject for relation in truly radical valences of solitude:

Antonio Entering, stage left:

But whose
Are these
Voices from open air
That seem to
Call me
From my chair
Accent from home
Scraps of
Our village speech
But other tongues as well
In other tones
Carry into my ears

Between the shifts
The great
In-drawing
And exhaling
Factory doors?

I feel myself a creature both
Of library and street
The fibers reach
And twist
In me
There is no
Singleness
Of mind
Possible
In Turin

Scene Three: Fascist Tribunal, Rome 1926
Prosecutor's Voice:
We must prevent this mind from functioning for twenty years.

*** *** ***

[The libretto breaks off here. As yet no musical score has been discovered.
Antonio Gramsci was released from prison only shortly before his death in
1937. His Prison Notebooks *and letters, along with his earlier political*
and critical writings, have become classics of European and Marxist
thought.]

Adrienne Rich 2010–2012

Coda

As I read and reread the late poems, scripts suffused in radical solitude, the outward designs of an inward openness, what Rich termed "A continuous dialectical motion," I return to the mission statement in "Endpapers" (2011), a poem placed at the very end of *Collected Poems*. The statement conveys the mutual gist of radical solitude, radiates back through all the eras of Rich's work, and, I hope, casts out into the future waiting to be made:

> What holds what binds is breath   is
> primal vision in a cloud's eye
> is gauze around a wounded head
> is bearing a downed comrade out beyond
> the numerology of vital signs
> into predictless space

So it is that Adrienne Rich's serial structure of morphing solitudes in poems comes to its final opening. Crafting her poems as sustained engagements with experience at many of its levels, she drew them out of individuated lyrical *ownership* and into outward-radiating frames of social and historical human and natural *relation*. As a result, people drawn into conflict with cultural and political forces aiming to prevail over their lives have a massive and intricate scaffold of alternatives to suffuse themselves with on their ways outward. Rich's poetry offers thousands of locations (relational, social, fugitive, dissident, radical) we can engage in lives of mutual suffusion, of survival. It is a radical threshold we arrive to: *mutual suffusion* is what it means "*to survive.*" That's where the record leaves off, the tone of its continued resonance outward. And that's where we take it up. As a result, in short, apropos the place of poetry in our resistance to forces that desiccate and isolate us, as workers, as parents, as people contending with our lives and each other's lives, we do not have to be any more—as Claudia Rankine puts it, quoting Adrienne— "sporadic, errant, orphaned" than we want to be. Peace.

Acknowledgments

I'd like to thank Doug Armato, Laura Westlund, and all at the University of Minnesota Press for their encouragement and support during the creation of this book. It has been a pleasure working with such a capable crew. In addition, many thanks to people who kept me company in various ways during the writing of this book in the United States and elsewhere, especially Craig Werner, Jeannette Riley, and Terrance Hayes, who read pieces of this work as it came into being. Thanks to Ed Pavlich, who was there every summer day at Dubec 26 in Omisalj, where my deepest reading of Adrienne's poems took shape. Thanks to Moleskine for unlined notebooks. Thanks to Zack Anderson for his keen eye and crucial help with permissions and in making sure the quotations from poems are correct. Thanks to Judy Selhorst for her close reading and copyediting expertise and to Denise Carlson for the great work on the index. Thanks to Stephen Corey and C. J. Bartunek, editors at the *Georgia Review,* and to Elizabeth Scanlon, editor at the *American Poetry Review,* who read and published pieces of what ultimately became the present study. Many thanks to Adrienne Rich Literary Estate and to Claire Reinertsen at W. W. Norton for working with my permissions requests. Thanks to the Willson Center for the Humanities and Arts at the University of Georgia for their generous support. Thanks to Stacey C. Barnum for traveling with me in all those ways visible and invisible. And, finally, *all* the thanks to Adrienne Rich for her career in the work and in the world and for those years of inimitable conversations—conversations that haven't ceased—that also accompanied the writing of this work and everything else.

Sources of Quotations

Introduction
"useless without the other end"
1 "I was like someone walking." Rich, *Collected Early Poems,* xx.
1 "neighborhoods already familiar." Rich, *Collected Early Poems,* xx.
1 "The medium is language intensified." Rich, *A Human Eye,* 96.
1 "poetic imagination," "radical, meaning root-tangled." Rich, *A Human Eye,* 96.

"radical, meaning root-tangled"
3 "Poetry, at least in our age." Keyes, *The Aesthetics of Power,* 162.
3 "trapped in a shared reality." Keyes, *The Aesthetics of Power,* 191.
4 "self-conscious individual assertion." Werner, *Adrienne Rich,* 107.
4 "an integrity based upon relationships." Werner, *Adrienne Rich,* 113.
4 "implies an alternative means of conceiving the self." Werner, *Adrienne Rich,* 127.
5 "Twitter feed," "heavy rhetorical baggage," "aesthetic toxicity." Haven, *Virginia Quarterly Review.*
5 "impact on poets of the last couple generations." Mlinko, *The Nation.*
6 "raised on a diet of negative capability," "should quiver with equivocation," Cathy Park Hong, quoted in Mlinko, *The Nation.*
6 "She grew as a poet by self-repudiation." Chiasson, *New Yorker.*
6 "powerful reminders that it is still possible." Tejada, *Virginia Quarterly Review,* 249.
6 "reclaim an exhausted body." Tejada, *Virginia Quarterly Review,* 249.
6 "The key to Rich's genius." Chiasson, *New Yorker.*
6 "For more than fifty years." Rich, *Arts of the Possible,* 8.
7 "her rejection of conventions." Werner, *Virginia Quarterly Review,* 243.
7 "physiologies . . . revolt against tamed sound." Koestenbaum, *New York Times Book Review.*

7 "She founded a perpetually astonishing." Koestenbaum, *New York Times Book Review.*

7 "long vowels and keen consonants." Koestenbaum, *New York Times Book Review.*

8 "in one woman the history." Ruth Whitman, quoted in Gilbert, *American Scholar.*

8 "own feminist awakening," "realize[d] how much of what she said." Gilbert, *American Scholar.*

8 "As a nineteen-year-old, I read." Rankine, *New Yorker.*

9 "questioned paternalistic, heteronormative." Rankine, *New Yorker.*

9 "experience their own work." Rich, *On Lies, Secrets, and Silence,* 11, quoted in Rankine, *New Yorker.*

9 "re-united the public poem." Boland, *New Republic.*

10 "moving relation between the individual consciousness." Rukeyser, *The Life of Poetry,* xi.

10 "from the motions of their own minds." Wordsworth, *Lyrical Ballads,* preface.

10 "especially those thoughts and feelings." Wordsworth, *Lyrical Ballads,* preface.

10 "unavailable to others." Rich, *On Lies, Secrets, and Silence,* 43.

11 "estranged intensity." Rich, *A Change of World,* 51; *Collected Poems,* 20.

11 "music of the entirely / isolated soul." Rich, *Diving into the Wreck,* 43; *Collected Poems,* 391.

11 "terribly alone." Rich, *The Fact of a Doorframe,* 201; *Collected Poems,* 409.

11 "each man she touches." Rich, *The Fact of a Doorframe,* 201; *Collected Poems,* 409.

11 "a world masculinity made." Rich, *Diving into the Wreck,* 36; *Collected Poems,* 386.

11 "I wonder if this is a white man's." Rich, *An Atlas of the Difficult World,* 19; *Collected Poems,* 722.

11 "I honor your truth." Rich, *An Atlas of the Difficult World,* 19; *Collected Poems,* 722.

12 "Rich took a woman's worldview." Hacker, *Virginia Quarterly Review,* 231.

12 "attention to the join between." Clark, *Cambridge Quarterly,* 48.

13 "Rich's poems do not tend to be narratives." Wallace, *Englewood Review of Books.*

14 "Mr. Pavlić has listened." Rich, Foreword, xi, in Pavlić, *Paraph of Bone & Other Kinds of Blue.*

"Our words misunderstand us."

"and we by now too wise"

17 "fogged-in." Rich, *Collected Early Poems,* xx.

17 "the world's corruption." Rich, *A Change of World,* 21; *Collected Poems,* 5.

17 "do the things left to be done." Rich, *A Change of World,* 21; *Collected Poems,* 5.

17 "Every navigator / Fares unwarned." Rich, *A Change of World*, 66; *Collected Poems*, 29.

17 "two furtive exiles," "the porcelain people." Rich, *A Change of World*, 29; *Collected Poems*, 8–9.

18 "And almost we imagine." Rich, *A Change of World*, 29; *Collected Poems*, 8–9.

18 "a socially responsible role to play." Ellison, *Invisible Man*, 581.

18 "But stones are thrown by children." Rich, *A Change of World*, 29–30; *Collected Poems*, 9.

"Dear fellow-particle"

19 "detachment from the self and its emotions." W. H. Auden, foreword to Rich, *A Change of World*, 10.

19 "Sigh no more, ladies." Rich, *Snapshots of a Daughter-in-Law*, 26; *Collected Poems*, 121.

19 "Reading while waiting." Rich, *Snapshots of a Daughter-in-Law*, 24; *Collected Poems*, 118.

19 "The present holds you like a raving wife." Rich, *Snapshots of a Daughter-in-Law*, 39; *Collected Poems*, 131.

19 "What are you now." Rich, *Snapshots of a Daughter-in-Law*, 39; *Collected Poems*, 131.

20 "They say the second's getting shorter—." Rich, *Snapshots of a Daughter-in-Law*, 47; *Collected Poems*, 138.

20 "Dear fellow-particle, electric dust." Rich, *Snapshots of a Daughter-in-Law*, 48; *Collected Poems*, 139.

21 "You see a man." Rich, *Snapshots of a Daughter-in-Law*, 60; *Collected Poems*, 147–48.

22 "I've said: I wouldn't ever." Rich, *Snapshots of a Daughter-in-Law*, 54; *Collected Poems*, 142–43.

22 "I'm older now than you." Rich, *Snapshots of a Daughter-in-Law*, 66; *Collected Poems*, 151–52.

23 "I now no longer think." Rich, *Snapshots of a Daughter-in-Law*, 36; *Collected Poems*, 128.

23 "unwittingly even." Rich, *Snapshots of a Daughter-in-Law*, 36; *Collected Poems*, 128.

23 "Marianne dangles barefoot." Rich, *Snapshots of a Daughter-in-Law*, 53; *Collected Poems*, 142.

24 "I used myself, let nothing use me." Rich, *Necessities of Life*, 9–10; *Collected Poems*, 168.

24 "to name / over the bare necessities." Rich, *Necessities of Life*, 10; *Collected Poems*, 168.

24 "touchingly desirable / a prize." Rich, *Necessities of Life*, 22; *Collected Poems*, 180.

24 "I'd call it love if love." Rich, *Necessities of Life*, 22; *Collected Poems*, 180.

24 "troubled regions." Rich, *A Change of World,* 17; *Collected Poems,* 3.

24 "truthful," "white orchid." Rich, *Snapshots of a Daughter-in-Law,* 36; *Collected Poems,* 128.

25 "Happiness! how many times." Rich, *Necessities of Life,* 12; *Collected Poems,* 170.

25 "my soul wheeled back." Rich, *Necessities of Life,* 12; *Collected Poems,* 170.

25 "You can feel so free, so free." Rich, *Necessities of Life,* 24; *Collected Poems,* 181.

25 "Barbed wire, dead at your feet." Rich, *Necessities of Life,* 24; *Collected Poems,* 181–82.

25 "Your eyes / spring open, still filmed." Rich, *Necessities of Life,* 25; *Collected Poems,* 182.

26 "sphinx, medusa?" Rich, *Necessities of Life,* 25; *Collected Poems,* 182.

26 "For years I never saw it." Rich, *Necessities of Life,* 41; *Collected Poems,* 196.

26 "bright enamel people." Rich, *A Change of World,* 30; *Collected Poems,* 9.

26 "there, all along." Rich, *Necessities of Life,* 41; *Collected Poems,* 196.

26 "Little wonder the eye, healing." Rich, *Necessities of Life,* 41; *Collected Poems,* 196.

26 "the sea . . . / grinding and twisting." Rich, *Necessities of Life,* 42; *Collected Poems,* 197.

26 "the pier stands groaning." Rich, *Necessities of Life,* 42; *Collected Poems,* 197.

26 "in aftercalm / . . . the black, blurred face." Rich, *Necessities of Life,* 42; *Collected Poems,* 197.

26 "I'm am gliding backward." Rich, *Necessities of Life,* 47; *Collected Poems,* 201.

27 "Thunder is all it is, and yet." Rich, *Necessities of Life,* 44; *Collected Poems,* 198.

27 "The power of the dinosaur." Rich, *Necessities of Life,* 45; *Collected Poems,* 199.

27 "power of dead grass." Rich, *Necessities of Life,* 45; *Collected Poems,* 199.

27 "a roof I can't live under?" *Snapshots of a Daughter-in-Law,* 68; *Collected Poems,* 154.

27 "No criminal, no hero." Rich, *Necessities of Life,* 45; *Collected Poems,* 200.

27 "Over him, over you." Rich, *Necessities of Life,* 46; *Collected Poems,* 200.

27 "It is the first flying cathedral." Rich, *Necessities of Life,* 46; *Collected Poems,* 200–201.

"all these destructibles"

28 "I find that I can no longer." Rich, quoted in Gelpi, *American Poetry since 1960,* 132–33.

28 "I needed a way of dealing with very complex." Rich, quoted in Ahmad, *Ghazals of Ghalib,* xxv–xxvi. For more information about Adrienne Rich's work in the SEEK program at CUNY, see Reed, *Jayne Cortez, Adrienne*

Rich, and the Feminist Superhero. See also Brown et al., *"What We Are Part Of."*

29 "the only thing I've ever done," "applied for the job." Rich, quoted in Dean, *New Republic.*

30 "down from that simplified west." Rich, *Leaflets,* 11; *Collected Poems,* 231.

30 "We stand in the porch." Rich, *Leaflets,* 15; *Collected Poems,* 234.

30 "the old masters, the old sources." Rich, *Leaflets,* 15; *Collected Poems,* 234.

30 "a railing on an icy night." Rich, *Leaflets,* 15; *Collected Poems,* 234.

30 "the point is, it's a shelter." Rich, *Leaflets,* 13; *Collected Poems,* 233.

30 "How long have I gone round." Rich, *Leaflets,* 34; *Collected Poems,* 251.

30 "They've supplied us with pills." Rich, *Leaflets,* 31; *Collected Poems,* 248.

31 "The fox, panting, fire-eyed." Rich, *Leaflets,* 31; *Collected Poems,* 248.

31 "No one tells the truth about truth." Rich, *Leaflets,* 31; *Collected Poems,* 248.

31 "being that / inanely single-minded." Rich, *Leaflets,* 31; *Collected Poems,* 248.

31 "There's a secret boundary hidden." Rich, *Leaflets,* 33; *Collected Poems,* 250.

31 "My hands are knotted in the rope." Rich, *Leaflets,* 42; *Collected Poems,* 260.

31 "and that poster streaking the opposite wall." Rich, *Leaflets,* 44; *Collected Poems,* 262.

32 "types out 'useless' as 'monster.'" Rich, *Leaflets,* 45; *Collected Poems,* 263.

32 "Is this all I can say of these." Rich, *Leaflets,* 45; *Collected Poems,* 263.

32 "alive, whatever it is." Rich, *Leaflets,* 44; *Collected Poems,* 262.

32 "What life was there, was mine." Rich, *Necessities of Life,* 10; *Collected Poems,* 168.

32 "There are no angels   yet." Rich, *Leaflets,* 50; *Collected Poems,* 267.

33 "bare apartment." Rich, *Leaflets,* 50; *Collected Poems,* 267.

33 "words stream past me." Rich, *Leaflets,* 50; *Collected Poems,* 267.

33 "I get your message Gabriel." Rich, *Leaflets,* 51; *Collected Poems,* 268.

33 "life without caution." Rich, *Leaflets,* 52; *Collected Poems,* 269.

34 "I want to hand you this." Rich, *Leaflets,* 55; *Collected Poems,* 272–73.

34 "I want this to be yours." Rich, *Leaflets,* 56; *Collected Poems,* 273.

35 "My *ghazals* are personal and public." Rich, *Leaflets,* 59; *Collected Poems,* 1126.

35 "When I look at that wall." Rich, *Leaflets,* 61; *Collected Poems,* 277.

35 "When you read these lines." Rich, *Leaflets,* 61; *Collected Poems,* 277.

36 "Sleeping back-to-back." Rich, *Leaflets,* 61; *Collected Poems,* 277.

36 "These words are vapor-trails." Rich, *Leaflets,* 61; *Collected Poems,* 277.

36 "For us the work undoes itself." Rich, *Leaflets,* 66; *Collected Poems,* 279.

36 "In Central Park we talked." Rich, *Leaflets,* 62; *Collected Poems,* 278.

36 "The friend I can trust." Rich, *Leaflets,* 65; *Collected Poems,* 281.

36 "gender was just beginning to be understood." Rich, *Arts of the Possible,* 4.

36 "white apparencies." Rich, *Necessities of Life,* 41; *Collected Poems,* 196.

36 "We are the forerunners." Rich, in Ahmad, *Ghazals of Ghalib,* 78.

37 "A dead mosquito, flattened against a door." Rich, *Leaflets,* 66; *Collected Poems,* 282.

37 "James Baldwin is as dead." Rich, quoted in Dean, *New Republic.*

37 "Maybe our perceptions are getting sharper." Rich, quoted in Dean, *New Republic.*

38 "When your sperm enters me." Rich, *Leaflets,* 64; *Collected Poems,* 280.

38 "own mind merely." Wordsworth, *Lyrical Ballads,* preface.

38 "owned no property." Rich, *Leaflets,* 59; *Collected Poems,* 1126.

38 "To resign *yourself*—what an act of betrayal!" Rich, *Leaflets,* 64; *Collected Poems,* 280.

38 "In the red wash of the darkroom." Rich, *Leaflets,* 62; *Collected Poems,* 278.

38 "If these are letters." Rich, *Leaflets,* 68; *Collected Poems,* 284.

38 "When they read this poem." Rich, *Leaflets,* 68; *Collected Poems,* 284.

38 "I long ago stopped dreaming." Rich, *Leaflets,* 67; *Collected Poems,* 283.

38 "There's a war on earth." Rich, *Leaflets,* 68; *Collected Poems,* 284.

39 "I'm speaking to you as a woman." Rich, *Leaflets,* 69; *Collected Poems,* 285.

39 "clogged and mostly / nothing." Rich, *Leaflets,* 50; *Collected Poems,* 267.

40 "Stripped / you're beginning to float." Rich, *The Will to Change,* 11; *Collected Poems,* 299.

40 "once the last absolutes were torn." Rich, *The Will to Change,* 11; *Collected Poems,* 299.

40 "my ignorance of you." Rich, *The Will to Change,* 11; *Collected Poems,* 299.

40 "was written after a visit." Rich, *On Lies, Secrets, and Silence,* 47.

40 "in her 98 years to discover." Rich, *The Will to Change,* 13; *Collected Poems,* 301.

41 "What we see, we see." Rich, *The Will to Change,* 14; *Collected Poems,* 302.

41 "I have been standing all my life." Rich, *The Will to Change,* 14; *Collected Poems,* 302.

41 "A woman in the shape of a monster." Rich, *The Will to Change,* 13; *Collected Poems,* 301.

41 "At last the woman in the poem." Rich, *On Lies, Secrets, and Silence,* 47.

41 "I am a galactic cloud so deep." Rich, *The Will to Change,* 14; *Collected Poems,* 302.

41 "I am an instrument in the shape." Rich, *The Will to Change,* 14; *Collected Poems,* 302.

42 "a scientist and art-collector." Rich, *The Will to Change,* 15; *Collected Poems,* 303.

42 "We lie under the sheet." Rich, *The Will to Change,* 17; *Collected Poems,* 305.

43 "sexual jealousy / outflung hand." Rich, *The Will to Change,* 17; *Collected Poems,* 305.

43 "*burn the texts* said Artaud." Rich, *The Will to Change*, 18; *Collected Poems*, 306.

43 "The burning of a book arouses." Rich, *The Will to Change*, 18; *Collected Poems*, 306.

43 "The typewriter is overheated." Rich, *The Will to Change*, 18; *Collected Poems*, 306.

43 "relief of the body," "reconstruction of the mind," "a woman trying to translate pulsations." Rich, *The Will to Change*, 14; *Collected Poems*, 302.

43 "People suffer highly in poverty." Rich, *The Will to Change*, 16; *Collected Poems*, 304.

44 "(the fracture of order." Rich, *The Will to Change*, 16; *Collected Poems*, 305.

44 "*send carbons* you said." Rich, *The Will to Change*, 31; *Collected Poems*, 319.

44 "City of accidents, your true map." Rich, *The Will to Change*, 24; *Collected Poems*, 312.

44 "oppressor's language." Rich, *The Will to Change*, 18; *Collected Poems*, 306.

44 "Our whole life a translation." Rich, *The Will to Change*, 37; *Collected Poems*, 324.

44 "Trying to tell the doctor." Rich, *The Will to Change*, 37; *Collected Poems*, 324.

45 "like the Algerian / who has walked." Rich, *The Will to Change*, 37; *Collected Poems*, 324–25.

45 "all those dead letters." Rich, *The Will to Change*, 37; *Collected Poems*, 324–25.

45 "Grief held back from the lips." Rich, *The Will to Change*, 54; *Collected Poems*, 340.

45 "battery of signals." Rich, *The Will to Change*, 14; *Collected Poems*, 302.

45 "all conversation / becomes an interview." Rich, *The Will to Change*, 14; *Collected Poems*, 302.

46 "To love, to move perpetually." Rich, *The Will to Change*, 48; *Collected Poems*, 336.

46 "the notes for the poem are the only poem." Rich, *The Will to Change*, 49; *Collected Poems*, 337–38.

46 "submarine echo." Rich, *Snapshots of a Daughter-in-Law*, 66; *Collected Poems*, 152.

"look at her closely if you dare"
"answer me / when I speak badly"

47 "look at her closely if you dare." Rich, *A Wild Patience Has Taken Me This Far*, 57; *Collected Poems*, 567.

48 "This is how it feels to do something." Rich, *Poems: Selected and New*, 139; *Collected Poems*, 293.

48 "tears of fear, of the child stepping." Rich, *Poems: Selected and New*, 139; *Collected Poems*, 293.

48 "and I am afraid." Rich, *Poems: Selected and New,* 139; *Collected Poems,* 293.

48 "coming back to something written years ago." Rich, *Poems: Selected and New,* 139; *Collected Poems,* 293.

48 "The will to change begins in the body." Rich, *Poems: Selected and New,* 140; *Collected Poems,* 294.

49 "I need a language to hear myself." Rich, *Poems: Selected and New,* 140; *Collected Poems,* 294.

49 "that things I have said." Rich, *Poems: Selected and New,* 141; *Collected Poems,* 295.

49 "these images are not what I mean." Rich, *Poems: Selected and New,* 141; *Collected Poems,* 295.

50 "How well we all spoke." Rich, *The Will to Change,* 18; *Collected Poems,* 306.

50 "I want you to answer me." Rich, *Poems: Selected and New,* 141; *Collected Poems,* 295.

50 "not in poems but in tears." Rich, *Poems: Selected and New,* 141; *Collected Poems,* 295.

50 "imaginative transformation," "a certain freedom of the mind." Rich, *On Lies, Secrets, and Silence,* 43.

50 "in no way passive," "become unavailable to others." Rich, *On Lies, Secrets, and Silence,* 43.

50 "mood of isolation," "male poetic." Rich, *On Lies, Secrets, and Silence,* 49.

50 "must be ways, and we will be finding out." Rich, *On Lies, Secrets, and Silence,* 43.

51 "another kind of action." Rich, *Poems: Selected and New,* 141; *Collected Poems,* 295.

"the truth / of the lies we were living"

51 "traditional female functions." Rich, *On Lies, Secrets, and Silence,* 43.

51 "the energy of creation." Rich, *On Lies, Secrets, and Silence,* 43.

51 "the only important subject for poetry." Seidman, *Virginia Quarterly Review,* 227.

51 "condemned scenery." Rich, *Diving into the Wreck,* 3; *Collected Poems,* 355.

51 "you look at me like an emergency," "I feel more helpless." Rich, *Diving into the Wreck,* 3; *Collected Poems,* 355.

52 "everything outside our skins." Rich, *Diving into the Wreck,* 5; *Collected Poems,* 356.

52 "even you, fellow-creature, sister." Rich, *Diving into the Wreck,* 5; *Collected Poems,* 357.

52 "The fact of being separate." Rich, *Diving into the Wreck,* 5; *Collected Poems,* 357.

52 "disproof of what we thought possible," "doubts of another's existence." Rich, *Diving into the Wreck,* 6; *Collected Poems,* 357.

52 "closer to the truth." Rich, *Diving into the Wreck,* 6; *Collected Poems,* 357.

52 "blue energy piercing." Rich, *Diving into the Wreck*, 6; *Collected Poems*, 358.

52 "the tragedy of sex." Rich, *Diving into the Wreck*, 8; *Collected Poems*, 359.

52 "—the hermit's cabin." Rich, *Diving into the Wreck*, 8; *Collected Poems*, 359.

52 "A man's world." Rich, *Diving into the Wreck*, 8; *Collected Poems*, 359.

52 "the unconscious forest." Rich, *Diving into the Wreck*, 8; *Collected Poems*, 359.

52 "Nothing will save this." Rich, *Diving into the Wreck*, 8; *Collected Poems*, 360.

53 "All night dreaming of a body." Rich, *Diving into the Wreck*, 10; *Collected Poems*, 361.

53 "go on / streaming through." Rich, *Diving into the Wreck*, 8; *Collected Poems*, 359.

53 "But this is the saying of a dream." Rich, *Diving into the Wreck*, 10; *Collected Poems*, 361–62.

53 "asleep in the next room," "sit up smoking." Rich, *Diving into the Wreck*, 11–12; *Collected Poems*, 363.

53 "He has spent a whole day." Rich, *Diving into the Wreck*, 12; *Collected Poems*, 363.

53 "hand in hand." Rich, *Diving into the Wreck*, 12; *Collected Poems*, 363.

53 "*cable of blue fire.*" Rich, *The Dream of a Common Language*, 6; *Collected Poems*, 445. For this image as an initial spark of relation, see also "the blue pulse of your life" in "The Alleged Murderess Walking in Her Cell." Rich, *Poems: Selected and New*, 226; *Collected Poems*, 418.

53 "She is the one you call sister." Rich, *Diving into the Wreck*, 15; *Collected Poems*, 365.

54 "knows what it is," "knows it's neither." Rich, *Diving into the Wreck*, 20; *Collected Poems*, 369.

54 "Underneath my lids another eye has opened." Rich, *Diving into the Wreck*, 17; *Collected Poems*, 367.

54 "detail not on TV," "the violence." Rich, *Diving into the Wreck*, 17; *Collected Poems*, 367.

54 "This eye." Rich, *Diving into the Wreck*, 17–18; *Collected Poems*, 367–68.

55 "Looking as I've looked before." Rich, *Diving into the Wreck*, 19; *Collected Poems*, 368.

55 " walking as I've walked before." Rich, *Diving into the Wreck*, 19; *Collected Poems*, 368.

55 "if they ask me my identity." Rich, *Diving into the Wreck*, 19; *Collected Poems*, 368.

55 "I cannot touch you." Rich, *The Will to Change*, 18; *Collected Poems*, 306.

55 "for hours our talk has beaten." Rich, *Diving into the Wreck*, 21; *Collected Poems*, 370.

56 "what makes the body shoot." Rich, *A Change of World*, 64; *Collected Poems*, 28.

56 "at the Berlin Olympics." Rich, *Diving into the Wreck*, 9; *Collected Poems*, 360.

56 "control; loss of control." Rich, *Diving into the Wreck*, 9; *Collected Poems*, 360.

56 "before the dark chambers." Rich, *Diving into the Wreck*, 9; *Collected Poems*, 360–61.

56 "A woman made this film." Rich, *Diving into the Wreck*, 9; *Collected Poems*, 361.

56 "another kind of action." Rich, *Poems: Selected and New*, 141; *Collected Poems*, 295.

57 "dead language." Rich, *Diving into the Wreck*, 19; *Collected Poems*, 368.

57 "I crawl like an insect." Rich, *Diving into the Wreck*, 22–23; *Collected Poems*, 371.

57 "the sea is another story." Rich, *Diving into the Wreck*, 23; *Collected Poems*, 371.

57 "a force beyond all bodily powers." Rich, *A Change of World*, 64; *Collected Poems*, 28.

57 "the law / of gravity." Rich, *Diving into the Wreck*, 9; *Collected Poems*, 361.

57 "to turn my body without force." Rich, *Diving into the Wreck*, 23; *Collected Poems*, 372.

57 "but here alone," "and there is no one," "I have to learn alone." Rich, *Diving into the Wreck*, 22–23; *Collected Poems*, 371–72.

57 "it is easy to forget." Rich, *Diving into the Wreck*, 22–23; *Collected Poems*, 371–72.

57 "in the prime of life, "babies are old enough." Rich, *Diving into the Wreck*, 13; *Collected Poems*, 364.

57 "a city where nothing is forbidden." Rich, *Diving into the Wreck*, 13; *Collected Poems*, 364.

57 "I stroke the beam of my lamp." Rich, *Diving into the Wreck*, 23; *Collected Poems*, 372.

57 "the wreck and not the story." Rich, *Diving into the Wreck*, 23; *Collected Poems*, 372.

57 "This is the place." Rich, *Diving into the Wreck*, 24; *Collected Poems*, 373.

57 "I am here, the mermaid." Rich, *Diving into the Wreck*, 24; *Collected Poems*, 373.

58 "We circle silently." Rich, *Diving into the Wreck*, 24; *Collected Poems*, 373.

58 "the intelligence of their mistakes," Shaughnessy, *Errors and Expectations*, 11.

58 "We are admitting minds." Rich, "Statement to C.C.N.Y. Faculty Meeting, Wednesday April 23," in Brown et al., *"What We Are Part Of."*

58 "strategies by which intelligence imprisoned." Rich, cover note for Shaughnessy, *Errors and Expectations*.

58 "a child steal because he did not," "(the fracture of order." Rich, *The Will to Change*, 16; *Collected Poems*, 304–5.

58 "How well we all spoke." Rich, *The Will to Change,* 18; *Collected Poems,* 306.

59 "I cannot touch you." Rich, *The Will to Change,* 18; *Collected Poems,* 306.

59 "We are, I am, you are." Rich, *Diving into the Wreck,* 24; *Collected Poems,* 373.

59 "I know it hurts to burn." Rich, *The Will to Change,* 18; *Collected Poems,* 306.

60 "sing hey nonny no." Hayden, *Collected Poems,* 95.

60 "how we are burning up our lives." Rich, *Diving into the Wreck,* 31; *Collected Poems,* 381.

60 "candles see themselves disembodied." Rich, *Diving into the Wreck,* 42; *Collected Poems,* 390.

60 "1. The freedom of the wholly mad." Rich, *Diving into the Wreck,* 27; *Collected Poems,* 377.

60 "huddled fugitive." Rich, *Diving into the Wreck,* 27; *Collected Poems,* 377.

60 "4. White light splits the room." Rich, *Diving into the Wreck,* 28; *Collected Poems,* 378.

61 "computing body counts." Rich, *Diving into the Wreck,* 28; *Collected Poems,* 377.

61 "Will the judges try to tell me." Rich, *Diving into the Wreck,* 28; *Collected Poems,* 377.

61 "I hate your words." Rich, *Diving into the Wreck,* 29; *Collected Poems,* 379–80.

61 "a conspiracy to coexist." Rich, *Diving into the Wreck,* 30; *Collected Poems,* 380.

61 "ignorant of the fact." Rich, *Diving into the Wreck,* 41; *Collected Poems,* 389.

61 "Walking Amsterdam Avenue." Rich, *Diving into the Wreck,* 36; *Collected Poems,* 386.

62 "I think of Norman Morrison." Rich, *Diving into the Wreck,* 36; *Collected Poems,* 386.

62 "Taking off in a plane." Rich, *Diving into the Wreck,* 36–37; *Collected Poems,* 386–87.

62 "a world masculinity made." "Merced," Rich, *Diving into the Wreck,* 36; *Collected Poems,* 386.

62 "white light." Rich, *Diving into the Wreck,* 28; *Collected Poems,* 378.

62 "music of the entirely / isolated," "where everything is silence." Rich, *Diving into the Wreck,* 43; *Collected Poems,* 391.

62 "machinery," "in the sickening light." Rich, *Diving into the Wreck,* 45; *Collected Poems,* 392.

63 "Will the judges try to tell me." Rich, *Diving into the Wreck,* 28; *Collected Poems,* 377.

63 "sweet simmer of the hay." Rich, *Diving into the Wreck,* 27; *Collected Poems,* 377.

63 "back so far there is another language." Rich, *Diving into the Wreck*, 58; *Collected Poems*, 402.

63 "repair of speech," "fracture of order." Rich, *The Will to Change*, 16; *Collected Poems*, 305.

63 "these scars bear witness." Rich, *Diving into the Wreck*, 58; *Collected Poems*, 403.

63 "Madness. Suicide. Murder." Rich, *Diving into the Wreck*, 28; *Collected Poems*, 378.

63 "I trust none of them." Rich, *Diving into the Wreck*, 48; *Collected Poems*, 395.

63 "the trained violence of doctors." Rich, *Diving into the Wreck*, 48; *Collected Poems*, 395.

63 "Only my existence." Rich, *Diving into the Wreck*, 28; *Collected Poems*, 395.

64 "no longer personal." Rich, *Diving into the Wreck*, 58; *Collected Poems*, 402.

64 "chance connections." Rich, *Diving into the Wreck*, 28; *Collected Poems*, 395.

64 "Little by little." Rich, *Diving into the Wreck*, 28; *Collected Poems*, 395.

64 "no longer personal." Rich, *Diving into the Wreck*, 58; *Collected Poems*, 402.

64 "We believe that we can enrich ourselves." Audre Lorde, Adrienne Rich, and Alice Walker, quoted in Rankine, *New Yorker*.

64 "As I type these words." Rich, *Poems: Selected and New*, xv–xvi.

"my own forces so taken up and shared"

65 "wounded herself." Rich, *The Fact of a Doorframe*, 200; *Collected Poems*, 409.

65 "that each man she touches." Rich, *The Fact of a Doorframe*, 200–201; *Collected Poems*, 409.

66 "terribly alone." Rich, *The Fact of a Doorframe*, 201; *Collected Poems*, 409.

66 "out like barbed wire." Rich, *The Fact of a Doorframe*, 201; *Collected Poems*, 409.

66 "if she takes," "will it slash." Rich, *The Fact of a Doorframe*, 201; *Collected Poems*, 409.

66 "if she passes it by." Rich, *The Fact of a Doorframe*, 201; *Collected Poems*, 410.

66 "a ward of amnesiacs," "create something." Rich, *Poems: Selected and New*, 221; *Collected Poems*, 410–11.

66 "I want to write." Rich, *Poems: Selected and New*, 221; *Collected Poems*, 410–11.

66 "the keepers of order." Rich, *Poems: Selected and New*, 221; *Collected Poems*, 410–11.

66 "inside the spider's body." Rich, *Diving into the Wreck*, 11; *Collected Poems*, 362.

66 "I am thinking / of films we have made." Rich, *Poems: Selected and New*, 222; *Collected Poems*, 411.

66 "Tonight I understand." Rich, *Poems: Selected and New,* 228; *Collected Poems,* 415.

67 "The woman / I needed to call." Rich, *Poems: Selected and New,* 228; *Collected Poems,* 415.

67 "But we were talking in 1952." Rich, *Poems: Selected and New,* 234; *Collected Poems,* 424.

67 "the energy it draws on." Rich, *Poems: Selected and New,* 228; *Collected Poems,* 415.

67 "For now, I am myself." Rich, *Poems: Selected and New,* 224; *Collected Poems,* 416.

67 "A city waits at the back of my skull." Rich, *Poems: Selected and New,* 225; *Collected Poems,* 416–17.

67 "beat a man to death." Rich, *Poems: Selected and New,* 226; *Collected Poems,* 417.

67 "I don't know what / it means." Rich, *Poems: Selected and New,* 226; *Collected Poems,* 418.

67 "more at peace." Rich, *Poems: Selected and New,* 226; *Collected Poems,* 418.

68 "the blue pulse of your life." Rich, *Poems: Selected and New,* 226; *Collected Poems,* 418.

68 "we have done our time." Rich, *Poems: Selected and New,* 242; *Collected Poems,* 434.

68 "near and yet above." Rich, *Poems: Selected and New,* 242; *Collected Poems,* 434.

68 "such women are dangerous." Rich, *Poems: Selected and New,* 244; *Collected Poems,* 437.

68 "yes, we will be dangerous." Rich, *Poems: Selected and New,* 244; *Collected Poems,* 437.

68 "Isolation, the dream." Rich, *Poems: Selected and New,* 244; *Collected Poems,* 437.

69 "—a suicidal leaf." Rich, *Poems: Selected and New,* 244; *Collected Poems,* 437.

69 "one of the oldest motions," "sings / a courage-song." Rich, *Poems: Selected and New,* 231; *Collected Poems,* 438.

69 "I have been standing." Rich, *The Will to Change,* 14; *Collected Poems,* 302.

69 "translate pulsations / into images." Rich, *The Will to Change,* 14; *Collected Poems,* 302.

69 "she must have known." Rich, *The Dream of a Common Language,* 3; *Collected Poems,* 443.

69 "She died a famous woman." Rich, *The Dream of a Common Language,* 3; *Collected Poems,* 443.

70 "If in this sleep I speak." Rich, "*The Dream of a Common Language,* 4; *Collected Poems,* 444.

70 "You climbed here for yourself." Rich, *The Dream of a Common Language,* 5; *Collected Poems,* 444.

70 "*I have never seen.*" Rich, *The Dream of a Common Language,* 5; *Collected Poems,* 445.

70 "*We know now we have always been.*" Rich, *The Dream of a Common Language,* 6; *Collected Poems,* 445.

70 "What life was there, was mine." Rich, *Necessities of Life,* 10; *Collected Poems,* 168.

70 "alive, whatever it is." Rich, *Leaflets,* 44; *Collected Poems,* 262.

70 "The fact of being separate." Rich, *Diving into the Wreck,* 5; *Collected Poems,* 357.

71 "I have lived in isolation." Rich, *Poems: Selected and New,* 239; *Collected Poems,* 430.

71 "*to survive.*" Rich, *The Dream of a Common Language,* 6; *Collected Poems,* 446.

71 "When you have buried us." Rich, *The Dream of a Common Language,* 5; *Collected Poems,* 445.

71 "*What does love mean.*" Rich, *The Dream of a Common Language,* 6; *Collected Poems,* 446.

71 "the language / is no longer personal." Rich, *Diving into the Wreck,* 58; *Collected Poems,* 403.

72 "I can't call it life." Rich, *The Dream of a Common Language,* 9; *Collected Poems,* 449.

72 "No one lives in this room." Rich, *The Dream of a Common Language,* 7; *Collected Poems,* 446.

72 "the true nature of poetry." Rich, *The Dream of a Common Language,* 7; *Collected Poems,* 446.

72 "did this. Conceived / of each other." Rich, *The Dream of a Common Language,* 9; *Collected Poems,* 448.

72 "How well we all spoke." Rich, *The Will to Change,* 18; *Collected Poems,* 306.

72 "givens," "the splitting / between love." Rich, *The Dream of a Common Language,* 11; *Collected Poems,* 451.

72 "I will not be divided   from her." Rich, *The Dream of a Common Language,* 11; *Collected Poems,* 450.

73 "blunted by malnutrition," "sharpened by the passion." Rich, *The Dream of a Common Language,* 13; *Collected Poems,* 452.

73 "no longer personal." Rich, *Diving into the Wreck,* 58; *Collected Poems,* 403.

73 "the so-called common language," "Inscribes with its unreturning stylus." Rich, *The Dream of a Common Language,* 16; *Collected Poems,* 455.

73 "loneliness of the liar." Rich, *The Dream of a Common Language,* 17; *Collected Poems,* 456.

74 "Silence can be a plan." Rich, *The Dream of a Common Language,* 17; *Collected Poems,* 457.

74 "If at the will of the poet." Rich, *The Dream of a Common Language,* 19; *Collected Poems,* 459.

74 "If it could simply look you in the face." Rich, *The Dream of a Common Language*, 19; *Collected Poems*, 459.

74 "as silence falls at the end." Rich, *The Dream of a Common Language*, 18; *Collected Poems*, 458.

74 "a process, delicate, violent." Rich, *Women and Honor*, n.p.

74 "not one thing." Rich, *Women and Honor*, n.p.

74 "are trying, all the time." Rich, *Women and Honor*, n.p.

75 "what in fact I keep choosing." Rich, *The Dream of a Common Language*, 20; *Collected Poems*, 460.

75 "We need to grasp our lives inseparable." Rich, *The Dream of a Common Language*, 25; *Collected Poems*, 465.

76 "the desire to show you to everyone." Rich, *The Dream of a Common Language*, 25; *Collected Poems*, 466.

76 "Did I ever walk the morning streets." Rich, *The Dream of a Common Language*, 26; *Collected Poems*, 466.

76 "I'm lugging my sack." Rich, *The Dream of a Common Language*, 26; *Collected Poems*, 466.

76 "I let myself into the kitchen." Rich, *The Dream of a Common Language*, 26; *Collected Poems*, 467.

76 "delicious coffee," "my body still both light." Rich, *The Dream of a Common Language*, 26; *Collected Poems*, 467.

76 "my mouth is burning." Rich, *The Will to Change*, 18; *Collected Poems*, 306.

77 "world masculinity made." Rich, *Diving into the Wreck*, 36; *Collected Poems*, 386.

77 "The mail / lets fall a Xerox." Rich, *The Dream of a Common Language*, 26–27; *Collected Poems*, 467.

77 "*Do whatever you can to survive.*" Rich, *The Dream of a Common Language*, 27; *Collected Poems*, 467.

77 "Our words misunderstand us." Rich, *Necessities of Life*, 17; *Collected Poems*, 176.

77 "This is the oppressor's language." Rich, *The Will to Change*, 18; *Collected Poems*, 306.

77 "lovers caught in the crossfire." Rich, *The Dream of a Common Language*, 14; *Collected Poems*, 454.

77 "both light and heavy." Rich, *The Dream of a Common Language*, 26; *Collected Poems*, 467.

77 "And my incurable anger." Rich, *The Dream of a Common Language*, 27; *Collected Poems*, 467.

77 "What kind of beast." Rich, *The Dream of a Common Language*, 28; *Collected Poems*, 468.

77 "yet, writing words like these." Rich, *The Dream of a Common Language*, 28; *Collected Poems*, 468.

78 "the failure to want our freedom." Rich, *The Dream of a Common Language*, 28; *Collected Poems*, 469.

78 "break open further." Rich, *The Dream of a Common Language*, 27; *Collected Poems*, 467.

78 "Your silence today is a pond." Rich, *The Dream of a Common Language*, 29; *Collected Poems*, 469.

78 "Whatever's lost there." Rich, *The Dream of a Common Language*, 29; *Collected Poems*, 469.

78 "show me what I can do." Rich, *The Dream of a Common Language*, 29; *Collected Poems*, 470.

78 "voices of the psyche drive through." Rich, *The Dream of a Common Language*, 30; *Collected Poems*, 470.

78 "and our bodies, so alike." Rich, *The Dream of a Common Language*, 30; *Collected Poems*, 471.

78 "*forces so taken up and shared.*" Rich, *The Dream of a Common Language*, 5; *Collected Poems*, 445.

79 "There are latitudes revealed." Rich, *A Change of World*, 66; *Collected Poems*, 29.

79 "out here I feel more helpless." Rich, *Diving into the Wreck*, 3; *Collected Poems*, 355.

79 "The rules break like a thermometer." Rich, *The Dream of a Common Language*, 31; *Collected Poems*, 471.

79 "pure invention," "the maps they gave us." Rich, *The Dream of a Common Language*, 31; *Collected Poems*, 471.

79 "the music on the radio." Rich, *The Dream of a Common Language*, 31; *Collected Poems*, 471–72.

79 "No one's fated or doomed." Rich, *The Dream of a Common Language*, 33; *Collected Poems*, 474.

79 "*the more I live the more I think.*" Rich, *The Dream of a Common Language*, 34; *Collected Poems*, 474.

79 "Am I speaking coldly." Rich, *The Dream of a Common Language*, 34; *Collected Poems*, 475.

79 "(I told you from the first." Rich, *The Dream of a Common Language*, 34; *Collected Poems*, 475.

79 "two women together is a work." Rich, *The Dream of a Common Language*, 35; *Collected Poems*, 475.

80 "where the fiercest attention." Rich, *The Dream of a Common Language*, 35; *Collected Poems*, 475.

80 "—look at the faces." Rich, *The Dream of a Common Language*, 35; *Collected Poems*, 475.

80 "I discern a woman / I loved." Rich, *The Dream of a Common Language*, 35; *Collected Poems*, 476.

80 "and soon I shall know." Rich, *The Dream of a Common Language*, 35; *Collected Poems*, 476.

80 "back to where her solitude." Rich, *The Dream of a Common Language*, 35; *Collected Poems*, 476.

80 "a cleft of light." Rich, *The Dream of a Common Language*, 35; *Collected Poems*, 476.

80 "I choose to be a figure." Rich, *The Dream of a Common Language*, 36; *Collected Poems*, 476.

81 "To have enough courage." Rich, *The Dream of a Common Language*, 39; *Collected Poems*, 479.

81 "it does not pay to feel." Rich, *The Dream of a Common Language*, 39; *Collected Poems*, 479.

81 "Her face   The fast rain tearing." Rich, *The Dream of a Common Language*, 39–40; *Collected Poems*, 479.

82 "Spilt love   seeking its level." Rich, *The Dream of a Common Language*, 40; *Collected Poems*, 480.

82 "I have written so many words." Rich, *The Dream of a Common Language*, 41; *Collected Poems*, 480.

82 "Now I must write for myself." Rich, *The Dream of a Common Language*, 41; *Collected Poems*, 480.

82 "I look at my hands." Rich, *The Dream of a Common Language*, 41; *Collected Poems*, 480–81.

82 "and I ask myself and you." Rich, *The Dream of a Common Language*, 46; *Collected Poems*, 485.

83 "*everything you feel is true.*" Rich, *The Dream of a Common Language*, 56; *Collected Poems*, 495.

83 "how the body tells the truth." Rich, *The Dream of a Common Language*, 58; *Collected Poems*, 497.

83 "Most of our love took the form." Rich, *The Dream of a Common Language*, 58; *Collected Poems*, 497.

83 "to extend herself," "miner is no metaphor," "goes / into the cage." Rich, *The Dream of a Common Language*, 60; *Collected Poems*, 498–99.

83 "is flung // downward by gravity," "must change / her body." Rich, *The Dream of a Common Language*, 60; *Collected Poems*, 499.

83 "turns a doorknob," "ascertains / how they sleep." Rich, *The Dream of a Common Language*, 61; *Collected Poems*, 499–500.

83 "It is only she who sees." Rich, *The Dream of a Common Language*, 61; *Collected Poems*, 500.

83 "But gentleness is active." Rich, *The Dream of a Common Language*, 63; *Collected Poems*, 502.

84 "*This is what I am.*" Rich, *The Dream of a Common Language*, 64; *Collected Poems*, 503.

84 "enormity of the simplest things." Rich, *The Dream of a Common Language*, 65; *Collected Poems*, 504.

84 "the fibers of actual life." Rich, *The Dream of a Common Language*, 66; *Collected Poems*, 505.

84 "this fraying blanket." Rich, *The Dream of a Common Language*, 66–67; *Collected Poems*, 505–6.

84 "vanished pride and care." Rich, *The Dream of a Common Language*, 67; *Collected Poems*, 506.

85 "theatricality, the false glamour." Rich, *The Dream of a Common Language*, 74; *Collected Poems*, 512.

85 "there are no prodigies." Rich, *The Dream of a Common Language*, 74; *Collected Poems*, 512.

85 "the truths we are salvaging." Rich, *The Dream of a Common Language*, 74; *Collected Poems*, 512.

85 "I have to cast my lot with those." Rich, *The Dream of a Common Language*, 67; *Collected Poems*, 506.

85 *"Can you imagine / a world."* Rich, *The Dream of a Common Language*, 61; *Collected Poems*, 500.

85 "(He believed / he was joking.)" Rich, *The Dream of a Common Language*, 61; *Collected Poems*, 500.

86 "There are words I cannot choose again." Rich, *The Dream of a Common Language*, 66; *Collected Poems*, 505.

86 "it sees // detail not on TV." Rich, *Diving into the Wreck*, 17; *Collected Poems*, 367.

86 *"What I am telling you."* Rich, *A Wild Patience Has Taken Me This Far*, 48; *Collected Poems*, 560.

87 "Your son is dead." Rich, *A Wild Patience Has Taken Me This Far*, 32; *Collected Poems*, 546.

87 "with no extraordinary power." Rich, *The Dream of a Common Language*, 67; *Collected Poems*, 506.

87 "Close to your body." Rich, *A Wild Patience Has Taken Me This Far*, 3; *Collected Poems*, 519.

87 "touch knows you before language." Rich, *A Wild Patience Has Taken Me This Far*, 3; *Collected Poems*, 519.

87 "a howl, police sirens," "registering pure force," "ripping the sheath of sleep." Rich, *A Wild Patience Has Taken Me This Far*, 3; *Collected Poems*, 519.

87 "drawn against fear and woman-loathing," "We are trying to live." Rich, *A Wild Patience Has Taken Me This Far*, 4; *Collected Poems*, 520.

87 "no-man's-land does not exist," "I can never romanticize language." Rich, *A Wild Patience Has Taken Me This Far*, 4; *Collected Poems*, 520.

87 "continually fail to ask." Rich, *A Wild Patience Has Taken Me This Far*, 4; *Collected Poems*, 520.

88 "Two women sleeping / together." Rich, *A Wild Patience Has Taken Me This Far*, 3; *Collected Poems*, 519.

88 "see our bodies strung." Rich, *A Wild Patience Has Taken Me This Far*, 3–4; *Collected Poems*, 519.

88 "all the lost / crumbled burnt smashed shattered." Rich, *A Wild Patience Has Taken Me This Far*, 5; *Collected Poems*, 521.

88 "could rise reassemble re-collect re-member." Rich, *A Wild Patience Has Taken Me This Far*, 5; *Collected Poems*, 521.

88 "as every night close to your body." Rich, *A Wild Patience Has Taken Me This Far*, 5; *Collected Poems*, 521.

89 "I recognize: the stand of pines." Rich, *A Wild Patience Has Taken Me This Far*, 8; *Collected Poems*, 524.

89 *"Nothing but myself?"* Rich, *A Wild Patience Has Taken Me This Far*, 8; *Collected Poems*, 524.

89 "my visionary anger cleansing." Rich, *Diving into the Wreck*, 19; *Collected Poems*, 368.

89 "Anger and tenderness." Rich, *A Wild Patience Has Taken Me This Far*, 9; *Collected Poems*, 524.

90 "and they have caught the baby leaping." Rich, *A Wild Patience Has Taken Me This Far*, 9; *Collected Poems*, 525.

90 "Orion plunges like a drunken hunter." Rich, *A Wild Patience Has Taken Me This Far*, 44; *Collected Poems*, 557.

90 "All the figures up there." Rich, *A Wild Patience Has Taken Me This Far*, 44; *Collected Poems*, 557.

90 "We are the thorn-leaf guarding." Rich, *A Wild Patience Has Taken Me This Far*, 5; *Collected Poems*, 521.

90 "run wild, 'escaped.'" Rich, *A Wild Patience Has Taken Me This Far*, 10; *Collected Poems*, 525.

90 "headlong, loved, escaping." Rich, *A Wild Patience Has Taken Me This Far*, 10; *Collected Poems*, 525.

91 "Upstairs, long silence." Rich, *A Wild Patience Has Taken Me This Far*, 11; *Collected Poems*, 526.

91 "An energy I cannot even yet." Rich, *A Wild Patience Has Taken Me This Far*, 11; *Collected Poems*, 526.

91 *"the home of the Brontë sisters."* Rich, *A Wild Patience Has Taken Me This Far*, 11; *Collected Poems*, 527.

91 *"short and ill-environed lives," "a most sad day."* Rich, *A Wild Patience Has Taken Me This Far*, 11; *Collected Poems*, 527.

91 *"the sisters walked up and down."* Rich, *A Wild Patience Has Taken Me This Far*, 11; *Collected Poems*, 527.

91 *"much the world of literature has lost."* Rich, *A Wild Patience Has Taken Me This Far*, 11; *Collected Poems*, 527.

91 "to settle for less." Rich, *The Dream of a Common Language*, 6; *Collected Poems*, 446.

91 *". . . and is it possible you think."* Rich, *A Wild Patience Has Taken Me This Far*, 13; *Collected Poems*, 528.

92 "leaflets / dissolving within hours." Rich, *A Wild Patience Has Taken Me This Far*, 14; *Collected Poems*, 529.

92 "The heavy volumes, calf." Rich, *A Wild Patience Has Taken Me This Far*, 14; *Collected Poems*, 529.

92 "I brush my hand across my eyes." Rich, *A Wild Patience Has Taken Me This Far*, 14; *Collected Poems*, 529.

92 "THE HISTORY OF HUMAN SUFFERING." Rich, *A Wild Patience Has Taken Me This Far*, 14; *Collected Poems*, 529.

92 "OF HUMAN SUFFERING." Rich, *A Wild Patience Has Taken Me This Far*, 14; *Collected Poems*, 529.

92 "the saying of a dream," "there were somewhere / actual." Rich, *Diving into the Wreck*, 10; *Collected Poems*, 361–62.

92 "How you have given back." Rich, *A Wild Patience Has Taken Me This Far*, 15; *Collected Poems*, 530.

93 "I slice the beetroots to the core." Rich, *A Wild Patience Has Taken Me This Far*, 15; *Collected Poems*, 531.

93 "Freedom. It isn't once." Rich, *A Wild Patience Has Taken Me This Far*, 22; *Collected Poems*, 537.

93 "detail not on TV." Rich, *Diving into the Wreck*, 17; *Collected Poems*, 367.

93 "male dominion, gangrape." Rich, *A Wild Patience Has Taken Me This Far*, 45; *Collected Poems*, 557.

93 "The world as it is." Rich, *A Wild Patience Has Taken Me This Far*, 45; *Collected Poems*, 557–58.

94 "The road to the great canyon." Rich, *A Wild Patience Has Taken Me This Far*, 59; *Collected Poems*, 568.

94 "I am traveling to the edge." Rich, *A Wild Patience Has Taken Me This Far*, 59; *Collected Poems*, 568.

94 "Today I turned the wheel." Rich, *A Wild Patience Has Taken Me This Far*, 59; *Collected Poems*, 568.

"solitude of no absence"
"a struggle at the roots of the mind"

97 "neighborhoods already familiar." Rich, *Collected Early Poems*, xx.

98 "Creative practice is thus of many kinds." Williams, *Marxism and Literature*, 212.

99 "the active struggle." Williams, *Marxism and Literature*, 212.

99 "struggle at the roots." Williams, *Marxism and Literature*, 212.

99 "practical substance." Williams, *Marxism and Literature*, 212.

99 "private castle in air," "most dangerous place." Rich, *Your Native Land, Your Life*, 8; *Collected Poems*, 576.

100 "All this in a castle of air." Rich, *Your Native Land, Your Life*, 9; *Collected Poems*, 577.

100 "After your death I met you." Rich, *Your Native Land, Your Life*, 9; *Collected Poems*, 577.

100 "practical substance." Williams, *Marxism and Literature*, 212.

100 "I saw the power and arrogance." Rich, *Your Native Land, Your Life*, 9; *Collected Poems*, 577.

100 "When my dreams showed signs." Rich, *Your Native Land, Your Life,* 33;
      Collected Poems, 594.

100 "Well, I am studying a different book." Rich, *Your Native Land, Your Life,*
      53; *Collected Poems,* 614.

101 "prepare to meet the unplanned." Rich, *Your Native Land, Your Life,* 53–54;
      Collected Poems, 614.

101 "a certain air of *populatedness.*" Wallace, *Englewood Review of Books.*

101 "try pretending." Rich, *Your Native Land, Your Life,* 34; *Collected Poems,*
      595.

102 "There is a *whom,* a *where.*" Rich, *Your Native Land, Your Life,* 6; *Collected
      Poems,* 575.

102 "If you have taken this rubble." Rich, *Time's Power,* 32; *Collected Poems,*
      683.

103 "out beyond / the numerology." Rich, *Collected Poems,* 1119.

"where the pattern . . . becomes a different pattern"

103 "refuse these givens," "the splitting." Rich, *The Dream of a Common Language,*
      11; *Collected Poems,* 451.

103 "lies outside those neighborhoods." Rich, *Collected Early Poems,* xx.

104 *"With whom do you believe."* Rich, *Your Native Land, Your Life,* 6; *Collected
      Poems,* 575.

104 "rootless ideology." Rich, *Your Native Land, Your Life,* 8; *Collected Poems,*
      576.

104 "The Jews I've felt rooted among." Rich, *Your Native Land, Your Life,* 18;
      Collected Poems, 583.

105 "The place where all tracks end." Rich, *Your Native Land, Your Life,* 20;
      Collected Poems, 584–85.

105 "from imaginations that have dwelt." Rich, *Your Native Land, Your Life,*
      cover.

105 "—who are not my people." Rich, *Your Native Land, Your Life,* 13; *Collected
      Poems,* 579.

106 "look becomes the bomb." Rich, *Your Native Land, Your Life,* 16; *Collected
      Poems,* 581.

106 "I can't stop seeing like this." Rich, *Your Native Land, Your Life,* 16; *Collected
      Poems,* 582.

106 "powerful, womanly," Rich, *Your Native Land, Your Life,* 9; *Collected Poems,*
      577.

106 "with no extraordinary power." Rich, *The Dream of a Common Language,*
      67; *Collected Poems,* 506.

106 "practical substance." Williams, *Marxism and Literature,* 212.

106 "following a track of freedom." Rich, *Your Native Land, Your Life,* 10;
      Collected Poems, 577.

106 "If I try to conjure their lives." Rich, *Your Native Land, Your Life,* 13;
      Collected Poems, 579.

107 "intense light of significance." Rich, *On Lies, Secrets, and Silence,* 24.

107 "vitality of pure conviction." Rich, *On Lies, Secrets, and Silence,* 25.

107 "to find room in that life." Rich, *On Lies, Secrets, and Silence,* 32.

107 "These upland farms are the farms." Rich, *Your Native Land, Your Life,* 12; *Collected Poems,* 578.

107 "the endless / purifications of self." Rich, *Your Native Land, Your Life,* 11; *Collected Poems,* 578.

107 "there being no distance." Rich, *Your Native Land, Your Life,* 11; *Collected Poems,* 578.

107 "has any of this to do." Rich, *Your Native Land, Your Life,* 14; *Collected Poems,* 580.

107 "the passion I connect with," "trace of the original." Rich, *Your Native Land, Your Life,* 14; *Collected Poems,* 580.

107 "is the region still trying to speak." Rich, *Your Native Land, Your Life,* 14; *Collected Poems,* 580.

108 "are signals also coming back." Rich, *Your Native Land, Your Life,* 14; *Collected Poems,* 580.

108 "through the immense silence." Rich, *Your Native Land, Your Life,* 7; *Collected Poems,* 575.

108 "private castle in air." Rich, *Your Native Land, Your Life,* 8; *Collected Poems,* 576.

108 "some special destiny." Rich, *Your Native Land, Your Life,* 7; *Collected Poems,* 575.

108 "growing up safe, American," "living in a bombed-out house." Rich, *Your Native Land, Your Life,* 7; *Collected Poems,* 575.

108 "an oldfashioned, an outrageous thing." Rich, *Your Native Land, Your Life,* 17; *Collected Poems,* 582.

109 "but there is something else." Rich, *Your Native Land, Your Life,* 17; *Collected Poems,* 582.

109 "have kept beyond violence the knowledge." Rich, *Your Native Land, Your Life,* 17; *Collected Poems,* 582.

109 "the Alabama quilt." Rich, *A Wild Patience Has Taken Me This Far,* 41; *Collected Poems,* 554.

110 "*to survive.*" Rich, *The Dream of a Common Language,* 6; *Collected Poems,* 446.

110 "the eldest daughter raised," "castle of air." Rich, *Your Native Land, Your Life,* 9; *Collected Poems,* 577.

110 "Sometimes I felt ideas that attracted me." Rich, *Arts of the Possible,* 6.

110 "faithful drudging child." Rich, *Your Native Land, Your Life,* 23; *Collected Poems,* 586.

110 "passion so unexpected." Rich, *Your Native Land, Your Life,* 13; *Collected Poems,* 579.

110 "boundaries of perfection." Rich, *Your Native Land, Your Life,* 23; *Collected Poems,* 586.

110 "neighborhoods already familiar." Rich, *Collected Early Poems*, xx.

110 "a struggle at the roots." Williams, *Marxism and Literature*, 212.

111 "Say that she grew up in a house." Rich, *Your Native Land, Your Life*, 23; *Collected Poems*, 586.

111 "had memorized the formula," "ended isolate." Rich, *Your Native Land, Your Life*, 19; *Collected Poems*, 584.

111 "bound by no tribe of clan." Rich, *Your Native Land, Your Life*, 18; *Collected Poems*, 583.

111 "formula you had found." Rich, *Your Native Land, Your Life*, 25; *Collected Poems*, 587.

111 "drove to Vermont." Rich, *Your Native Land, Your Life*, 19; *Collected Poems*, 584.

111 "no person, trying to take responsibility." Rich, *Your Native Land, Your Life*, 25; *Collected Poems*, 588.

111 "I have wished I could rest." Rich, *Your Native Land, Your Life*, 27; *Collected Poems*, 589.

112 "where the context is never given." Rich, *Your Native Land, Your Life*, 35; *Collected Poems*, 597.

112 "You sleep in a room with bluegreen curtains." Rich, *Your Native Land, Your Life*, 56; *Collected Poems*, 616.

112 "the family coil so twisted." Rich, *Your Native Land, Your Life*, 56; *Collected Poems*, 616.

112 "You who did and had to do." Rich, *Your Native Land, Your Life*, 59; *Collected Poems*, 619.

113 "where the context is never given." Rich, *Your Native Land, Your Life*, 35; *Collected Poems*, 597.

113 "What if I told you your home." Rich, *Your Native Land, Your Life*, 59–60; *Collected Poems*, 620.

113 "What if I tell you." Rich, *Your Native Land, Your Life*, 59–60; *Collected Poems*, 620.

113 "no person, trying to take responsibility." Rich, *Your Native Land, Your Life*, 25; *Collected Poems*, 588.

113 "held in a DC-10." Rich, *Your Native Land, Your Life*, 41; *Collected Poems*, 602.

113 "dreaming of innocence." Rich, *Your Native Land, Your Life*, 41; *Collected Poems*, 602.

113 "no one can reach her." Rich, *Your Native Land, Your Life*, 41; *Collected Poems*, 602.

113 "what if forever after." Rich, *Your Native Land, Your Life*, 42; *Collected Poems*, 603.

114 "does not want to hear." Rich, *Your Native Land, Your Life*, 42; *Collected Poems*, 604.

114 "This woman I have been." Rich, *Your Native Land, Your Life*, 41; *Collected Poems*, 603.

114 "Because I have sometimes been her." Rich, *Your Native Land, Your Life*, 41; *Collected Poems*, 603.

114 "I am tired of innocence." Rich, *Your Native Land, Your Life*, 41; *Collected Poems*, 603.

114 "what protections / has she traded." Rich, *Your Native Land, Your Life*, 42; *Collected Poems*, 604.

114 "contort and twist." Rich, *Your Native Land, Your Life*, 41; *Collected Poems*, 603.

114 "stop dreaming the dream." Rich, *Your Native Land, Your Life*, 43; *Collected Poems*, 604.

114 "grasp [their] lives inseparable." Rich, *The Dream of a Common Language*, 25; *Collected Poems*, 465.

115 "the energy of creation." Rich, *On Lies, Secrets, and Silence*, 43.

115 "What is a Jew in Solitude?" Rich, *Your Native Land, Your Life*, 75; *Collected Poems*, 633.

115 "the quilt of whiteness," "rough earth," "hated nation." Rich, *Your Native Land, Your Life*, 41; *Collected Poems*, 603.

115 "To love the Stranger." Rich, *Your Native Land, Your Life*, 77; *Collected Poems*, 635.

115 "Close to the center, safety," "Solitude, O taboo." Rich, *Your Native Land, Your Life*, 76; *Collected Poems*, 635.

115 "new consciousness through new relationships." Williams, *Marxism and Literature*, 212.

116 "The glassy, concrete octagon." Rich, *Your Native Land, Your Life*, 75; *Collected Poems*, 633.

116 "Three thousand miles." Rich, *Your Native Land, Your Life*, 75; *Collected Poems*, 633.

116 "Robinson Jeffers, multitude." Rich, *Your Native Land, Your Life*, 76; *Collected Poems*, 634.

116 "neighborhoods already familiar." Rich, *Collected Early Poems*, xx.

116 "Must I argue for the love of multitude." Rich, *Your Native Land, Your Life*, 76; *Collected Poems*, 634.

117 "Find someone like yourself." Rich, *Your Native Land, Your Life*, 76; *Collected Poems*, 634.

117 "the energy of creation." Rich, *On Lies, Secrets, and Silence*, 43.

118 "when we refuse to be women and men." Rich, *Your Native Land, Your Life*, 78; *Collected Poems*, 636.

118 "practical substance." Williams, *Marxism and Literature*, 212.

118 "*I have never seen.*" Rich, *The Dream of a Common Language*, 5; *Collected Poems*, 445.

118 "Close to the center, safety." Rich, *Your Native Land, Your Life*, 76–77; *Collected Poems*, 635.

119 "I hear myself stuttering these words." Rich, *Your Native Land, Your Life*, 77; *Collected Poems*, 635.

119 "Did anyone ever know who we were." Rich, *Your Native Land, Your Life,* 107; *Collected Poems,* 653.

119 "*I stopped letting him do it.*" Rich, *Your Native Land, Your Life,* 86; *Collected Poems,* 642.

119 "*brother-in-law,*" "*a shrink / with the State,*" "*I have to watch my step.*" Rich, *Your Native Land, Your Life,* 86; *Collected Poems,* 642.

120 "I'm afraid of prison." Rich, *Your Native Land, Your Life,* 90; *Collected Poems,* 645.

120 "I have my fears." Rich, *Your Native Land, Your Life,* 90; *Collected Poems,* 645.

120 "Unable one day to get up." Rich, *Your Native Land, Your Life,* 90; *Collected Poems,* 645.

120 "I came out of the hospital." Rich, *Your Native Land, Your Life,* 93; *Collected Poems,* 646.

120 "from the center of my body." Rich, *Your Native Land, Your Life,* 94; *Collected Poems,* 647.

120 "Violence as purification." Rich, *Your Native Land, Your Life,* 94; *Collected Poems,* 647.

120 "Trapped in one idea." Rich, *Your Native Land, Your Life,* 95; *Collected Poems,* 647.

121 "If to feel is to be unreliable." Rich, *Your Native Land, Your Life,* 101; *Collected Poems,* 650.

121 "burning of a book arouses." Rich, *The Will to Change,* 18; *Collected Poems,* 306.

121 "win prizes / but to change." Rich, *Your Native Land, Your Life,* 23; *Collected Poems,* 586.

122 "the problem, unstated till now." Rich, *Your Native Land, Your Life,* 100; *Collected Poems,* 650.

122 "You for whom I write this." Rich, *Your Native Land, Your Life,* 111; *Collected Poems,* 656.

122 "because jazz finds its very life." Ellison, *Collected Essays,* 267.

123 "the sickening light of the precinct." Rich, *Diving into the Wreck,* 45; *Collected Poems,* 392.

123 "a hated nation." Rich, *Your Native Land, Your Life,* 41; *Collected Poems,* 603.

123 "If you think you can grasp me." Rich, *Time's Power,* 32; *Collected Poems,* 683.

"forbidden face-to-face"

123 "thinking was unable to fulfill itself." Rich, *Arts of the Possible,* 1.

124 "neighborhoods already familiar." Rich, *Collected Early Poems,* xx.

124 "when we refuse to be women and men." Rich, *Your Native Land, Your Life,* 78; *Collected Poems,* 636.

124 "*movement* was being parochialized." Rich, *Arts of the Possible,* 5.

124 "who we were / if *we* means more." Rich, *Your Native Land, Your Life*, 107;
      Collected Poems, 653.

124 "wonder / what that keyboard meant," "the hours of solitude," "prize-
      recitals." Rich, *Time's Power*, 3; *Collected Poems*, 659.

125 "Freedom: what could that mean." Rich, *Time's Power*, 4; *Collected Poems*,
      660.

125 "what I remember isn't lessons." Rich, *Time's Power*, 4; *Collected Poems*, 660.

125 "And so you played, evenings." Rich, *Time's Power*, 4; *Collected Poems*, 660.

125 "the articulate message of the slave." Du Bois, *The Souls of Black Folk*, 733.

125 "tell of death and suffering." Du Bois, *The Souls of Black Folk*, 733–34.

126 "of the songs of white America." Du Bois, *The Souls of Black Folk*, 735.

126 "Mine Eyes Have Seen the Glory." Stauffer and Soskis, *The Battle Hymn
      of the Republic*, 21. On Julia Ward Howe's involvement with the song, see
      Williams, *Hungry Heart*, 208. On John Brown's Secret Six, see Linder,
      "The Trial of John Brown."

126 "merely the sum / of the damages." Rich, *Your Native Land, Your Life*, 17;
      Collected Poems, 582.

127 "What would it mean to think." Rich, *Time's Power*, 29–30; *Collected
      Poems*, 681–82.

127 "where drought is the epic." Rich, *Time's Power*, 27; *Collected Poems*, 679.

127 "who persist, not by species-betrayal." Rich, *Time's Power*, 27; *Collected
      Poems*, 679.

127 "the energy of creation." Rich, *On Lies, Secrets, and Silence*, 43.

127 "Upstairs, long silence." Rich, *A Wild Patience Has Taken Me This Far*, 111;
      Collected Poems, 526.

128 "How you have given back." Rich, *A Wild Patience Has Taken Me This Far*,
      15; *Collected Poems*, 530.

128 "*Yes, our work is one.*" Rich, *A Wild Patience Has Taken Me This Far*, 15;
      Collected Poems, 531.

128 "our blood is mixed in." Rich, *Time's Power*, 26; *Collected Poems*, 678.

128 "dark blood under gold skin," "to your mud-river flashing." Rich, *Time's
      Power*, 7; *Collected Poems*, 663.

128 "more I cannot know." Rich, *Time's Power*, 7; *Collected Poems*, 663.

128 "All winter you went to bed early." Rich, *Time's Power*, 11; *Collected Poems*,
      665.

129 "All winter you asked nothing." Rich, *Time's Power*, 11; *Collected Poems*,
      666.

129 "you felt the pages thickening." Rich, *Time's Power*, 11; *Collected Poems*,
      666.

129 "For I mean to meet you." Rich, *Time's Power*, 17; *Collected Poems*, 670.

129 "If you wrote me." Rich, *Time's Power*, 18; *Collected Poems*, 670.

129 "Every stone around your neck." Rich, *Time's Power*, 18; *Collected Poems*,
      671.

130 "own, unwritten life." Rich, *Time's Power,* 11; *Collected Poems,* 666.

130 "Calmly you look over my shoulder." Rich, *Time's Power,* 19; *Collected Poems,* 672.

130 "many waited to cross over." Rich, *Time's Power,* 19; *Collected Poems,* 672.

130 "women, in pairs, strolling." Rich, *Time's Power,* 19; *Collected Poems,* 672.

130 "Many thousands go," "I stood by the river." Rich, *Time's Power,* 19; *Collected Poems,* 672.

130 "the notes for the poem," "the mind of the poet," "the moment of change." Rich, *The Will to Change,* 49; *Collected Poems,* 337–38.

130 "The practical nurse is the only nurse." Rich, *Time's Power,* 20; *Collected Poems,* 672.

131 "it will be a long day." Rich, *Time's Power,* 20; *Collected Poems,* 673.

131 "Will you let her touch you." Rich, *Time's Power,* 20; *Collected Poems,* 673.

131 "I'm afraid of the border patrol." Rich, *Time's Power,* 20; *Collected Poems,* 673.

131 "the failure to want our freedom." Rich, *The Dream of a Common Language,* 28; *Collected Poems,* 469.

131 "I want five hours with you." Rich, *Time's Power,* 21; *Collected Poems,* 673.

132 "I promise I won't fall asleep." Rich, *Time's Power,* 21; *Collected Poems,* 673–74.

132 "our story is not about women." Rich, *Time's Power,* 34; *Collected Poems,* 684.

132 "moments / when even slow motion." Rich, *Time's Power,* 34; *Collected Poems,* 684.

133 "candle-stumps," "on ledges by fugitives." Rich, *Time's Power,* 38; *Collected Poems,* 688.

133 "Whatever gave the girl the idea." Rich, *Time's Power,* 39; *Collected Poems,* 689.

133 "this girl is expert." Rich, *Time's Power,* 39; *Collected Poems,* 689.

133 "a strategy of mass flight." Rich, *Time's Power,* 40; *Collected Poems,* 690.

133 "*No more   Many thousand go.*" Rich, *Time's Power,* 41; *Collected Poems,* 690.

133 "the cotton swells in its boll." Rich, *Time's Power,* 41; *Collected Poems,* 690.

134 "ready for more than solitary defiance." Rich, *Time's Power,* 41; *Collected Poems,* 691.

134 "The men are dark." Rich, *Time's Power,* 38; *Collected Poems,* 688.

134 "This would be my scenario." Rich, *Time's Power,* 41; *Collected Poems,* 691.

134 "*to survive.*" Rich, *The Dream of a Common Language,* 6; *Collected Poems,* 446.

134 "a *whom,* a *where.*" Rich, *Your Native Land, Your Life,* 6; *Collected Poems,* 575.

134 "who we were / if *we* means more." Rich, *Your Native Land, Your Life,* 107; *Collected Poems,* 653.

134 "the hard practical substance." Williams, *Marxism and Literature,* 212.
134 "the active struggle," "casting off an ideology." Williams, *Marxism and Literature,* 212.
134 "What would you bring along." Rich, *Time's Power,* 51; *Collected Poems,* 699.
135 "where swimming against the current." Rich, *Time's Power,* 53; *Collected Poems,* 701.
135 "the prickle of memory." Rich, *Time's Power,* 52; *Collected Poems,* 700.
135 "This eyeflash, / this touch." Rich, *Time's Power,* 53; *Collected Poems,* 701.
135 "how to break a mold of discourse." Rich, *Time's Power,* 54; *Collected Poems,* 702.
135 "how little by little minds change." Rich, *Time's Power,* 54; *Collected Poems,* 702.
135 "our changes of mind have come." Rich, *Time's Power,* 54; *Collected Poems,* 702.
135 "solitude of no absence." Rich, *Time's Power,* 55; *Collected Poems,* 703.
136 "so I have thought of you." Rich, *Time's Power,* 54–55; *Collected Poems,* 702–3.
136 "go where no song has ever gone." Rich, *Time's Power,* 26; *Collected Poems,* 678.
136 "more than a handful." Rich, *Your Native Land, Your Life,* 107; *Collected Poems,* 653.

"take the mirrors and turn them outward"

136 "take the mirrors and turn them outward." Rich, *An Atlas of the Difficult World,* 48; *Collected Poems,* 744.
137 "neither unique nor universal." Rich, *The Fact of a Doorframe,* xv.
137 "Increasingly . . . has meant hearing." Rich, *The Fact of a Doorframe,* xv–xvi.
137 "the artist," "she got away." Rich, *An Atlas of the Difficult World,* 31; *Collected Poems,* 732.
137 "Clogged, the fine nets bulge." Rich, *An Atlas of the Difficult World,* 29; *Collected Poems,* 731.
137 "I know the power you thought you had." Rich, *An Atlas of the Difficult World,* 33; *Collected Poems,* 735.
137 "the fibres of the self," "practical substance." Williams, *Marxism and Literature,* 212.
137 "hating and loving come down." Rich, *An Atlas of the Difficult World,* 31; *Collected Poems,* 732.
138 "This is not the father's kiss," "unsweetened taste." Rich, *An Atlas of the Difficult World,* 30; *Collected Poems,* 732.
138 "the sweep of the great ocean." Rich, *An Atlas of the Difficult World,* 5; *Collected Poems,* 710–11.

138 "a woman of sixty," "eyes open." Rich, *An Atlas of the Difficult World,* 41; *Collected Poems,* 739.

138 "the young who do not wander." Rich, *An Atlas of the Difficult World,* 41; *Collected Poems,* 739–40.

138 "neighborhoods already familiar." Rich, *Collected Early Poems,* xx.

138 "refuse . . . the splitting." Rich, *The Dream of a Common Language,* 11; *Collected Poems,* 451.

138 "left for another generation's." Rich, *An Atlas of the Difficult World,* 41; *Collected Poems,* 739–40.

139 "I'm nothing if I'm just a roll of film." Rich, *An Atlas of the Difficult World,* 41; *Collected Poems,* 739–40.

139 "I can't be restored." Rich, *An Atlas of the Difficult World,* 41; *Collected Poems,* 741.

139 *"what does it mean 'to survive.'"* Rich, *The Dream of a Common Language,* 6; *Collected Poems,* 446.

139 *"burning together in the snow."* Rich, *The Dream of a Common Language,* 6; *Collected Poems,* 446.

139 *"own forces,"* "*so taken up and shared.*" Rich, *The Dream of a Common Language,* 5; *Collected Poems,* 445.

139 "it's as if part of you had died." Rich, *An Atlas of the Difficult World,* 47; *Collected Poems,* 743.

139 "what do you know." Rich, *An Atlas of the Difficult World,* 48; *Collected Poems,* 744.

139 "What does it mean to say." Rich, *An Atlas of the Difficult World,* 48; *Collected Poems,* 744.

140 "That light of outrage." Rich, *An Atlas of the Difficult World,* 49; *Collected Poems,* 744.

140 "in history." Rich, *The Fact of a Doorframe,* xv.

140 "*forces taken up and shared.*" Rich, *The Dream of a Common Language,* 5; *Collected Poems,* 445.

140 "take the mirrors and turn them outward." Rich, *An Atlas of the Difficult World,* 48; *Collected Poems,* 744.

140 "neighborhoods already familiar." Rich, *Collected Early Poems,* xx.

140 "if *we* means more than a handful." Rich, *Your Native Land, Your Life,* 107; *Collected Poems,* 653.

140 "that those we love / be well." Rich, *An Atlas of the Difficult World,* 49; *Collected Poems,* 744.

140 "whatever that means." Rich, *An Atlas of the Difficult World,* 49; *Collected Poems,* 744.

140 "to say *I have survived.*" Rich, *An Atlas of the Difficult World,* 48; *Collected Poems,* 744.

140 "Outrage: who dare claim protection." Rich, *An Atlas of the Difficult World,* 49; *Collected Poems,* 744.

140 "solitude of no absence." Rich, *Time's Power*, 55; *Collected Poems*, 703.

141 "I am *not* the victim here." James Baldwin, in Moore, *Take This Hammer*.

141 "will occupy your thought." Rich, *An Atlas of the Difficult World*, 57; *Collected Poems*, 749.

141 "You are coming into us." Rich, *An Atlas of the Difficult World*, 57; *Collected Poems*, 749.

141 "you are taking parts of us." Rich, *An Atlas of the Difficult World*, 57; *Collected Poems*, 750.

141 "turn [the mirrors] outward," "outraged light," "the light of history." Rich, *An Atlas of the Difficult World*, 48–49; *Collected Poems*, 744.

"fathoming what it means / to love my country"

142 "fathoming what it means." Rich, *An Atlas of the Difficult World*, 22; *Collected Poems*, 725.

142 "A dark woman, head bent." Rich, *An Atlas of the Difficult World*, 3; *Collected Poems*, 709.

142 "night after night." Rich, *An Atlas of the Difficult World*, 3; *Collected Poems*, 709.

142 "the haunted river flowing." Rich, *An Atlas of the Difficult World*, 3; *Collected Poems*, 709.

142 "past eucalyptus, cypress." Rich, *An Atlas of the Difficult World*, 3; *Collected Poems*, 709.

142 "What is a Jew in Solitude?" Rich, *Your Native Land, Your Life*, 75; *Collected Poems*, 633.

143 "One says: 'I never knew." Rich, *An Atlas of the Difficult World*, 3; *Collected Poems*, 709.

143 "I fix on the land," "I am stuck to earth." Rich, *An Atlas of the Difficult World*, 5; *Collected Poems*, 711.

143 "I don't want to hear," "I don't want to think," "I don't want to know." Rich, *An Atlas of the Difficult World*, 4; *Collected Poems*, 710.

143 "wreckage, dreck, and waste," "these are the materials." Rich, *An Atlas of the Difficult World*, 4; *Collected Poems*, 710.

143 "and so are the slow lift." Rich, *An Atlas of the Difficult World*, 4; *Collected Poems*, 710.

143 "a woman dreaming," "a map of variations, "the material and the dream." Rich, *Time's Power*, 35; *Collected Poems*, 685.

144 "I promised to show you a map." Rich, *An Atlas of the Difficult World*, 6; *Collected Poems*, 712.

144 "practical substance." Williams, *Marxism and Literature*, 212.

144 "Where do we see it from." Rich, *An Atlas of the Difficult World*, 6; *Collected Poems*, 712.

144 "*with their arms around,*" "*short and ill-environed lives.*" Rich, *A Wild Patience Has Taken Me This Far*, 11; *Collected Poems*, 527.

144 "One hot afternoon I sat there." Rich, *An Atlas of the Difficult World*, 8; *Collected Poems*, 713.

144 "—trying to enfigure such a life." Rich, *An Atlas of the Difficult World*, 8; *Collected Poems*, 713.

145 "intrusive inappropriate bitter flashing." Rich, *An Atlas of the Difficult World*, 43; *Collected Poems*, 741.

145 "nothing comes without labor." Rich, *An Atlas of the Difficult World*, 10; *Collected Poems*, 715.

145 "Was it worth while to lay." Rich, *Snapshots of a Daughter-in-Law*, 68; *Collected Poems*, 154.

145 "But how do I know." Rich, *An Atlas of the Difficult World*, 10; *Collected Poems*, 715.

146 "Waste.   Waste." Rich, *An Atlas of the Difficult World*, 11; *Collected Poems*, 716.

146 "views of the Palace of Fine Arts." Rich, *An Atlas of the Difficult World*, 13; *Collected Poems*, 717.

146 "*With whom do you believe.*" Rich, *Your Native Land, Your Life*, 6; *Collected Poems*, 575.

147 "Where are we moored?" Rich, *An Atlas of the Difficult World*, 12; *Collected Poems*, 717.

147 "but this is not a bad dream." Rich, *An Atlas of the Difficult World*, 14; *Collected Poems*, 718.

147 "It was New York." Rich, *An Atlas of the Difficult World*, 16; *Collected Poems*, 720.

147 "bodies young and ordinary." Rich, *An Atlas of the Difficult World*, 16; *Collected Poems*, 720.

147 "as darkly we felt our own blood." Rich, *An Atlas of the Difficult World*, 16; *Collected Poems*, 720.

148 "A crosshair against the pupil." Rich, *An Atlas of the Difficult World*, 14; *Collected Poems*, 718.

148 "with your best friend," "in the prairie classroom." Rich, *An Atlas of the Difficult World*, 19; *Collected Poems*, 722.

148 "is a white man's madness." Rich, *An Atlas of the Difficult World*, 19; *Collected Poems*, 722.

148 "I honor your truth." Rich, *An Atlas of the Difficult World*, 19; *Collected Poems*, 722.

148 "*I have never seen.*" Rich, *The Dream of a Common Language*, 5; *Collected Poems*, 445.

148 "*But the significant feature.*" Rich, *An Atlas of the Difficult World*, 21; *Collected Poems*, 724.

149 "neighborhoods already familiar." Rich, *Collected Early Poems*, xx.

149 "—power and powerlessness run amuck." Rich, *An Atlas of the Difficult World*, 23; *Collected Poems*, 725.

150 "some who have learned to handle." Rich, *An Atlas of the Difficult World*, 23;
     Collected Poems, 725–26.
150 "refuse . . . the splitting." Rich, *The Dream of a Common Language*, 11;
     Collected Poems, 451.
150 "a beauty built to last." Rich, *An Atlas of the Difficult World*, 24; *Collected
     Poems*, 726.
150 "clouds an arm's reach away." Rich, *An Atlas of the Difficult World*, 24;
     Collected Poems, 727.
150 "in outraged light." Rich, *An Atlas of the Difficult World*, 48; *Collected Poems*,
     744.
150 "practical substance." Williams, *Marxism and Literature*, 212.
150 "drinking the spaces." Rich, *An Atlas of the Difficult World*, 24; *Collected
     Poems*, 727.
151 "I know you are reading this poem." Rich, *An Atlas of the Difficult World*,
     25; *Collected Poems*, 728.

"So we are thrown together"
"dissimilar / yet unseparate   that's beauty"

153 "I need to understand." Rich, *Arts of the Possible*, 64.
153 "as a woman, a Jew," "trying to create." Rich, *Arts of the Possible*, 64.
153 "even if nation-states are now." Rich, *Arts of the Possible*, 64.
153 "as a great geographer." Rich, *Arts of the Possible*, 4.
154 "In a society in such extreme pain." Rich, *Arts of the Possible*, 149.
155 "flashes of insight that came through." Rich, *Blood, Bread, and Poetry*, 3.
155 "moonlight picking at small stones." Rich, *Dark Fields of the Republic*, 8;
     Collected Poems, 758–59.
156 "I tried to listen." Rich, *Dark Fields of the Republic*, 31; *Collected Poems*, 776.
156 "precisely how the air moved." Rich, *Dark Fields of the Republic*, 31; *Collected
     Poems*, 776.
157 "to feel with a human stranger." Rich, *Dark Fields of the Republic*, 31;
     Collected Poems, 776.
157 "this is not somewhere else but here." Rich, *Dark Fields of the Republic*, 3;
     Collected Poems, 755.
157 "this isn't a Russian poem," "its own ways of making." Rich, *Dark Fields of
     the Republic*, 3; *Collected Poems*, 755.
157 "I know already who wants." Rich, *Dark Fields of the Republic*, 3; *Collected
     Poems*, 755.
157 "that living human individual." Rich, *Arts of the Possible*, 64.
157 "the empirical witch." Rich, *Arts of the Possible*, 65.
157 "all physical and intellectual senses." Karl Marx, quoted in Rich, *Arts of the
     Possible*, 2.
157 "buy it, sell it." Rich, *Dark Fields of the Republic*, 3; *Collected Poems*, 755.

158 "we found ourselves." Rich, *Dark Fields of the Republic*, 4; *Collected Poems*, 755.

158 "we lost track / of the meaning of *we*." Rich, *Dark Fields of the Republic*, 4; *Collected Poems*, 755.

158 "if *we* means more than a handful." Rich, *Your Native Land, Your Life*, 107; *Collected Poems*, 653.

158 "practical substance." Williams, *Marxism and Literature*, 212.

159 "Upstairs, long silence." Rich, *A Wild Patience Has Taken Me This Far*, 11; *Collected Poems*, 526.

159 *"Yes, our work is one."* Rich, *A Wild Patience Has Taken Me This Far*, 15; *Collected Poems*, 531.

159 "passionate factuality," "Black feminists, *But you don't know us!"* Rich, *Blood, Bread, and Poetry*, x.

160 "Calmly you look over my shoulder." Rich, *Time's Power*, 21; *Collected Poems*, 672.

160 "wheeling," "steadily rising." Rich, *Dark Fields of the Republic*, 5; *Collected Poems*, 756.

160 "A typewriter's torrent." Rich, *Dark Fields of the Republic*, 5; *Collected Poems*, 756.

160 "scrub oak and cactus." Rich, *Dark Fields of the Republic*, 11; *Collected Poems*, 759.

161 "Not what you thought." Rich, *Dark Fields of the Republic*, 11; *Collected Poems*, 759.

161 "this is your room." Rich, *Dark Fields of the Republic*, 11; *Collected Poems*, 760.

161 "Calle Visión   wounded knee." Rich, *Dark Fields of the Republic*, 14; *Collected Poems*, 761.

161 "your heart beats on unbroken." Rich, *Dark Fields of the Republic*, 14; *Collected Poems*, 761.

161 "how is this possible." Rich, *Dark Fields of the Republic*, 14; *Collected Poems*, 761.

161 "simultaneity of oppressions." Rich, *Blood, Bread, and Poetry*, xii.

162 "O sister of nausea." Rich, *Your Native Land, Your Life*, 87; *Collected Poems*, 643.

162 "The problem, unstated till now." Rich, *Your Native Land, Your Life*, 100; *Collected Poems*, 650.

162 "The problem is / to connect." Rich, *Your Native Land, Your Life*, 100; *Collected Poems*, 650.

162 "remember: the body's pain." Rich, *Your Native Land, Your Life*, 111; *Collected Poems*, 656.

162 "but you can learn." Rich, *Your Native Land, Your Life*, 111; *Collected Poems*, 656.

162 "Poetry, like silk or coffee or oil." Rich, *Poetry and Commitment*, 21.

162 *"to survive."* Rich, *The Dream of a Common Language,* 6; *Collected Poems,* 446.

162 "Whatever you bring." Rich, *Dark Fields of the Republic,* 5; *Collected Poems,* 756.

163 "Calle Visión   never forget." Rich, *Dark Fields of the Republic,* 14; *Collected Poems,* 762.

163 "the gasses that rise." Rich, *Dark Fields of the Republic,* 15; *Collected Poems,* 762.

163 *"And the fire shall try."* Rich, *Dark Fields of the Republic,* 15; *Collected Poems,* 762.

163 *"With whom do you believe."* Rich, *Your Native Land, Your Life,* 6; *Collected Poems,* 575.

163 "powerful;   womanly." Rich, *Your Native Land, Your Life,* 27; *Collected Poems,* 589.

163 "are queer, outside, and out of bounds." Rich, *Time's Power,* 38; *Collected Poems,* 688.

164 "repetitive motions," "fire in the chicken factory." Rich, *Dark Fields of the Republic,* 16; *Collected Poems,* 763.

164 *"fire ropes our bodies," "will not live."* Rich, *The Dream of a Common Language,* 6; *Collected Poems,* 446.

164 "some fleeing to the freezer." Rich, *Dark Fields of the Republic,* 16; *Collected Poems,* 763.

164 "The burning of a book arouses." Rich, *The Will to Change,* 18; *Collected Poems,* 306.

165 "once we were dissimilar." Rich, *Dark Fields of the Republic,* 17; *Collected Poems,* 763.

165 "My verse works." Dennis Brutus, quoted in Rich, *Poetry and Commitment,* 13.

165 "would act as part of the world." James Scully, quoted in Rich, *Poetry and Commitment,* 14.

165 "creative practice." Williams, *Marxism and Literature,* 212.

165 "The place is alive with the dead." Rich, *Dark Fields of the Republic,* 17; *Collected Poems,* 765.

165 "to connect, without hysteria." Rich, *Your Native Land, Your Life,* 100; *Collected Poems,* 650.

165 *"It's all about you."* Rich, *Time's Power,* 21; *Collected Poems,* 672.

166 "You were telling a story." Rich, *Dark Fields of the Republic,* 49; *Collected Poems,* 783.

166 "active struggle for new consciousness." Williams, *Marxism and Literature,* 212.

166 "I was telling you a story." Rich, *Dark Fields of the Republic,* 51; *Collected Poems,* 784.

166 "Yes . . . but the larynx is bloodied." Rich, *Dark Fields of the Republic,* 51; *Collected Poems,* 784.

166 "Well I said love is hated." Rich, *Dark Fields of the Republic*, 51; *Collected Poems*, 784.

166 "No . . . you are talking." Rich, *Dark Fields of the Republic*, 51; *Collected Poems*, 784.

166 "So we are thrown together." Rich, *Dark Fields of the Republic*, 52; *Collected Poems*, 784.

"the light we stand under when we meet"

167 "dissimilar / yet unseparate." Rich, *Dark Fields of the Republic*, 17; *Collected Poems*, 763.

167 "Little as I knew you." Rich, *Dark Fields of the Republic*, 59; *Collected Poems*, 791.

167 "My testimony." Rich, *Dark Fields of the Republic*, 59; *Collected Poems*, 791.

168 "news of an awareness." Rich, *Poetry and Commitment*, 25.

168 "The self unlocked to many selves." Rich, *Dark Fields of the Republic*, 60; *Collected Poems*, 791–92.

168 "Times of walking across a street." Rich, *Dark Fields of the Republic*, 61; *Collected Poems*, 792.

168 "When does a life bend." Rich, *Dark Fields of the Republic*, 61; *Collected Poems*, 792.

169 "someone with facts with numbers." Rich, *Dark Fields of the Republic*, 61; *Collected Poems*, 792.

169 "Your journals Patricia." Rich, *Dark Fields of the Republic*, 61; *Collected Poems*, 793.

169 "—And now she turns her face." Rich, *Dark Fields of the Republic*, 62; *Collected Poems*, 793.

169 "the repeti- / tive blows." Rich, *Dark Fields of the Republic*, 61; *Collected Poems*, 793.

169 "She's a mermaid." Rich, *Dark Fields of the Republic*, 62; *Collected Poems*, 793.

169 "That year I began to understand." Rich, *Dark Fields of the Republic*, 66; *Collected Poems*, 795.

170 "I started feeling in my body." Rich, *Dark Fields of the Republic*, 66; *Collected Poems*, 795.

170 "the active struggle." Williams, *Marxism and Literature*, 212.

170 "and the talk goes on." Rich, *Dark Fields of the Republic*, 66; *Collected Poems*, 796.

170 "(Knotted crowns of asparagus." Rich, *Dark Fields of the Republic*, 66; *Collected Poems*, 796.

170 "the photographer's / darkroom." Rich, *Dark Fields of the Republic*, 66; *Collected Poems*, 796.

170 "laboring under that burden." Rich, *Dark Fields of the Republic*, 66; *Collected Poems*, 796.

171 "two phantoms caught." Rich, *Dark Fields of the Republic*, 66; *Collected Poems*, 796.

171 "In the heart of the capital." Rich, *Dark Fields of the Republic*, 68; *Collected Poems*, 798.

171 "I had been wondering why." Rich, *Dark Fields of the Republic*, 68; *Collected Poems*, 798.

171 "[W]andering among white monuments," "I found myself there." Rich, *Dark Fields of the Republic*, 68; *Collected Poems*, 798.

171 "A strangely focused many-lumened glare." Rich, *Dark Fields of the Republic*, 69; *Collected Poems*, 798.

172 "One keen as mica, glittering." Rich, *Dark Fields of the Republic*, 70; *Collected Poems*, 799.

172 "The bright planet that plies." Rich, *Dark Fields of the Republic*, 71; *Collected Poems*, 800.

172 "spiritual and moral vision," "have been explored." Rich, *Blood, Bread, and Poetry*, 165.

173 "acknowledge a precious resource." Rich, *Blood, Bread, and Poetry*, 165.

173 "You   who sees me." Rich, *Dark Fields of the Republic*, 71; *Collected Poems*, 800.

173 "sixty-fifth year." Rich, *Dark Fields of the Republic*, 71; *Collected Poems*, 800.

173 "*these vivid stricken cells.*" Rich, *Dark Fields of the Republic*, 72; *Collected Poems*, 801.

173 "edgelight from the high desert." Rich, *Dark Fields of the Republic*, 72; *Collected Poems*, 801.

173 "There are the extremes I stoke." Rich, *Dark Fields of the Republic*, 73; *Collected Poems*, 802.

174 "dark's velvet dialectic." Rich, *Midnight Salvage*, 51; *Collected Poems*, 836.

"we are not a little / cell, but we are like a little cell"

174 "[T]hat was a mission, surely." Rich, *Midnight Salvage*, 3; *Collected Poems*, 805.

174 "daunting and dauntless." Rich, *Midnight Salvage*, 3; *Collected Poems*, 805.

174 "to lift toward home." Rich, *Midnight Salvage*, 3; *Collected Poems*, 805.

174 "back to [her] country," "bearing [her colleague's]." Rich, *Midnight Salvage*, 3; *Collected Poems*, 805.

174 "the translators stopped." Rich, *Midnight Salvage*, 6; *Collected Poems*, 806.

174 "That the books are for personal use." Rich, *Midnight Salvage*, 6; *Collected Poems*, 806.

174 "Like a thief I would deny." Rich, *Midnight Salvage*, 5; *Collected Poems*, 806.

175 "the active struggle." Williams, *Marxism and Literature*, 212.

175 "the hard practical substance." Williams, *Marxism and Literature*, 212.

175 "not with each other exactly," "known and unknown." Rich, *Dark Fields of the Republic*, 59; *Collected Poems*, 791.

175 "It's only a branch like any other." Rich, *Midnight Salvage*, 4; *Collected Poems*, 805.

175 "nest on Tomales Bay," "The left wing shouldered." Rich, *Midnight Salvage*, 7; *Collected Poems*, 807.

176 "thought's blood ebb between." Rich, *Midnight Salvage*, 8; *Collected Poems*, 808.

176 "Under the conditions of my hiring." Rich, *Midnight Salvage*, 9; *Collected Poems*, 808. ˙

176 "could not any more // peruse." Rich, *Midnight Salvage*, 9; *Collected Poems*, 808.

176 "active struggle," "not casting off." Williams, *Marxism and Literature*, 212.

176 "swift reading and current thinking." Rich, *Midnight Salvage*, 9; *Collected Poems*, 808.

176 "a process often described." Williams, *Marxism and Literature*, 212.

177 "Had never expected hope would form." Rich, *Midnight Salvage*, 10; *Collected Poems*, 809.

177 "But neither was expecting in my time." Rich, *Midnight Salvage*, 11; *Collected Poems*, 809–10.

178 "I am concerned about what it means." Rich, in "Poet Adrienne Rich."

179 "Old walls the pride of architects." Rich, *Midnight Salvage*, 15; *Collected Poems*, 812.

179 "*This war will prolong itself.*" Rich, *Midnight Salvage*, 17; *Collected Poems*, 813.

180 "knowing the end of war." Rich, *Midnight Salvage*, 17; *Collected Poems*, 814.

180 "Hermetic guide in resistance." Rich, *Midnight Salvage*, 18; *Collected Poems*, 814.

180 "enjoying every bright day." Rich, *Dark Fields of the Republic*, 76; *Collected Poems*, 1135.

180 "To be human, said Rosa—." Rich, *Dark Fields of the Republic*, 5; *Collected Poems*, 756.

181 "The difficulty of proving." Rich, *Midnight Salvage*, 31; *Collected Poems*, 823.

181 "measure happiness." Rich, *Midnight Salvage*, 32; *Collected Poems*, 824.

181 "happiness is not to be / mistrusted." Rich, *Midnight Salvage*, 32; *Collected Poems*, 824

181 "at the end of a day." Rich, *Midnight Salvage*, 33; *Collected Poems*, 824.

181 "that somewhere there." Rich, *Diving into the Wreck*, 36–37; *Collected Poems*, 386.

182 "Imagine a city." Rich, *Midnight Salvage*, 51; *Collected Poems*, 836.

182 "This *I*—must she, must she lie." Rich, *Midnight Salvage*, 52; *Collected Poems*, 837.

183 "queer, outside, and out of bounds." Rich, *Time's Power*, 38; *Collected Poems*, 688.

183 "that is ransacking this region." Rich, *Midnight Salvage*, 57; *Collected Poems*, 839.

183 "as if we are a class." Rich, *Midnight Salvage*, 59; *Collected Poems*, 840.

183 "Like a little cell." Rich, *Midnight Salvage*, 57; *Collected Poems*, 839.

183 "*whole relations of society*," "must *sell themselves piecemeal*." Rich, *Midnight Salvage*, 58; *Collected Poems*, 840.

183 "Someone:—Technology's changing," "But technology is nothing." Rich, *Midnight Salvage*, 59; *Collected Poems*, 840.

183 "Someone, I say, makes a killing." Rich, *Midnight Salvage*, 59; *Collected Poems*, 841.

183 "Now someone gets up and leaves." Rich, *Midnight Salvage*, 59; *Collected Poems*, 841.

184 "All kinds of language fly." Rich, *Midnight Salvage*, 60; *Collected Poems*, 841.

184 "*At the risk of appearing ridiculous*." Rich, *Midnight Salvage*, 64; *Collected Poems*, 844.

184 "*we* [that] means more than a handful." Rich, *Your Native Land, Your Life*, 107; *Collected Poems*, 653.

184 "I can imagine a sentence." Rich, *Midnight Salvage*, 64; *Collected Poems*, 844.

184 "we wanters we unwanted." Rich, *Midnight Salvage*, 15; *Collected Poems*, 812.

184 "We want to be part of the future." Rich, *Fox*, 39; *Collected Poems*, 876.

185 "I needed fox." Rich, *Fox*, 25; *Collected Poems*, 865.

185 "For a human animal." Rich, *Fox*, 25; *Collected Poems*, 866.

185 "Go back far enough." Rich, *Fox*, 25; *Collected Poems*, 866.

185 "back far enough it blurts." Rich, *Fox*, 25; *Collected Poems*, 866.

185 "instruments of force," "cameras / for the desouling." Rich, *Fox*, 26; *Collected Poems*, 866–67.

186 "If you want to feel the true time." Rich, *Fox*, 26; *Collected Poems*, 867.

186 "When does a life bend." Rich, *Dark Fields of the Republic*, 61; *Collected Poems*, 792.

186 "My name is a prisoner." Rich, *Fox*, 49; *Collected Poems*, 882.

186 "She says: When my life depended." Rich, *Fox*, 49; *Collected Poems*, 882.

186 "Sick of my old poems," "Pier Paolo," "that vernacular voice." Rich, *Fox*, 50; *Collected Poems*, 882–83.

186 "a bite of bitter chocolate." Rich, *Fox*, 51; *Collected Poems*, 883.

186 "pale dreams," "deep current." Rich, *Dark Fields of the Republic*, 61; *Collected Poems*, 792.

187 "a public privacy . . . a public happiness." Rich, *Fox*, 46; *Collected Poems*, 880.

187 "without them we're prey." Rich, *Fox*, 51; *Collected Poems*, 883.

187 "How I've hated speaking." Rich, *Fox*, 52; *Collected Poems*, 884.

187 "our shadows   reindeer-huge." Rich, *Fox,* 53; *Collected Poems,* 884–85.

188 "*In response to your inquiry.*" Rich, *The School among the Ruins,* 43; *Collected Poems,* 918–19.

"Voices from open air"
"suffused / by what it works in"

189 "Pain made her conservative." Rich, *The Will to Change,* 24; *Collected Poems,* 312.

189 "Remember: the body's pain." Rich, *Your Native Land, Your Life,* 111; *Collected Poems,* 656.

189 "Pain taught her the language / root." Rich, *Tonight No Poetry Will Serve,* 46; *Collected Poems,* 1073.

190 "poetic imagination," "is never merely unto itself." Rich, *A Human Eye,* 96.

190 "head, heart, perforated / by raw." Rich, *Dark Fields of the Republic,* 71; *Collected Poems,* 799–800.

190 "Thence comes it that my name." William Shakespeare, Sonnet 111, quoted in Rich, *Dark Fields of the Republic,* 79; *Collected Poems,* 1137–38.

190 "I have kept 'suffused' here." Rich, *Dark Fields of the Republic,* 79; *Collected Poems,* 1137–38.

190 "*to survive.*" Rich, *The Dream of a Common Language,* 6; *Collected Poems,* 446.

190 "There's a permeable membrane," "A continuous dialectical motion." Rich, *A Human Eye,* 99.

191 "Say a pen must write underground." Rich, *Collected Poems,* 1115.

191 "Throw the handwritten scraps." Rich, *Collected Poems,* 1117.

191 "My hands under your buttocks." Rich, *Collected Poems,* 1116.

191 "*liquefaction* is a word I might use." Rich, *Telephone Ringing in the Labyrinth,* 70; *Collected Poems,* 1015.

191 "Tenant already of the disensoulment projects." Rich, *Telephone Ringing in the Labyrinth,* 93; *Collected Poems,* 1034.

192 "the idea of perpetual war." Rich, *Muriel Rukeyser,* xxv.

192 "Historian's voice." Rich, "Fragment of a Libretto," author's files. Printed with permission from the Adrienne Rich Literary Estate.

193 "Antonio Entering, stage left." Rich, "Fragment of a Libretto," author's files.

Coda

195 "A continuous dialectical motion." Rich, *A Human Eye,* 99.

195 "What holds what binds is breath." Rich, *Collected Poems,* 1119.

195 "*to survive.*" Rich, *The Dream of a Common Language,* 6; *Collected Poems,* 446.

196 "sporadic, errant, orphaned." Rich, *On Lies, Secrets, and Silence,* 11, quoted in Rankine, *New Yorker.*

Bibliography

Works by Adrienne Rich
Poetry

A Change of World, foreword by W. H. Auden. New Haven, Conn.: Yale University Press, 1951.

The Diamond Cutters and Other Poems. New York: Harper, 1955.

Snapshots of a Daughter-in-Law: Poems, 1954–1962. New York: Harper & Row, 1963.

Necessities of Life: Poems 1962–1965. New York: W. W. Norton, 1966.

Leaflets: Poems 1965–1968. New York: W. W. Norton, 1969.

The Will to Change: Poems 1968–1970. New York: W. W. Norton, 1971.

Diving into the Wreck: Poems 1971–1972. New York: W. W. Norton, 1973.

Poems: Selected and New, 1950–1974. New York: W. W. Norton, 1975.

The Dream of a Common Language: Poems 1974–1977. New York: W. W. Norton, 1978.

A Wild Patience Has Taken Me This Far: Poems 1978–1981. New York: W. W. Norton, 1981.

The Fact of a Doorframe: Poems Selected and New 1950–1984. New York: W. W. Norton, 1984.

Your Native Land, Your Life: Poems. New York: W. W. Norton, 1986.

Time's Power: Poems 1985–1988. New York: W. W. Norton, 1989.

An Atlas of the Difficult World: Poems 1988–1991. New York: W. W. Norton, 1991.

Collected Early Poems: 1950–1970. New York: W. W. Norton, 1993.

Dark Fields of the Republic: Poems 1991–1995. New York: W. W. Norton, 1995.

Midnight Salvage: Poems 1995–1998. New York: W. W. Norton, 1999.

Fox: Poems 1998–2000. New York: W. W. Norton, 2001.

The School among the Ruins: Poems 2000–2004. New York: W. W. Norton, 2004.

Telephone Ringing in the Labyrinth: Poems 2004–2006. New York: W. W. Norton, 2007.

Tonight No Poetry Will Serve: Poems 2007–2010. New York: W. W. Norton, 2011.

Later Poems: Selected and New, 1971–2012. New York: W. W. Norton, 2012.
Collected Poems: 1950–2012. New York: W. W. Norton, 2016.

Prose

Of Woman Born: Motherhood as Experience and Institution. New York: W. W. Norton, 1976.
Women and Honor: Some Notes on Lying. Pittsburgh: Motheroot Publications/ Pittsburgh Women Writers, 1977.
On Lies, Secrets, and Silence: Selected Prose 1966–1978. New York: W. W. Norton, 1979.
Blood, Bread, and Poetry: Selected Prose 1979–1985. New York: W. W. Norton, 1986.
What Is Found There: Notebooks on Poetry and Politics. New York: W. W. Norton, 1993.
Arts of the Possible: Essays and Conversations. New York: W. W. Norton, 2001.
Foreword to *Paraph of Bone and Other Kinds of Blue,* by Ed Pavlić. Port Townsend, Wash.: Copper Canyon Press, 2001.
Introduction to *Muriel Rukeyser: Selected Poems,* edited by Adrienne Rich. New York: Library of America, 2004.
Poetry and Commitment. New York: W. W. Norton, 2007.
A Human Eye: Essays on Art in Society, 1997–2008. New York: W. W. Norton, 2009.

Critical Texts

Ahmad, Aijaz, ed. *Ghazals of Ghalib: Versions from the Urdu by Aijaz Ahmad, W. S. Merwin, Adrienne Rich, William Stafford, David Ray, Thomas Fitzsimmons, Mark Strand, and William Hunt.* New York: Columbia University Press, 1971.
Alexander, Mabel. *Via Oklahoma: And Still the Music Flows.* Oklahoma City: Oklahoma Heritage Association, 2004.
Andrea, Meredith. "Too Reflective, Too Fierce, Too Engaging." *Stride Magazine,* February 2008. http://stridebooks.co.uk/archive.htm.
Bennett, Paula. *My Life, a Loaded Gun: Female Creativity and Feminist Poetics.* Boston: Beacon Press, 1986.
Boland, Eavan. "When a Couplet Caught Fire—The Poetry of Adrienne Rich." *New Republic,* November 8, 2012. https://newrepublic.com.
Brown, Iemanjá, Stefania Heim, erica kaufman, Kristin Moriah, Conor Tomás Reed, Talia Shalev, and Wendy Tronrud, eds. *"What We Are Part Of": Teaching at CUNY, 1968–1974; Adrienne Rich.* Lost and Found, series 4, no. 3 (Fall), 2 pts. New York: CUNY Poetics Document Initiative, 2013.
Chiasson, Dan. "Boundary Conditions: Adrienne Rich's Collected Poems." *New Yorker,* June 20, 2016. https://www.newyorker.com.
Clark, Miriam Marty. "Human Rights and the Work of Lyric in Adrienne Rich." *Cambridge Quarterly* 38, no. 1 (2009): 45–65.
Cook, Christina. "Poverties and Protest: *Tonight No Poetry Will Serve: Poems*

2007–2010 by Adrienne Rich." *Cerise Press: A Journal of Literature, Arts and Culture* 3, no. 7 (2011). http://www.cerisepress.com.

Dean, Michelle. "The Wreck: Adrienne Rich's Feminist Awakening, as Glimpsed through Her Never-Before-Published Letters." *New Republic,* April 3, 2016. https://newrepublic.com.

DeShazer, Mary K. "'The End of a Century': Feminist Millennial Vision in Adrienne Rich's *Dark Fields of the Republic.*" *NWSA Journal* 8, no. 3 (1996): 36–62.

De Veaux, Alexis. *Warrior Poet: A Biography of Audre Lorde.* New York: Norton, 2004.

Du Bois, W. E. B. *The Souls of Black Folk.* In *The Norton Anthology of African American Literature,* edited by Henry Louis Gates Jr. and Nellie Y. McKay, 613–740. New York: W. W. Norton, 1997.

DuPlessis, Rachel Blau. *Writing beyond the Ending: Narrative Strategies of Twentieth-Century Women Writers.* Bloomington: Indiana University Press, 1985.

Eagleton, Mary. "Adrienne Rich, Location and the Body." *Journal of Gender Studies* 9, no. 3 (2000): 299–312.

Ellison, Ralph. *Invisible Man.* 1952. New York: Vintage International, 1990.

———. "The Charlie Christian Story." In *Collected Essays.* New York: Modern Library, 1995.

Erickson, Peter. "Singing America: From Walt Whitman to Adrienne Rich." *Kenyon Review* 17, no. 1 (1995): 103–19.

———. Review of *Tonight No Poetry Will Serve: Poems 2007–2010,* by Adrienne Rich. *Women's Studies* 41, no. 1 (2012): 105–8.

Flickinger, Robert Elliott. *The Choctaw Freedmen and the Story of Oakhill Industrial Academy.* Berwyn Heights, Md.: Heritage Books, 2002.

Franzek, Phyllis. "Adrienne Rich's *An Atlas of the Difficult World*: Strategic Interference, Articulate Response." In *"Catch If You Can Your Country's Moment": Recovery and Regeneration in the Poetry of Adrienne Rich,* edited by William S. Waddell, 64–80. Cambridge: Cambridge Scholars, 2007.

Gelpi, Albert. "Adrienne Rich: The Poetics of Change." In *American Poetry since 1960,* edited by Robert Shaw. Cheadle, Cheshire: Carcanet Press, 1973.

Gelpi, Barbara Charlesworth, and Albert Gelpi, eds. *Adrienne Rich's Poetry and Prose.* New York: W. W. Norton, 1993.

Gilbert, Sandra M. "A Life Written in Invisible Ink." *American Scholar,* September 6, 2016. https://theamericanscholar.org.

Gwiazda, Piotr. "'Nothing Else Left to Read': Poetry and Audience in Adrienne Rich's 'An Atlas of the Difficult World.'" *Journal of Modern Literature* 28, no. 2 (2005): 165–88.

Hacker, Marilyn. "The Mimesis of Thought." *Virginia Quarterly Review* 82, no. 2 (2006): 230–35.

Haven, Cynthia. "The Suffering of Others: On Adrienne Rich." *Virginia Quarterly Review* 89, no. 3 (2013). https://www.vqronline.org.

Hayden, Robert. *Collected Poems*. New York: W. W. Norton, 1985.

Hinton, Laura, ed. *Jayne Cortez, Adrienne Rich, and the Feminist Superhero: Voice, Vision, Politics, and Performance in U.S. Contemporary Women's Poetics*. New York: Lexington Books, 2016.

Jacobs, Joshua S. "'An Atlas of the Difficult World': Adrienne Rich's Countermonument." *Contemporary Literature* 42, no. 4 (Winter 2001): 727–49.

Keyes, Claire. *The Aesthetics of Power: The Poetry of Adrienne Rich*. Athens: University of Georgia Press, 1986.

Knutson, Lin. "Broken Forms: Land, History, and National Consciousness in Adrienne Rich's Poetry: 1989–1995." In *"Catch If You Can Your Country's Moment": Recovery and Regeneration in the Poetry of Adrienne Rich,* edited by William S. Waddell, 101–20. Cambridge: Cambridge Scholars, 2007.

Koestenbaum, Wayne. "Adrienne Rich's Poetry Became Political, but It Remained Rooted in Material Fact." *New York Times Book Review,* July 15, 2016. https://www.nytimes.com.

Langdell, Cheri Colby. *Adrienne Rich: The Moment of Change*. Westport, Conn.: Praeger, 2004.

Linder, Douglas O. "The Trial of John Brown: The Secret Six." Famous Trials. Accessed December 4, 2020. https://www.famous-trials.com.

Mlinko, Ange. "Diagram This: On Adrienne Rich," *The Nation,* February 18, 2013. https://www.thenation.com.

Montenegro, David. *Points of Departure: International Writers on Writing and Politics*. Ann Arbor: University of Michigan Press, 1991.

Moore, Richard O., dir. *Take This Hammer*. Film. San Francisco: KQED, 1964. https://diva.sfsu.edu.

Nowak, Mark. "Notes toward an Anti-capitalist Poetics." *Virginia Quarterly Review* 82, no. 2 (2006): 236–40.

Perreault, Jeanne. *Writing Selves: Contemporary Feminist Autobiography*. Minneapolis: University of Minnesota Press, 1995.

"Poet Adrienne Rich Refuses to Accept National Medal for the Arts." Interview of Adrienne Rich by Amy Goodman. Democracy Now!, July 16, 1997. https://www.democracynow.org.

Prince, Ruth E. C. "The Possibilities of an Engaged Art: An Interview with Adrienne Rich." *Radcliffe Quarterly* (Fall 1998): 36–37.

Rankine, Claudia. "Adrienne Rich's Poetic Transformations." *New Yorker,* May 12, 2016. https://www.newyorker.com.

Reed, Conor Tomás. "Diving into SEEK: Adrienne Rich and Social Movements at the City College of New York, 1968–1974." In *Jayne Cortez, Adrienne Rich, and the Feminist Superhero: Voice, Vision, Politics, and Performance in U.S. Contemporary Women's Poetics,* edited by Laura Hinton, 91–116. New York: Lexington Books, 2016.

Rehm, Maggie. "'try telling yourself / you are not accountable': Adrienne Rich as Citizen Poet." *Women's Studies* 46, no. 7 (2017): 684–703.

Riley, Jeannette E. *Understanding Adrienne Rich*. Columbia: University of South Carolina Press, 2016.

———. "'questing toward what might otherwise be': Adrienne Rich's Later Work." *Women's Studies* 46, no. 7 (2017): 704–17.

Rukeyser, Muriel. *The Life of Poetry*. Hanover, N.H.: Wesleyan University Press, 1996.

Schoerke, Meg. "Backward Glances." *Hudson Review* 66, no. 2 (2013): 423–31.

Seidman, Hugh. "Will, Change, and Power in the Poetry of Adrienne Rich." *Virginia Quarterly Review* 82, no. 2 (2006): 224–29.

Shaughnessy, Mina. *Errors and Expectations: A Guide for the Teacher of Basic Writing*. New York: Oxford University Press, 1977.

Sontag, Susan. "Fascinating Fascism." *New York Review of Books,* February 6, 1975. https://www.nybooks.com.

Stauffer, John, and Benjamin Soskis. *The Battle Hymn of the Republic: A Biography of the Song That Marches On*. New York: Oxford University Press, 2013.

Tejada, Roberto. "As in Tendrils a Transparency." *Virginia Quarterly Review* 82, no. 2 (2006): 247–51.

Templeton, Alice. "Contradictions: Tracking Adrienne Rich's Poetry." *Tulsa Studies in Women's Literature* 12, no. 2 (Autumn 1993): 333–40.

———. *The Dream and the Dialogue: Adrienne Rich's Feminist Poetics*. Knoxville: University of Tennessee Press, 1995.

Valentine, Jean. "A Change of World: A Friendship." *Virginia Quarterly Review* 82, no. 2 (2006): 221–23.

Waddell, William S. "Where We See It From: Adrienne Rich and a Reconstruction of American Space." In *"Catch If You Can Your Country's Moment": Recovery and Regeneration in the Poetry of Adrienne Rich,* edited by William S. Waddell, 81–100. Cambridge: Cambridge Scholars, 2007.

Waldman, Kate. "Adrienne Rich on 'Tonight No Poetry Will Serve.'" *Paris Review,* March 2, 2011. https://www.theparisreview.org.

Wallace, Cynthia R. "Adrienne Rich: *Later Poems*." *Englewood Review of Books,* January 4, 2013, https://englewoodreview.org.

Werner, Craig. *Adrienne Rich: The Poet and Her Critics*. Chicago: American Library Association, 1988.

———. "Trying to Keep Faith: Adrienne Rich's 'Usonian Journals 2000.'" *Virginia Quarterly Review* 82, no. 2 (2006): 241–46.

Williams, Gary. *Hungry Heart: The Literary Emergence of Julia Ward Howe*. Amherst: University of Massachusetts Press, 1999.

Williams, Raymond. *Marxism and Literature*. New York: Oxford University Press, 1977.

Wojan, David. "*An Atlas of the Difficult World*: 'Where Are We Moored? What Are the Bindings? What Behooves Us?'" *Field: Contemporary Poetry and Poetics* 77 (Fall 2007): 67–71.

Wordsworth, William. *Lyrical Ballads*. 3rd ed. (London, 1802). https://www.sas.upenn.edu.

Index

26, 44, 51; visionary, 55, 93. *See also* images; perceptions
"Voices," 169–70

Waddell, William S., 9
"Waking in the Dark," 52–53, 56
Walker, Alice, 12, 64
Wallace, Cynthia R., 9, 13, 101
war/warfare, 38, 111, 126, 142, 166, 171, 191–92. *See also* "Eastern War Time"; Rich, Adrienne, poetry of: warfare in; Vietnam War; violence; World War II
Werner, Craig, 3, 4, 7, 9
"What Does a Woman Need to Know?," 155
"What Kind of Times Are These," 157–58, 180
"When We Dead Awaken: Writing as Re-Vision," 40–41, 50, 51–52, 70–71, 90, 115, 127–28, 159
whiteness, 26, 112, 115; Rich's identity of, 86, 97, 99, 113–14, 119, 137; threat of, 72, 170; white men's madness, 11, 148
white supremacy, 7, 119. *See also* racism; segregation
Whitman, Ruth, 8
Whitman, Walt, 86, 142
Wild Patience Has Taken Me This Far, A: Poems 1978–1981, 3, 5, 12, 65, 86–87, 90, 93–94, 97, 104, 109, 123, 127, 128, 144, 159
Williams, Raymond, *Marxism and Literature*, 98–99, 104, 110, 115, 118, 134–35, 137, 144, 154, 158, 165, 175, 176
Willis, Wallace and Minerva, 126

"Will to Change, The," 39
Will to Change, The: Poems 1968–1970, 3, 23, 35, 39–46, 47, 69
Wittgenstein, Ludwig, 183
Wollstonecraft, Mary, 20
"Woman Dead in Her Forties, A," 82–83
women: bodies of, 66, 83; consciousness of, 3, 113; conversations between, 51, 57; erotic relations between, 73, 75–80, 87, 118, 140; experience of, 64, 68, 82, 89, 104; images of, 26, 41; interacting with men, 39, 70, 151; labor of, 27, 87–88, 92–93, 145, 159; liberation movement, 32, 45, 90–92, 104, 106, 109–10, 123–24, 141; life of, 19–20, 25–26; nature of, 21–22; patience of, 85, 87, 89, 93; relationships between, 64–65, 69, 72, 81–85, 88–89; transformations of, 41, 43. *See also* feminism/feminists; *and individual women*
Women and Honor: Some Notes on Lying, 73–74
Woolf, Virginia, 94
Wordsworth, William, 10, 38, 103
World War II, 56, 104–5, 108, 121, 164, 179
Wright, Richard, "The Man Who Lived Underground," 59

Yeats, William Butler, 6
"Yom Kippur," 115, 118–19, 124, 142–43
Your Native Land, Your Life: Poems, 12, 99–100, 103, 104, 105, 112, 119–20, 122–23, 124, 127, 137, 154

Ed Pavlić is Distinguished Research Professor of English and African American Studies at the University of Georgia. He is author of several books, including *Let It Be Broke*; *Another Kind of Madness*; *Who Can Afford to Improvise? James Baldwin and Black Music, the Lyric and the Listeners*; and *Crossroads Modernism: Descent and Emergence in African-American Literary Culture* (Minnesota, 2002).